THE HOLSTEIN PAPERS

THE MEMOIRS, DIARIES AND
CORRESPONDENCE OF
FRIEDRICH VON HOLSTEIN
1837–1909

I

MEMOIRS
AND POLITICAL OBSERVATIONS

Due Return Date Date	Due Return Date Date

THE
HOLSTEIN PAPERS

EDITED BY

NORMAN RICH & M. H. FISHER

VOLUME I

*

MEMOIRS

AND

POLITICAL OBSERVATIONS

CAMBRIDGE
AT THE UNIVERSITY PRESS
1955

PUBLISHED BY
THE SYNDICS OF THE CAMBRIDGE UNIVERSITY PRESS
London Office: Bentley House, N.W. 1
American Branch: New York

Agents for Canada, India, and Pakistan: Macmillan

Printed in Great Britain at the University Press, Cambridge
(Brooke Crutchley, University Printer)

CONTENTS

PLATES

PREFACE

THE editors have made every effort to include in the present volumes all that is of historical significance in the Holstein Papers. The sheer bulk of the material made it necessary to make a rigid selection of the documents to be printed.

The memoirs and diaries have been cut very little; only repetitions and anecdotes of little historical interest have been omitted. A large proportion of the letters written by Holstein has also been selected for publication. On the other hand, the majority of the letters written to Holstein have been omitted. For the most part these were letters from friends in diplomatic posts outside the main stream of policy, including the small German states, or letters which add nothing further to our knowledge of the period. From the letters selected for publication, details of private life (when these did not affect policy) have usually been omitted, as well as some material that is fully covered by other document publications, such as the *Grosse Politik*. Even so, we have tried to err on the side of a generous selection. All omissions have been marked thus: [...]. Spelling and punctuation have been standardized. The correspondence has been arranged chronologically, and the date has been uniformly written at the head of each document for the sake of clarity.

We have refrained from any attempt to correct interpretations of Holstein's policy or personality current in other historical literature. Wherever necessary, we have elucidated the text by reference to the files of the German Foreign Ministry, to printed documents or memoir literature, or to works based on unpublished documents. We have tried to correct errors of fact, but apart from that, Holstein and his correspondents have been allowed to speak for themselves.

We have included in the present publication all Holstein documents of historical interest which we have found in the files of the German Foreign Ministry or in other collections deposited in the Foreign Ministry archives. When the originals of documents were found, of which there were only copies in the Holstein Papers, the text of the original has been printed. Any important textual differences have been footnoted. Whenever such documents have been used, their origin has been indicated.

In addition to the volumes here presented, we have prepared a corrected typewritten transcript of all the Holstein Papers. This, together with the original documents, has been microfilmed, and the films will be placed at the disposal of scholars by the Foreign Office in the Public Record Office in England and by the Department of State in the National Archives in the United States by stages as the material is published.

NORMAN RICH
M. H. FISHER

WHADDON HALL
BUCKINGHAMSHIRE
1954

FRIEDRICH VON HOLSTEIN IN 1906

INTRODUCTION

I. FRIEDRICH VON HOLSTEIN

FEW men in recent times can have given rise to so much speculation based on so little fact as Friedrich von Holstein. In the flood of memoir literature which swept over Germany after the First World War, there was remarkable unanimity in the way writers singled out Holstein as the evil genius in the development which culminated in Germany's defeat. The choice of scapegoat was an excellent one. The picture of a sinister intriguer, motivated by personal vindictiveness and ambition, who retained office and influence by an uncanny knowledge of diplomatic secrets if not by downright blackmail of his superiors, appealed to the popular imagination. Moreover, Holstein was dead and his papers, on which a more balanced interpretation of his policy might have been based, were not available. Historians like Johannes Haller, in his effort to restore Eulenburg's reputation,[1] or Adalbert Wahl, in his attempt to explain the downfall of the German Empire,[2] lost what remnants of impartiality and detachment they tried to preserve when writing about Holstein. G. P. Gooch's study of Holstein,[3] though free from invective and wild speculation, could not but reflect the mass of memoir evidence against him.

It was not until 1932, when Helmuth Rogge published the letters from Holstein to his cousin Ida von Stülpnagel, that reliable evidence became available for long periods of Holstein's life and work.[4] As Rogge pointed out in his introduction, a final assessment of Holstein could only become possible if his personal papers, at that time in the possession of Paul von Schwabach, were made available to historians. It is these papers which the present editors now bring before the public. Not all questions are answered

---

[1] *Aus dem Leben des Fürsten Philipp zu Eulenburg-Hertefeld* (Berlin-Leipzig, 1926).

[2] *Deutsche Geschichte. Von der Reichsgründung bis zum Ausbruch des Weltkriegs* (1871 *bis* 1914), 4 vols. (Stuttgart, 1926–36).

[3] 'Holstein: Oracle of the Wilhelmstrasse,' *Studies in German History* (London, New York, Toronto, 1948: first published 1931).

[4] *Friedrich von Holstein, Lebensbekenntnis in Briefen an eine Frau* (Berlin, 1932). The reader is referred to Rogge for a more detailed account of Holstein's life.

by them. Two sources in particular must still be fully exploited, provided they have survived the Second World War: the letters written by Holstein to Herbert and Wilhelm von Bismarck, and his letters to Paul von Hatzfeldt. But the interpretation of the material here presented can henceforth only be affected in some points of detail. It should put an end both to irresponsible and unfruitful speculation and to downright travesty of fact to which Holstein's personality and policy have been so long subjected.

Friedrich von Holstein was born in 1837 at Schwedt au der Oder, the son of a retired Prussian officer, who after the death of his first wife, the daughter of a wealthy landed family, had married her elder sister. It was this second wife who at the age of 46 gave birth to Friedrich, the only child.

For the first eleven years of his life Holstein lived in the country, with some sojourns in Berlin at the time of the 'season'. The outbreak of the revolution of 1848 caused the family to travel for several years in France, Switzerland and Italy. It was there that Holstein, privately tutored until he went to university, learned to speak and write French and Italian fluently.

In 1853 he began his studies at Berlin University, where he read law. He was rejected in his army medical examination because of a 'weak chest and general bodily weakness'.[1] The only career now open to one of his background was in the service of the Prussian state. After his final law examination, he automatically entered the civil service.

In 1860 Holstein applied for a transfer from the home civil to the diplomatic service. Bismarck already knew Holstein at this time and was prepared to further his career. Holstein's transfer was opposed by the Foreign Minister, von Schleinitz, but, supported by Bismarck, he addressed a successful appeal to the Prince Regent (the later Kaiser Wilhelm I) and in December 1860 was appointed Attaché at the Prussian Legation in St Petersburg, where Bismarck was Minister. There is no doubt that Holstein was on excellent terms with Bismarck, for the latter spoke highly of him in his correspondence;[2] in his report to the Foreign Ministry

---

[1] From the personnel files of the German Foreign Ministry.
[2] Otto von Bismarck, *Die gesammelten Werke* (Berlin, 1923–35), vol. XIV/I, nos. 815, 827, pp. 567–8, 576.

on the young attaché, he recommended him as a young man who promised to be of great use in the foreign service.[1]

Holstein left St Petersburg in 1862, passed his examinations for the diplomatic service in 1863, and was posted to Rio de Janeiro. It was Bismarck's intervention which brought him back to Europe from the unpromising South American post. He participated as a Foreign Ministry attaché in the early part of the Danish campaign, and was then sent to the London Conference, called to settle the Schleswig-Holstein question, as a member of the Prussian delegation. He remained in London on the regular Prussian diplomatic staff for over a year. From August 1865 to June 1867 he stayed in the United States, first in a private capacity, later as a member of the Prussian Legation in Washington. After his return to Europe he held several temporary posts of minor importance.

From April 1868 to 1870 Holstein took leave from the service in order to devote his time to an undertaking to provide a mechanized towing system for canal transport. In this enterprise he appears to have invested heavily. The success of the venture cannot be discovered from Holstein's papers, although his simple way of life later and the fact that he died penniless tend to show that his experiment in the world of commerce proved financially fruitless.

The outbreak of the Franco-Prussian War brought Holstein back to the diplomatic service. His duties during the war afford evidence of the high regard in which Bismarck held him, for he was immediately sent on a confidential and delicate mission to Italy, and was later attached to the diplomatic staff attending Bismarck at his headquarters in France. After the end of the war, he remained in France with the occupation authorities until, in November 1871, he became Second Secretary at the newly established German Legation in Paris under Count Harry von Arnim.

While Holstein served under him in Paris, Arnim became one of Bismarck's bitterest rivals for imperial favour, and at the same time tried to pursue an independent foreign policy with regard to France. Bismarck eventually persuaded Wilhelm I to transfer Arnim to Constantinople. Arnim was recalled from Paris in

[1] Johann Sass, 'Bismarcks Petersburger Bericht über Holstein vom 28. April 1862.' *Preussische Jahrbücher*, vol. CCXIX, pp. 232–4.

February 1874, but before leaving he removed secret diplomatic documents from the archives, which he subsequently allowed to be used in the press to attack Bismarckian policy. In the ensuing trial of Arnim for unauthorized removal of official documents, Holstein was called upon to give evidence.

Holstein's role in the Arnim case is usually described as a turning-point in his career. He is alleged to have played the part of Bismarck's spy in Paris, and the evidence he gave against Arnim is cited as the reason which caused him to be shunned henceforth by decent society. The Arnim case is said to have turned Holstein into a bitter recluse for the rest of his life.

There is no evidence in the published records of the Arnim trials[1] or in the relevant Foreign Ministry files[2] to show that Holstein's part in the affair was dishonourable, nor is there any indication that his life was much affected thereby. Holstein continued in his Paris post and enjoyed the high regard of the new Ambassador, Prince Hohenlohe. His social difficulties were no greater than those of any other German in Paris after the Franco-Prussian War, or of other convinced adherents of Bismarck at the time of the *Kulturkampf*. It was not so much that society shunned him, but that he shunned society, an attitude his father had already deplored when Holstein was Attaché in St Petersburg.

When Bismarck recalled Holstein in 1876 to work in the Foreign Ministry in Berlin, where he was to serve until the end of his career, it was not to save him from social disgrace, but because of his appreciation of Holstein's outstanding gifts. It must not be forgotten that Bismarck's bitter strictures of Holstein came from the time after his resignation, when he was savagely attacking all whom he suspected of bringing about that event. Throughout the 1870's and the early 1880's Holstein was on terms of friendship and intimacy with the whole Bismarck family. He was full of

---

[1] *Darstellung der in der Untersuchungssache wider den Wirklichen Geheimen Rath Grafen von Arnim vor dem Königlichen Stadtgericht zu Berlin im Dezember* 1874 *stattgehabten öffentlichen Verhandlungen* (Berlin, 1875).

[2] Akta betr. das gegen den K. Botschafter Grafen Harry von Arnim eingeleitete Verfahren, 9 Bde., Generalia I.A. A.a. 52; Akta betr. das Verfahren gegen den eheml. Botschafter Wirkl. Geh. Rath Grafen Harry von Arnim aus Anlass der Herausgabe der Denkschrift 'Pro Nihilo', 6 Bde. Generalia I.A. A.a. 58; I.A. A.a. 58 adhibend I & II; Akta betr. die Diziplinar-Untersuchung gegen den eheml. Botschafter Wirkl. Geh. Rath Grafen Harry von Arnim, 1 Bd., Generalia I.A. A.a. 59; Akta betr. des Verhalten des Botschafters Gf. Arnim, I.A. B.c. 75 & 78 adhibend.

admiration for the Chancellor's policy and recognized his greatness. He was trusted by Bismarck, in so far as Bismarck ever trusted anyone. The Arnim affair had not made Holstein unacceptable abroad, as has been often maintained, for he was subsequently proposed for foreign posts; but he preferred to stay in Berlin, at the centre of affairs. He had few but good friends, and he was contented in his work.

It was in the mid-1880's that Holstein's attitude toward the Bismarck family underwent a change. He was unable to understand Bismarck's policy in these years. He saw only the complication of Bismarck's structure of treaties and alliances, the apparent fickleness and rapid change in method and tactics; he failed to appreciate the singleness of purpose which lay behind them. As Holstein's respect for Bismarck's political ability waned, so his criticism of the policies as well as the personalities of Bismarck and his son Herbert sharpened. By 1886, as Helmut Krausnick has shown for the first time,[1] he had arrived at the stage where he was prepared to pursue an independent policy, in the firm belief that he was actually carrying out the Chancellor's inmost wishes, and that Bismarck, in his dotage and under the fanatically Russophile influence of Herbert, did not realize the full implications of his actions. In this activity Holstein enjoyed not only the approval but the steady support of Count Paul von Hatzfeldt in London, whom Bismarck regarded as his best ambassador. Holstein and Hatzfeldt are striking examples of Bismarck's failure to give his subordinates insight into his policy.

By this time Holstein had become the most important man in the Foreign Ministry apart from the State Secretary, Herbert von Bismarck. His voluminous private correspondence, conducted with the Chancellor's approval and often submitted to him, kept him excellently informed on matters which did not always find their way into the files. During leave periods he regularly deputised for the Under State Secretary and on occasion for the State Secretary, a sure sign of Bismarck's confidence, and he continued to do so until the latter's resignation.

To what extent Holstein contributed to Bismarck's fall is difficult to assess. As has been stated, he had gone so far in Bismarck's later years of office as to pursue an independent policy on

[1] *Holsteins Geheimpolitik in der Ära Bismarck*, 1886–1890 (Hamburg, 1942).

a number of questions. According to Waldersee and Eulenburg, Holstein had tried to obtain their help to persuade Kaiser Wilhelm II to rectify what Holstein considered to be Bismarck's mistakes.[1] Both Waldersee and Eulenburg are hostile witnesses, however, and it must be remembered that Holstein also attempted to enlist the influence of Herbert and Wilhelm von Bismarck on the Chancellor. It seems fairly certain that Holstein never systematically plotted or even desired the complete exclusion of Bismarck from all affairs of state, especially from foreign policy. After the Chancellor's fall, he tried unsuccessfully to maintain Herbert von Bismarck in his position of State Secretary.

With the increase in Holstein's personal power and influence after 1890, it was inevitable that he should have come to be regarded as one of the men primarily responsible for Bismarck's fall. Perhaps with a view to allaying such suspicions, Holstein stated at the time of Bismarck's resignation that he would never accept any advancement in rank, that is, to the posts of Under State Secretary or State Secretary in the Foreign Ministry.

The situation was thereby created that the man who was generally regarded as the only person capable of maintaining the Bismarckian diplomatic tradition, the man, in fact, who was largely responsible for the planning and direction of German foreign policy from 1890 to 1906, remained in a subordinate position. Holstein was not responsible either to the Reichstag or to public opinion. Even more important, he was in the last resort unable to control the execution of the policy he had planned or to defend it before the Kaiser.

The files of the Foreign Ministry as well as the *Grosse Politik*[2] show with what devotion and capacity for work Holstein applied himself to his task. His position was no easy one. He himself points out in his memoirs how difficult it sometimes was to curb the fantastic and at the same time infinitely dangerous ideas of Wilhelm II. Time and again he despaired of stiffening the back of responsible ministers or men who enjoyed the Kaiser's confidence sufficiently to prevent irretrievable disasters to Germany's inter-

---

[1] The evidence has been well summarized by Krausnick (*Holsteins Geheimpolitik* pp. 242–58, 271–89).

[2] *Die Grosse Politik der Europäischen Kabinette*, 1871–1914, 40 vols. (Berlin, 1922–27).

national position; and frequently he failed. He was not an easy man to work with and his personal relations with his superiors and colleagues were often strained. Successes in foreign policy were usually claimed by those nominally responsible for them; whereas failures, particularly in his later years, were attributed to Holstein. Thus grew the myth of the sinister figure behind the scenes. Yet nothing, neither advancing age nor two cataract operations, seemed to affect his industry or his will to work. The historian may frequently criticize Holstein's policies; his selfless devotion to his task must go unchallenged.

Holstein's resignation came at a time when he appeared to have reached the height of his power. Early in 1906 Chancellor Bülow agreed to make him Director of the Political Department in the Foreign Ministry, a position he had long held in fact if not in name. More important, he was given control of the Press Division. Holstein directed all the more important problems of foreign policy in close co-operation with Bülow, almost to the complete exclusion of State Secretary von Richthofen.

It was the Morocco question that brought about Holstein's downfall. He had tried to use the Morocco crisis to drive a wedge in the recently formed Anglo-French entente, but the resulting threat of war had frightened both the Kaiser and Bülow.

Holstein tendered his resignation, for he had been forced to assume from the attitude of the newly appointed State Secretary, Heinrich von Tschirschky, a temporary favourite of the Kaiser, that he had lost the Kaiser's confidence. The threat of resignation was a method Holstein had frequently used in the past to assert his influence, and, to judge from his later behaviour, he evidently did not expect his resignation to be accepted. Instead, Bülow, while confined to his bed after a collapse in the Reichstag, transmitted instructions to Tschirschky to bring Holstein's resignation before the Kaiser with the recommendation that it be accepted. On 19 April 1906 Holstein left the Foreign Ministry for ever.

Suspiciously he cast about for some explanation for his dismissal. Bülow, realising the continued value of Holstein's advice, constantly sought and freely offered until his death, managed to persuade Holstein that he had been in no way responsible. Holstein's suspicions had in any case fallen on Prince Philipp zu Eulenburg, at one time one of his closest friends, who enjoyed the confidence of the Kaiser. Many authorities have suspected that it was Holstein who subsequently furnished Maximilian Harden, editor of the political journal *Die Zukunft*, with material for his attacks on the Kaiser's entourage culminating in the celebrated Eulenburg and Moltke trials. The Holstein papers show the close relationship existing between Holstein and Harden in the last three years before Holstein's death, but there is no positive evidence that it was Holstein who provided Harden with the inspiration or material to launch his journalistic campaign.

The years after Holstein's retirement were spent, as had been almost all his life, in concentration on problems of foreign policy. Both Bülow and Kiderlen-Wächter were constant visitors and correspondents. Holstein lived long enough to witness Germany's 'triumph' in the Bosnian crisis. He died on 9 May 1909.

II. HISTORY OF THE PAPERS[1]

After Holstein's death, his collection of personal papers passed to the friend and confidante of his later years, Helene von Lebbin, née von Brandt.

'I leave no negotiable assets,' Holstein wrote in his last will and testament,[2] 'they have either been spent or become worthless. All that remains is the furniture in my flat and whatever I possess in the way of books, documents of various kinds, notebooks and memoranda; all this is left to Frau von Lebbin. To the best of my knowledge, this includes nothing that should be returned to the Foreign Ministry. On my retirement I removed everything that should have been returned. A case containing papers (letters) is in the safe-keeping of my cousin Frau von Stülpnagel-Dargitz at Karlstein bei Zehden (Neumark). Frau von Lebbin will have to claim this if it has not been sent to me in the meantime.'

Already during his lifetime Holstein had put a great many of his private papers into the hands of Frau von Lebbin for safe-keeping. It is not possible to determine the exact date when he began this practice, but his letters to Frau von Lebbin show that he was certainly doing so by 1897.[3]

[1] When not otherwise stated, this section is based on documents in a secret file of the Archives Division of the German Foreign Ministry, Pol. Archiv No. 55g, and on documents in vol. 22/15 of the Holstein Papers.

[2] The will is dated 29 December 1908, and is printed in Rogge, *Friedrich von Holstein*, p. 342.　　　　　　[3] Papers, vol. 79.

Frau von Lebbin had not been the only guardian of Holstein's papers. As early as 1884 he had begun sending his diary as well as part of his personal correspondence to his cousin, Ida von Stülpnagel. Eight days before his death Holstein had asked Frau von Stülpnagel for the return of these papers, together with a large suitcase containing letters which he had left at Karlstein since 1893.[1] These documents came into Frau von Lebbin's possession a few weeks after Holstein's death.[2]

In March 1910, the German Foreign Ministry handed over to Frau von Lebbin some letters written to Holstein while he was Attaché in St Petersburg in 1861. These had recently been found in the archives of the St Petersburg Embassy, locked in a metal box—probably the box given to Holstein by his father for his birthday in 1861.[3]

On 24 May 1913, Frau von Lebbin gave the Holstein Papers to the banker Paul von Schwabach. In her deed of donation she wrote that Holstein had made her the heiress of his 'collected manuscripts'.[4]

'Herewith I make over to you as a gift these same papers, the ones already in your keeping as well as those documents preserved elsewhere. At the same time I stipulate that a publication of Herr von Holstein's papers in whole or in part shall not take place. You will please confirm that you accept the gift on this condition.'[5]

Paul von Schwabach already had an extensive archive collection, and he had the means to take proper care of the documents. It may have been partly with this in mind that Frau von Lebbin put the Holstein Papers into his hands. In the cover letter[6] to the deed of donation, quoted above, she wrote:

'My Dear Paul,
I enclose the deed of donation duly signed. May you be granted long life and good health in order to sift these documents, sort them and put them in good order. May the task revive many happy memories. That is my sincere and heartfelt wish.'

---

[1] Rogge, *Friedrich von Holstein*, p. 340.   [2] *Ibid.* p. 343, n. 2.
[3] See August von Holstein's letter of 18 April 1861 (*Correspondence*).
[4] The original deed of donation is in vol. 17 of the Holstein Papers.
[5] Schwabach's letter of 20 May 1913 (quoted in Friedrich von Trotha, *Fritz von Holstein als Mensch und Politiker* (Berlin, 1931), p. 27) probably expresses thanks for the promise of the gift of the papers. It cannot be the acknowledgement of the gift itself, as Trotha assumes.   [6] Papers, vol. 17.

The entire collection of Holstein Papers did not pass at once into the hands of Paul von Schwabach. Frau von Lebbin, who was paralysed, had overlooked the fact that some of the letters had been left behind in a cupboard.[1] When Frau von Lebbin died, these papers, which contained the Holstein-Bülow correspondence of 1908 on the naval programme, came into the possession of her nephew, Friedrich von Trotha. Schwabach purchased these letters in order to complete his collection.[2]

The German Foreign Ministry itself was not unconcerned about the Holstein Papers. In 1913 the Japanese newspaper *Jiji* published two articles, based on the papers of the former Japanese Ambassador in London, Count Hayashi, which contained revelations on the British-Japanese negotiations leading to the alliance of 1902. The articles showed that Eckardstein, Counsellor at the German Embassy in London at that time, had been working for a German-British-Japanese alliance, directed against France and Russia. The resulting investigation in the German Foreign Ministry and in the archives of the London Embassy showed that numerous documents relating to negotiations between London and Berlin in 1901 were missing from the files. Minister von Stumm, who was conducting the search, thought that they might be found in the Holstein Papers. To Stumm's enquiries, Paul von Schwabach replied, according to Stumm's memorandum of 5 January 1914, 'that the Holstein Papers now in the possession of Frau v. Lebbin contain no documents of an official nature'.

On 3 January 1915, State Secretary Jagow ordered all papers left by Frau von Lebbin to be taken into official custody. Schwabach replied on January 15:

'Simson [Frau von Lebbin's brother-in-law and executor of her will] has written to say that he found a number of papers amongst Frau von Lebbin's effects, but he burned every single one. Will you please inform Herr von Mühlberg of this. That is the best

---

[1] This information comes from a copy of a letter of 5 July 1937 from Schwabach's lawyer, Dr Rudolf Dix, to the Gestapo.

[2] Trotha does not mention this transaction in his book *Fritz von Holstein*. In his introduction, page x, he only acknowledges the kindness of Paul von Schwabach in putting certain Holstein papers at his disposal. The information about the purchase from Trotha comes from Schwabach's widow. (Foreign Ministry Memorandum of 11 March 1941; Letter of Frau von Schwabach to State Secretary von Weizsäcker of 24 July 1942.)

solution. People have probably more urgent matters to worry about, otherwise we could perhaps make it known by a notice in one of the newspapers that no Lebbin Papers exist.'[1]

For the next twenty years Schwabach was no longer disturbed by official enquiries about the Holstein Papers.

In December 1925, the *Berliner Tageblatt* published several letters, supposedly written by Holstein,[2] which showed that Holstein had used official information to speculate on the stock exchange. Schwabach's name was unpleasantly linked with Holstein's in the affair. Schwabach made no public denial, but in a private letter to State Secretary Dr von Schubert he described his relations to Holstein—and to the Holstein Papers:[3]

'It is a fact that for some time I was very closely associated with Herr von Holstein. Before the war I kept up a regular correspondence with a number of foreign friends; we discussed important business matters, and occasionally political events. Some of these friends were in more or less close touch with their own governments. Herr von Holstein made use of this circumstance to convey unofficially to the desired quarter the German attitude on pending questions and to obtain information in return by the same method. In this he was continuing an established custom; it is well known that Prince Bismarck used my predecessors, Herr G. von Bleichröder and my father, in the same way. This was no secret between Herr von Holstein and myself; on the contrary the other responsible officials in the Foreign Ministry were aware of what went on and not infrequently called on my services in the same way [...].
There has, moreover, been a good deal of discussion, some of it quite unnecessarily heated, about the Holstein Papers, which are in my possession. The truth of the matter is: for many years Herr von Holstein was on terms of friendship with the late Colonel von Brandt and Geheimrat von Lebbin, and transferred this friendship to the lady whose name has been so often mentioned, Frau von Lebbin, who was the Colonel's daughter and von Lebbin's wife. He constituted her his heir; i.e. in addition to some household

---

[1] This information and the quotations come from two memoranda of 29 August and 14 September 1942 by Professor Rheindorf, temporarily attached to the Foreign Ministry. The original documents have not been found.

[2] The Holstein Papers throw no light on this incident, but see Thimme's view in his introduction to Trotha's book on Holstein, pp. xvi–xvii.

[3] Letter of 22 January 1926. Printed in Paul von Schwabach, *Aus meinen Akten* (Berlin, 1927), pp. 446–8.

effects of no great value he left her his Papers. Frau von Lebbin, who was already a close friend of my parents when I was still a child, and always remained a friend of mine, was worried about the fate of these letters after her death, particularly as she herself fell seriously ill soon after Holstein died and was bedridden for the rest of her days. She finally decided, in view of my connections with Herr von Holstein, to rely on my friendship and hand over the Papers to me, whilst stipulating certain conditions to govern the possible use of the Papers. These conditions I accepted on behalf of myself and my heirs. Meanwhile the news had gradually leaked out that I was the owner, or as I would prefer to put it, the custodian, and I have been repeatedly requested by publishers, historians and journalists, to allow them to make use of the Papers. It has been frequently pointed out to me that even though I may formerly have been justified in refusing, this was no longer the case now that conditions were totally different. I am myself aware that times have changed. In my opinion, however, my obligation to keep my promises has remained unchanged. Any talk there may be of memoirs written by Holstein is based on idle specula-tion. I think it highly improbable that Holstein wrote his memoirs. The fact is that I have never come across them and there is no trace of them in the above-mentioned Papers. So far as the corre-spondence is concerned, a moment's consideration and a little good-will should suffice to make it clear that I can hardly possess the letters Holstein wrote, for they are in the hands of the recipients, but only the ones sent to him. Naturally many of the writers of these letters are dead, but others are still alive, as are some of the people mentioned in the letters. I have been on friendly terms for years with so many of the correspondents and the people they mention, that I should find it most repugnant to hand over to any third party documents of this kind which were given to me on a confidential basis. I am therefore determined, in spite of friendly or unfriendly approaches, to leave things exactly as they are.'

Paul von Schwabach did indeed observe the conditions of Frau von Lebbin's bequest until 1930. In that year he gave access to the Holstein Papers to Friedrich von Trotha, the nephew of Frau von Lebbin, and to Dr Friedricn Thimme, the chief editor of the *Grosse Politik*. The documents published in Trotha's *Fritz von Holstein als Mensch und Politiker* came from the Holstein Papers, as Trotha acknowledged.[1] Thimme, in his introduction to Trotha's

---

[1] Trotha, *Fritz von Holstein*, pp. x, 27.

book, stated that he (Thimme) had been allowed to have access to the greater part of the Holstein letters, and that he hoped soon to publish Holstein's correspondence with Paul von Hatzfeldt.[1]

In 1932, Helmuth Rogge published Holstein's personal letters to Frau von Stülpnagel in *Friedrich von Holstein, Lebensbekenntnis in Briefen an eine Frau*. This book was composed of the letters addressed to Frau von Stülpnagel which she had not considered herself obliged to hand over to Frau von Lebbin in 1909.[2] In his introduction Rogge pointed out that many problems connected with Holstein remained to be solved:

'Herr von Schwabach holds the key. May he follow up this first step with a second and thus restore that significant unity which existed for decades between the contents of this volume and his Holstein treasures. Only then will the man and the part he played in Germany's fortunes be revealed.'[3]

Shortly afterward Schwabach granted Rogge's request, and in 1932 Rogge began the preparation of a complete edition of the Holstein Papers with the aid of Schwabach's daughter, Baroness Vera von der Heydt. While this work was in progress, the Nazis came to power. In 1934 Baroness von der Heydt emigrated to England, taking with her typed transcripts of some of the letters in the Holstein Papers.

On 30 April 1935 the Holstein Papers were seized by the Gestapo. Paul von Schwabach was given a receipt which read:

'Dr von Schwabach today handed over to me 210 notebooks and portfolios, which are his property and contain the Papers left by the late *Wirkliche Geheime Rat* von Holstein. I have taken over this material by order of the Secret State Police, which desires to examine it from one particular aspect. I promised that these documents would be returned to the owner as soon as they had been examined.

Berlin, 30 April 1935   TAPLICK
                                                        Krim. Ass.'[4]

---

[1] *Ibid.* p. xii.
[2] See Frau von Lebbin's letter to Frau von Stülpnagel of 11 June 1909, Rogge, *Friedrich von Holstein*, p. 343.   [3] *Ibid.* p. vi.
[4] From the private papers of Baroness von der Heydt.

In a letter of 12 July 1935, Schwabach asked for the return of the Papers:

'Dear Herr Taplick,

You obtained from me the Holstein Papers in my possession in order to discover whether they throw any light on the problem of Freemasonry. Two and a half months have elapsed since then; I therefore assume that the task is concluded, particularly as your interest was limited to the above-mentioned problem and did not extend to the remaining contents of the documents. I should be most grateful if the Papers were returned to me as soon as possible [. . .].'[1]

Schwabach was informed that the Holstein Papers were still being examined; another query by Schwabach in July 1936 seems never to have been answered.[2]

In 1937 Schwabach's legal representative, Dr Rudolf Dix, addressed a further enquiry to the Gestapo about the Holstein Papers. He was informed 'that the Holstein Papers belonging to Dr Paul Schwabach appear to the Secret State Police to be of importance, not only as historical source material but also because of the political use to which they could be put. Moreover, the systematic examination and evaluation of this material, taken over on 30 April 1935, is in no way completed, but will on the contrary still take a considerable time.' Dr Dix pointed out that these Papers represented a valuable asset, and that Schwabach (who was 'non-Aryan') had never in any way threatened the interests of the German Government by the use he had made of them. He therefore voiced Schwabach's plea 'to restore the Papers to him after the completion of this task and meanwhile to give him an assurance that there shall be no publication or commercial exploitation of these Papers without his consent.'

The Foreign Ministry does not seem to have had any knowledge of the action taken by the Gestapo until, in April 1939, it received a letter from the publishing firm of E. S. Mittler and Son asking permission for Rogge to finish his edition of the Holstein Papers.

'Ever since 1933 the publishing firm of E. S. Mittler and Son has been negotiating with Dr Paul von Schwabach, owner of the Papers left by the *Wirkliche Geheime Rat* von Holstein. It

---

[1] From the private papers of Baroness von der Heydt.   [2] *Ibid.*

was intended to publish these Papers, edited by Reichsarchivrat Dr Helmuth Rogge. The preliminary work for this publication had reached the stage at which Dr Rogge had made a complete set of transcripts of these Papers.[1] As has been established, these Papers were confiscated by the Secret State Police during the lifetime of Dr Paul von Schwabach, who has since died. Presumably the documents are still in their custody [...].'

The Foreign Ministry now asked the Gestapo to hand over the Holstein Papers in their custody, in view of their close connection with secret diplomatic documents. The Secret State Police acknowledged the Foreign Ministry's claim and in August 1939 placed at its disposal the confiscated documents. There never seems to have been any intention of handing the Papers over to Dr Rogge, although the suggestion was put forward that an official publication of the Holstein Papers be made.

Meanwhile Paul von Schwabach's widow, who was 'Aryan', tried to get compensation for the Holstein Papers from the Foreign Ministry. She based her claim on the expenses which had been incurred by her husband while the Papers were in his possession. According to Frau von Schwabach, 10,000 marks had been paid to Trotha for his part of the Bülow-Holstein correspondence, and an annual pension of 12,000 marks had been paid to Frau von Lebbin. The claim lapsed with the death of Frau von Schwabach. Her heirs were 'non-Aryan' and to them there could be no question of payment by the Nazi Government.

After the capture of the files of the German Foreign Ministry by the Allied armies in 1945, the Holstein Papers were claimed by Baroness von der Heydt and were made available to the present editors.

III. THE DOCUMENTS IN THE HOLSTEIN PAPERS

The Holstein Papers may be roughly divided into four parts: memoirs and political observations; diaries; political memoranda; and correspondence.

MEMOIRS AND POLITICAL OBSERVATIONS

Holstein seems to have begun his memoirs with the idea of an autobiography in mind, but personal history soon gave way to

---

[1] The copies made by Dr Rogge were never found, and it is unlikely that a complete set of transcripts was ever made. The copies in the possession of Baroness von der Heydt form only a small part of the complete Papers.

Holstein's real muse, politics. The greater part of the memoirs is therefore not an account of Holstein's career, or personal memoirs at all, but rather a collection of recollections and reflections on politics and political personalities.

The Papers contain memoirs written during three periods of Holstein's life. The earliest memoir, dated 26 January 1883, is only a fragment which begins a description of Holstein's career as Attaché in St Petersburg. The later memoirs are much more substantial bodies of material. The second group, according to internal evidence, must have been written in 1898, and the final group was written after Holstein's dismissal in 1906.

There is considerable repetition in the memoirs, due no doubt to the long intervals between their composition. There are, for instance, three separate accounts of Holstein's service in St Petersburg. Holstein's several versions of an incident differ factually very little from one another. The most significant variation is the change in the point of view toward Bismarck. The tone of admiration of 1883 had changed to one of bitter criticism in 1898. This in turn gave way to a more balanced judgement after 1906. (See Appendix I.)

The various essays which make up Holstein's memoirs are anything but closely knit, and the essays themselves are nothing like the tightly reasoned memoranda Holstein used to prepare for official use. Holstein himself best described them while apologizing for a long excursus in one of his later writings: 'These essays of mine do not treat one single theme; they aim at reproducing, not in any logical sequence, but simply as they come into my head, those impressions of my life which have remained clear in my memory [...].'

DIARIES

When Holstein began his diplomatic career as Attaché in St Petersburg, Bismarck warned him that keeping a diary was incompatible with diplomatic discretion. For this reason, Holstein says, he kept no diary during the early part of his career.

In 1881 Holstein jotted down some of Bismarck's anecdotes in a bound notebook. By 1882 he had begun to use this notebook to record day-to-day events. There are large gaps in the entries. Nothing was written from April to November, 1882, and there are no entries at all after 27 March 1883. Only about half of the notebook was ever filled.

In 1884 Holstein began the custom of sending his diaries to his cousin, Ida von Stülpnagel. These diaries were written on loose sheets of paper, and continue reasonably consecutively from January 1884 through 1887, when they gradually thin out. There are no entries after 11 November 1888. In the letters written by Holstein to Ida von Stülpnagel during the years 1884 to 1888, references are made to these diaries.[1] After 1888 these references cease, and it seems probable that none were written after that date.

The Papers contain a second set of what might be called diaries, dating from 10 December 1901 to 13 November 1902, and 27 October 1906 to 14 December 1907. These are much more fragmentary than the earlier diaries and consist largely of political jottings. Since they lack all continuity in themselves, they have not been published as a body, but, in so far as they are of historical interest, under the appropriate dates with the correspondence.

POLITICAL MEMORANDA

The great bulk of Holstein's writing was for official use. His official memoranda went into the files of the German Foreign Ministry, as would be expected, and many of them have been printed in the *Grosse Politik*. A few which apparently did not pass through the official channels of the Foreign Ministry were found in the Papers. Those of historical interest have been printed under the appropriate dates with the correspondence.

CORRESPONDENCE

Letters form the largest part of the Holstein Papers (70 out of 91 volumes as filed by the Foreign Ministry). At the time the Foreign Ministry took over the Papers they contained 2809 letters and telegrams addressed to Holstein, and 275 drafts or copies of letters and telegrams sent by him. The Papers contain no letters preserved by Holstein himself earlier than 1880. The editors have found no explanation for this gap.

The greater part of the letters in the Holstein Papers come from regular correspondents like Paul von Hatzfeldt, Herbert and Wilhelm von Bismarck, or Bernhard von Bülow. From this

---

[1] Rogge, *Friedrich von Holstein*, pp. 135, 144, 148.

regular correspondence it is possible to see that the collection of letters in the Papers is by no means complete. Nearly all of Holstein's correspondence was political, and much of it was passed into the files of the Foreign Ministry. Some of this correspondence was printed in the *Grosse Politik*, but a great deal remains buried in the Foreign Ministry archives. The editors have searched these archives for Holstein letters, but owing to the enormous mass of the material cannot be sure that all of them have been found.

Many letters in the Papers bear the request 'burn' or 'destroy after reading'. It seems certain that some letters were in fact destroyed. There is also the obvious gap which occurred when the presence of the correspondent in Berlin made letter-writing unnecessary.

Not all the gaps can be accounted for by natural reasons. Some sections of the Holstein correspondence were removed by historians before the Papers were confiscated by the Gestapo. Thimme, for instance, probably removed the Hatzfeldt-Holstein letters of 1897–9 when working on his study of Hatzfeldt.[1] Attempts by the German Foreign Ministry to recover this correspondence after Thimme's death remained fruitless. In view of Thimme's publication in the *Berliner Monatshefte*,[2] it is possible that the Radolin-Holstein correspondence during the first Morocco Crisis shared the fate of the Hatzfeldt-Holstein letters.

Finally the possibility must be reckoned with that Holstein himself edited his Papers. After his dismissal he spent considerable time in going through them. In the process he may have destroyed many letters or even entire segments of correspondence. The document collection as left by Holstein may consist only of what he wished to be found.

[1] See above, p. xxi.
[2] 'Aus dem Nachlass des Fürsten Radolin. Fürst Radolin, Holstein und Friedrich Rosen,' *Berliner Monatshefte*, vol. xv, pp. 725 ff., 844 ff.

ACKNOWLEDGEMENTS

We wish to thank:

Baroness Vera von der Heydt, the daughter of Paul von Schwabach, for permission to publish the Holstein Papers on her behalf, and for turning over to us those transcripts of the Holstein documents she had placed for safe-keeping in the hands of Sir Harold Nicolson and Mr John W. Wheeler-Bennett.

Mr E. J. Passant, Director of Research, Librarian and Keeper of the Papers at the Foreign Office, and Dr G. Bernard Noble, Chief of the Historical Division of the State Department, who obtained the consent of their respective Governments as joint custodians of the German Foreign Ministry documents, amongst which the Holstein Papers were found, for us to have access to them in order to prepare this edition.

The Honourable Margaret Lambert, British Editor-in-Chief of the *Documents on German Foreign Policy*, Dr Paul R. Sweet, American Editor-in-Chief, and Mr K. H. M. Duke, head of the British team engaged on the publication, for much encouragement and valuable advice.

Mr John W. Wheeler-Bennett for bringing us into contact with Baroness von der Heydt and for his constant support; Dr G. P. Gooch for his advice and great kindness to us; Professors Raymond J. Sontag, Conyers Read, Bernadotte Schmitt and William L. Langer, who have given us valuable support and encouragement.

Mr R. J. L. Kingsford, Secretary to the Syndics of the Cambridge University Press.

Among those who actively assisted us in the preparation of this work, we thank especially Dr Fritz Fischer for his help in preparing the German edition; Mrs Joan Rich, who made the index; Mr R. W. Tillack for his work in preparing the typescript; Mr G. K. Meister, head archivist for the German Foreign Ministry documents, who helped us to search the files for additional Holstein material; and the American Philosophical Society for a grant which materially assisted in the publication of these volumes.

We particularly wish to thank Mrs Joan Spencer for her work and co-operation in preparing the English translation.

MEMOIRS AND POLITICAL OBSERVATIONS

THE FIRST PAGE OF THE MEMOIRS

The writing habits of a whole official career are carried over even into this personal composition; a wide margin has been left blank for annotation by a ministerial hand.

CHAPTER I

ST PETERSBURG
1861-1862[1]

Meeting with Cavour. Journey to St Petersburg. Bismarck. Frau von Bismarck. Bear-hunting. Bismarck's status at the Court of the Tsars. The function of the Prussian Legation. Count Adlerberg. Schlözer, Croy and Loen. Social unrest in Russia. The Russian Court. Nesselrode. Goltz.

AT the beginning of December 1860, while I was travelling in Italy, news reached me of my appointment as an Attaché to our Legation in St Petersburg. On my way back to Berlin I stayed a few days at Turin where I had friends. I was introduced to Cavour,[2] a short, thick-set, bull-necked man with a faintly sarcastic expression and a pair of spectacles which would have incurred Goethe's disapproval. The shape and carriage of his head, and the searching glance he gave you over the top of his spectacles, occasionally resembled Bill Bismarck[3] in later life.[4] [...]

---

[1] The chapter-heading is the editors'. See Appendix I.

[2] Camillo, Count Cavour. Head of the Sardinian Government, 1852–9, 1860–1.

[3] Wilhelm, Count von Bismarck. In the Prussian Judiciary Service, 1874–9; temporarily attached to the office of the Governor of Alsace-Lorraine, September 1879–80; an official in the Reich Chancellery, 1881–2; *Regierungsrat*, mostly on the staff of the Chancellor, October 1882–4; *Vortragender Rat* in the Prussian Ministry of State, May 1884–5; *Landrat* in Hanau, August 1885–9; Head of the administration of Hanover, March 1889–95, for the province of East Prussia, 1895–1901.

[4] In a letter to Giovanni Lanza of 8 December 1860 Cavour wrote of Holstein's visit: 'Il barone Holstein, giovane diplomatico prussiano che farà parte della Legazione prussiana a Pietroburgo, ottene il permesso di fare un viaggio in Italia prima di recarsi in Russia, e sta compilando un rapporto sulle nostre condizioni attuali. Non potendo recarsi a Napoli, egli manifestò il desiderio d'esser posto in relazione con lei, per conoscere il vero stato delle cose colà [...]. Importa che il barone Holstein riporti a Berlino ed a Pietroburgo giudizi rassicuranti sulla possibilità di fondare nella penisola un ordine di cose regolare e durevole. A ciò gioveranno moltissimo i discorsi ch'egli terrà con una persona così autorevole come il Presidente della Camera dei deputati; ed è questo principalmente il motivo che mi induce a recarle questo disturbo, e ad avvertirla confidenzialmente delle tendenze aristocratiche e dei pregiudizi germanici del barone Holstein. [...]' Luigi Chiala, *Lettere edite ed inedite di Camillo Cavour* (Turin, 1885), vol. IV, pp. 111–12. There are a number of Holstein's notes on political and economic conditions in Italy in 1860 amongst the Holstein Papers. They contain no personal reminiscences.

On 2 January 1861 I set out from Karlstein[1] and, together with my late father, returned to Berlin before travelling to St Petersburg to take up my duties as an attaché. At the station we learnt that the King was dead.[2]

A few days later I took my departure. An hour or two before I started, my manservant left me in the lurch. He told me he was afraid the climate would be too much for him, and that he preferred to remain behind and get married.

In those days the railway went no further than Stallupönen, so from there to Wirballen I took the usual yellow postchaise.

As I was sitting in the custom-house at Wirballen with my eight pieces of luggage, feeling rather bewildered and helpless, I noticed a pleasant-looking gentleman who spoke both Russian and German and appeared very inclined to make my acquaintance. I placed no obstacles in his way, and he turned out to be Herr Alex von Harder, Stieglitz's[3] nephew. We decided to join forces, which proved an excellent arrangement for us both. He enjoyed the advantage of riding in my special courier's compartment, *podoroschny*, and I was even more fortunate in that he made all arrangements for interpreters and so forth at the halts. I subsequently found that an interpreter was not so absolutely indispensable as I had imagined. At each posting station, even if we arrived in the middle of the night, there would appear from nowhere one or more of those inevitable Jews with a knowledge of German and a readiness to perform any service required.

In Wirballen I realized I had entered a new world. I felt I had left Europe far behind. Our luggage was tastefully arranged on the sleigh, with my largest trunk serving as a seat. In front stood the *Jämschtschik* in his long sheepskin coat, urging on the four galloping horses with words and with blows. By the same means, his voice and his stick, he cleared the peasants out of our way. They obeyed readily enough; only on one occasion, when we had a really tiny *Jämschtschik*—he looked like a boy of thirteen—did a peasant decide to give a rude reply. We drove fast, about twelve and a half miles an hour, but this was offset by a considerable waste of time at the halts. There are no buckles on Russian har-

---

[1] Karlstein near Zehden-on-the-Oder. The estate owned by Holstein's aunt, Minna von Holtzendorff.

[2] Friedrich Wilhelm IV, King of Prussia, died on 2 January 1861.

[3] Alexander, Baron von Stieglitz. Director of the Russian Imperial Bank.

nesses; everything is knotted. The posting stations, like the railway stations, are nearly always outside the towns. Both highways and railroads in Russia are perfectly straight.

For the first few hours the motion of the sleigh along the undulating track made me seasick. Then I felt tired. With no support to my back I should have slipped off my trunk time and again if Herr von Harder had not held on to me. This monotonous journey started at midnight and lasted until 2 p.m. a couple of days later. After thirty-eight hours we stopped outside Dünaburg station. The only incident I recall is a halt towards 10 p.m. to order a drink of tea and a bite of food at a reasonably respectable inn at Wilkomir. Harder conversed in Russian with the Polish landlady. I could tell by his expression that she had made some unpleasant remark. She had in fact replied to his request for some tea: 'You can make it yourselves.'

When Harder translated this to me I immediately declared we could not possibly let such a brazen creature serve us with supper. So we drove on. At the next halt there was nothing to be had. On reaching the next halt at three in the morning, absolutely famished, we ate black bread with butter tasting like axle-grease, and washed it down with a schnapps.

Later, when going on leave at Christmas, 1861, I had a similar experience to that in Wilkomir. I was staying at the inn at Kovno, and sent for the barber early in the morning. The boots came back with the message: 'Barber says he not go to Prussian man, Prussian man can come to him.' Both episodes revealed the attitude of the Poles, which was to find expression in the insurrection.

During the railway journey from Dünaburg to St Petersburg I found myself for the first time in my life in a train blocked by the snow. But not for long. In just under an hour the track was cleared. As we were sitting there helplessly I heard a peasant make some remark as he went by which caused amusement. Harder translated it as: 'Yes, mate, I mayn't go so fast but I get there in the end.'

At eight in the morning I reached St Petersburg and drove to the Pension Benson on the English quay, close by Stenbock House, where Herr von Bismarck[1] lived.

[1] Otto von Bismarck-Schönhausen, Count in 1865, Prince in 1871. Prussian Minister to the Federal Diet in Frankfurt, August 1851–9; Minister in St Petersburg, April 1859–62, in Paris, May–September 1862; Minister-President and Foreign Minister, 1862–71; Chancellor of the German Reich, 1871–90.

I well remember announcing my arrival. As a child I had seen Bismarck once or twice at my parents' home. He was young and jovial then. Later I met him in Wiesbaden in 1859 when he was recuperating from a severe illness. In 1860 my father, who had been against my choosing a military career and realized I was not cut out for the law, asked me whether I would like to be a diplomat. I answered, 'Yes, if Bismarck will take me on as an attaché.' He was approached, gave his consent, and subsequently pushed through my appointment in defiance of von Schleinitz's wishes.[1]

Now, when I presented myself, he held out his hand and said, 'You are welcome.' As he stood there, tall, erect, unsmiling, I saw him as he was later to appear to his family and the rest of the world: 'A man who allows no one to know him intimately.'

Bismarck then introduced me to Schlözer,[2] the Second Secretary, who was sitting at a table working. A spare man of about forty with a sharp nose and little beady eyes. He has since told me that I asked him what he was doing. When he said he was ciphering I replied, 'I hope I don't have much of that to do.' I have forgotten all this, but I do remember how Schlözer's face took on an even more mournful expression than usual.

As I walked back from the Legation to my pension along the quay, I was conscious perhaps for the only time in my life of a feeling of homelessness, or homesickness, as they say. In front of me stretched the broad Neva, with the east wind driving across its frozen surface flurries of finely powdered snow that gave a slight tinkle as it fell. That oddly pale Nordic light, making the gilded cupolas on the churches look like silver. Instead of human forms, walking sheepskins. An un-European quality in much that met the eye. And then the cold; not merely the thirty degrees out of doors but also the frosty welcome of my chief, which I, young,

---

[1] Alexander von Schleinitz, Count in 1879. Prussian Foreign Minister, summer 1848, 1849–50, 1858–61; Minister of the Royal Household, 1861–85. Schleinitz had refused Holstein's request for a transfer from the judiciary to the diplomatic service. The transfer was finally granted after an appeal to the Prince Regent. (Cf. Rogge, *Friedrich von Holstein*, pp. 17–18.)

[2] Kurd von Schlözer. Secretary of the Legation in St Petersburg, 1857–62; temporary Chargé d'Affaires in Copenhagen, 1863; Secretary of the Legation to the Holy See, 1864–9; Consul-General of the North German Federation in Mexico, 1869–71; Minister in Washington, 1871–82, to the Holy See, 1882–92. (Cf. his *Petersburger Briefe* (Stuttgart and Berlin, 1921), p. 187.)

inexperienced, straight from home, had imagined would be totally different.

At that time Bismarck was forty-five, slightly bald, with fair hair turning grey; not noticeably corpulent; sallow complexion. Never gay, even when telling amusing anecdotes, a thing he did only occasionally, in particularly congenial company. Total impression one of a dissatisfied man, partly a hypochondriac, partly a man insufficiently reconciled to the quiet life led in those days by the Prussian representative in St Petersburg. His every utterance revealed that for him action and existence were one and the same thing. 'The 1848 revolution must have been a harassing time for you', I once said to him. 'There was so much to do that there was no time to feel harassed', was the reply. On another occasion he recalled the parliamentary struggles of that period and said: 'Yes, in the days when you appeared every week in the *Kladderadatsch*[1] you really were somebody.'

The main attraction of this Frankfurt period for him had been the fact that it was one of constant strife.

His behaviour in public is perhaps best illustrated by the following little incident, which I may as well mention here. One day Herr von Bismarck and I had been out hunting and arrived at the Peterhof station just as the train was about to move off. The officials made signs to us and shouted 'Hurry up there!'. I, in obedience to authority, at once started to run. On reaching the carriage door and looking round I saw the Minister approaching at a most leisurely pace. The train waited. As he got in, Bismarck said, 'I'd rather be late ten times over than have to run once.' Bismarck's whole person was calculated to impress, and he knew it. The idea that his behaviour might give offence to those of his colleagues of less prepossessing appearance did not trouble him in the least. 'Your chief always reminds me of an ancient Roman; all he wants is a toga', I was told one day by the Vicomte Moira, the Portuguese Minister, an amiable but entirely insignificant-looking fat man, who can certainly never have impressed anyone.

Bismarck's attitude to the diplomatic corps as such was one of indifference. He probably found most of his *confrères* boring; at all events he reduced his points of contact with them by usually spending his evenings at home. [...]

[1] A humorous German weekly, devoting considerable space to politics.

He certainly did not lead a healthy life. He ate only one meal a day, but then, as is well known, he ate and drank very heavily. The fact that he was able to continue this mode of life up to about 1880, that is, until he was over sixty-five, shows how well equipped he was, physically as well as mentally, to sustain exceptional demands. But there is no doubt that the black moods to which Bismarck was so frequently a prey were due as much to physical as to mental strain. I have scarcely ever known anyone so joyless as Bismarck. When he was at the height of his intellectual powers one received the impression that he was always striving towards some goal, and putting behind him all past achievements. In earlier life, particularly in his Frankfurt days, he used to be passionately fond of hunting. When I went to St Petersburg he would still hunt, but not often, and when he became Minister-President his other interests gradually obliged him to give it up altogether.

He kept a peculiar household. During the year and a quarter I served under him, Bismarck gave not one single dinner. Schlözer, at that time a perpetual fault-finder, declared that a dinner Bismarck had given shortly before my arrival, in honour of the Saxon and Danish Ministers, had been a complete failure. Plessen, the Dane, a notorious gourmet, scarcely touched anything, but at the end of the meal he said, 'Please may I have some more cheese.' But this was one of Schlözer's pieces of exaggeration. I can well believe that the dinner was ill-balanced, because Bismarck took no interest in food and Princess Bismarck,[1] although she looked like a cook all her life, had not the slightest knowledge of how to cook, or at any rate how to give dinner parties. But they had quite a good chef, and their everyday diet was more copious than that of any other household I know, in fact they ate more than was good for the average digestion. There was so much food that one or two guests could arrive at the last minute without causing any embarrassment. A limited number of people, including Captain (now General) Erckert, the young Württemberg Minister, Spitzenberg, and any of the Balts who happened to be in St Petersburg—Keyserlingk, Üxküll, Öftingen, Hase—had a standing invitation; one or two others, e.g. Fieldmarshal Count Berg,[2] were asked to a meal when they came on a visit, without neces-

[1] Johanna von Bismarck, *née* von Puttkammer.
[2] Friedrich, Count Berg. Governor of Finland.

sitating any alteration in the arrangements. In those days I was young and a hearty eater, but I was amazed at the amount Bismarck could eat, and still more at what he could drink; I was also astonished at the time we spent at table.

When the conversation turned on political questions past or present, I listened with uncritical attention, without grasping their inner connection. But Bismarck was also fond of speaking about his youth and his student days, about his experiences in 1848 and the Frankfurt period. One listened to the same stories over and over again. They were always stories in which Bismarck figured as the hero, while the other characters usually appeared in a ridiculous, and at times a despicable light.

The note of true gaiety was lacking, so that the laughter was always at someone's expense. Once, for example, a passing cavalry officer was billeted on Bismarck in Kniephof, and was invited out to dine with a neighbour. But beforehand Bismarck had a few drinks with the lieutenant who, being unable to carry his liquor as well as his host, was soon three-quarters drunk. Description of their appearance at the party, Bismarck cool and correct, the officer reeling from side to side. Description of the hospitable neighbour's look of reproach and the horror displayed by his wife. The fact that the day had been ruined for several people was not of the slightest importance to Bismarck. All he saw was his own triumphant progress.

But his flow of speech became positively vitriolic if the story concerned someone he disliked, as for example the Hanoverian Minister Count Münster.[1] The latter had once reported to his government a politically indiscreet remark made to him by Bismarck when out hunting. From Hanover the remark had been passed on to Berlin, and Bismarck had received a reprimand from Schleinitz, which, though not comparable in form and content with the subsequent 'rockets' of the Bismarckian era, was nevertheless bitterly resented by its recipient, who became Münster's enemy. From that day Bismarck painted Münster in the darkest colours, and in particular declared he was a traitor and a liar. As

[1] Georg Herbert, Count Münster, Baron Grothaus; from 1899 Prince Münster von Derneburg. Hanoverian Minister in St Petersburg, 1856–64; from 1867 hereditary Member of the Prussian Upper House; Member of the Reichstag, 1867–73 (*Deutsche Reichspartei*); German Ambassador in London, 1873–85, in Paris, 1885–1900.

evidence of his falsehoods Bismarck would quote a hunting tale worthy of Baron Münchhausen, which Münster was supposed to have told of himself. When Bismarck told this story for the second time to the English First Secretary, Savile Lumley, whom he knew from Frankfurt days, Lumley screwed his monocle more firmly into position and said, 'The story has improved.' It is typical of Princess Bismarck that, quite unaware of its sting, she repeated Lumley's remark and thought it very witty, as indeed it was. [...]

He said quite openly that his salary did not permit him to do much entertaining. Consequently he would hardly ever accept luncheon invitations himself. Similarly he was seldom out in the evening. The only Russian salon he frequented now and again was the one held by Countess Antoinette Bludov,[1] where the guests talked politics. Otherwise he held himself strictly aloof from Russian society. After dining at five o'clock he usually remained at home reading newspapers or studying maps. I can only speak from personal observation, but I rarely saw him reading a serious book. Once, I remember, he read a volume of eighteenth-century memoirs with which I too was familiar. For some time he quoted from it constantly without acknowledging his source, with the result that he gave the impression of having studied a complete body of literature. Even so he had certainly retained a great deal from that single book.

Abeken says in his memoirs[2] that Prince Bismarck must at some period of his life have read very widely. And Bucher[3] told me that when Bismarck was living in solitude in the country he read Spinoza and various similar authors. But one day Bucher expressed a different view: 'Bismarck obtained most of his solid political knowledge from the memoranda and the protocols of the Federal Diet and the Prussian Ministry of State. They contain a great deal of information, if only you can remember it.' Bismarck possessed a prodigious memory and also accomplished much by solitary reflection. Since his assumption of office he read very few serious works but read novels for mental relaxation.

---

[1] Daughter of Count Dmitri Bludov, President of the Russian Senate.
[2] Heinrich Abeken. In the Prussian Foreign Ministry from 1848; *Vortragender Rat*, 1853–71. See *Heinrich Abeken, Ein schlichtes Leben in bewegter Zeit, aus Briefen zusammengestellt*, edited by Hedwig Abeken (Berlin, 1898).
[3] Lothar Bucher. *Vortragender Rat* in the Foreign Ministry, 1864–86.

He was not understood by St Petersburg society; it occasionally made fun of his striking stiffness of manner and resultant air of constraint which formed such a contrast to the Russian ease and urbanity, and it dismissed him as *peu homme du monde*. One day Frau von Bismarck said to him, 'Otto dear, whatever was the Tsar saying to you yesterday evening? You were standing there looking so worried.' 'I was not aware I was worried', he replied, evidently upset by her remark.

Frau von Bismarck, like her husband, was a peculiar person. The only attraction she could boast was a pair of arresting dark eyes. She had dark hair too, which revealed the Slav origins of the Puttkamer family. She was entirely devoid of feminine charm, attached no importance to dress, and only lived for her family. She exercised her quite considerable musical talent merely for her own enjoyment, though Bismarck liked to listen when she played classical music such as Beethoven. In society her speech and behaviour were doubtless not always appropriate, but she moved with a calm assurance which prevented her from ever appearing ill at ease or uncertain of herself. Her husband let her go her own way; I never once saw him take her to task. During the thirty years of our acquaintance I heard him rebuke her only twice. On the first occasion she had invited to Countess Rantzau's[1] wedding two ladies whom he considered socially unsuitable. The second incident occurred soon after, about 1880. The Chancellor, on coming in to a meal, was met by his wife with the words, 'What *do* you think, Otto dear! X—I can't remember the name—has just called and said I shouldn't have repeated certain things, because it may cause trouble.' Prince Bismarck answered indifferently, almost with a smile, 'It's not the first time people have said you sometimes render my task even more difficult.' She made no reply and the subject was dropped.

Bismarck displayed considerable nobility of character in the way he bore with his wife's inept behaviour, which was at times appalling. He never winced at it, but would on rare occasions gently admonish her. Even though he did not move much in society it seems hardly credible that he can have failed to notice his wife's blunders. It was most probably the conviction that he

[1] Marie, Otto von Bismarck's daughter, was married in November 1878 to Kuno, Count zu Rantzau.

could never bring his wife to mend her ways, coupled with his disdain for mankind, which determined him to let well alone. And it was part of Bismarck's strength of character to remain true to that decision.

When she lived in St Petersburg, Frau von Bismarck (as she was then) was a great friend of a certain Frau Berteau. (Despite the French name her husband was a German from the Baltic provinces.) She and Frau von Bismarck would drive round in a little droshky every morning to buy their household provisions. This was thought odd and no doubt raised a smile, but the complete indifference displayed by the Bismarcks impressed people nevertheless, particularly as they knew how high the Minister ranked in the Tsar's estimation. On Bismarck's arrival in St Petersburg Alexander II began to invite him to a small bear-hunt he held every week during the winter; he was the only diplomat included in the party.

These bear-hunts had first come into fashion with the opening of the railway linking St Petersburg and Moscow. Work on it was begun in the days of the Tsar Nicholas I. Taking a pencil and ruler—I have often heard Bismarck tell the story—the Tsar drew a straight line from Moscow to St Petersburg, thus marking out its course. The greater part of it, to the north, ran through marshy woodland. The cost of construction was so enormous that after its completion the accounts were burnt by order of the Tsar. This railway opened up a vast hunting ground and there arose among the peasants living in those lonely forests a new branch of commerce—bear-trading. With the first fall of snow the bear, as is well known, seeks out a place to hibernate in the dense undergrowth, and if disturbed only moves a mile or two away, so that it is not difficult to encircle him in his second lair. Here he remains until the thaw, and thus becomes a commodity with a market price, which is governed by the proximity of the lair to the railway and by the size of the bear's footprint. The deal is concluded either in the villages by means of a travelling agent, or in St Petersburg if some enterprising peasant makes his way there at his village's expense. The customers are the Court Hunt and various diplomats or foreign merchants; the Russians themselves, with their dislike of any kind of physical exertion, find bear-hunting too arduous. Between paying for your bear and hunting him there may well be a lapse of some months. During this interval the Court usually assigns, or rather used to assign, one Court huntsman to every bear purchased. He took up his quarters in the nearest village and from there he had to keep a close watch all round the lair to make sure the bear had not been disturbed and broken away. Provided the bear remained where it was until the thaw it fetched its price, even though no hunt took place. I was able to establish from an isolated case that honesty was not always the rule. Shortly before the end of the winter of 1862 the Master of the Imperial Hunt, Count Fersen, offered me the right to hunt a bear which the Court Hunt was no longer interested in. If the bear was sighted I was to pay for it; I was also to pay the beaters but of course not the Court huntsman in charge. Being of a suspicious nature I took with me a Russian servant with some knowledge of hunting. After the beaters had vainly attempted to rouse the animal my man went right round the lair on snow-shoes, and proved beyond a doubt that there had never been a bear inside at all. So no bear was paid for. My putting a stop to this trickery just before the end of the season was particularly unfortunate for the Court huntsman and the villagers concerned, who would have divided between them the price of the bear a few weeks later.

The Tsar set out for the hunt once a week on Tuesday evenings with a small retinue in attendance. On Wednesdays they encircled two lairs as a rule, and the Tsar usually shot the bears himself. Sometimes, when there was no bear available, a lynx brought for the purpose in a sack was let loose and shot down from a tree. When Bismarck was first in St Petersburg he received invitations to these hunts as a mark of the Tsar's particular favour. But they ceased when the heads of other missions, especially the French Ambassador,[1] complained to Gorchakov[2] about the way Prussia was singled out.

The discrepancy between Bismarck's actual status in St Petersburg and the conception formed of it in Berlin on the strength of his dispatches seemed to me remarkable. It was thought in Berlin —indeed the notion persists to this day—that Bismarck enjoyed the personal favour of Alexander II and that of the Court in general.

[1] Count Montebello. French Ambassador in St Petersburg, 1858–64.

[2] Alexander, Prince Gorchakov. Russian plenipotentiary at the German Federal Diet in Frankfurt, 1850–4; Minister in Vienna, 1854–6; Foreign Minister, 1856–82; Chancellor, 1870–82.

11

This was by no means the case. It is true that immediately after his arrival in St Petersburg the Tsar invited him once or twice to the Imperial Hunt on Tuesdays. But the French and Spanish[1] Ambassadors immediately lodged a complaint and from that time Bismarck was treated strictly in accordance with the rules of etiquette, which were nowhere applied more rigidly than in St Petersburg at that period. Bismarck saw the Tsar just as often as the other Ministers; whether at these encounters the Tsar spoke to him longer than he did to the rest I cannot say. [...]

Now, as I set it down, I find it barely comprehensible that the Danish, Saxon and Hanoverian Ministers should have aroused if not greater respect, at any rate greater attention in Russian society than Bismarck—and yet it was so. The main reason was that all three were married to Russian women of rank, whereas Frau von Bismarck's personality was an effective barrier to any kind of social intimacy. [...]

There was a complete transformation in Bismarck's status the day a report from the Russian Legation in Berlin proclaimed him as 'the coming man'. From that time the rigidly impartial code of diplomatic etiquette ceased to apply in his case. He assumed a position apart and suddenly found himself in the full blaze of Court favour.

Bismarck made a point of taking daily exercise, either on foot or on horseback. The Russians dislike both riding and walking. The climate, the snow and the mud all have contributed to this distaste for physical exercise felt by the inhabitants of the Empire of the Tsars. Certainly the young Horse-Guards officers of my day usually kept more coach-horses than saddle-horses in their stables. It never occurred to the common people, either, that anyone could take a walk for his health, still less for pleasure. One evening I was walking home from the theatre with Schlözer, who entirely shared my views on exercise, when a droshky travelling in the opposite direction turned round on seeing us and pulled up beside us by the kerb. The coachman undid the covers without saying a word; he took it for granted that we would get in. As we walked by, the coachman called something after us in a politely ironic tone. Schlözer translated it as: 'Have you two fellows gambled away all your money?'

[1] Duke of Ossuna. From 1858 Spanish Minister, then Ambassador in St Petersburg.

When I arrived in St Petersburg our Legation there had far more work to cope with than any of the other Prussian missions. The bulk of this work was non-political. As there was no consulate *de carrière* we were also responsible for most of the work normally dealt with by a consul. In addition there were far more reclamations in Russia than elsewhere. These were protests lodged by Prussian subjects who felt they had been unfairly or unlawfully used. [...]

Bismarck's predecessor,[1] so I was told, used to treat these complaints from Prussian subjects as a very secondary matter, but he himself took up the cudgels for every single case regardless of whose susceptibilities he offended. In this way he antagonized Grand Marshal Count Adlerberg, one of the most powerful figures at Court. Count Adlerberg senior was a perfect example of the licentious old man. Opposite the Adlerberg palace stood Madame Burkov's house. She was a German whom the old man had picked up in Hamburg and had married to a Captain Burkov; on the wedding-day he was promoted major and posted to Siberia. She had set up a glove-shop somewhere in the town and spent part of each day there. If anyone had a request to make of Count Adlerberg he first went and bought a pair of gloves from Madame Burkov at fifty roubles—or even more, according to circumstances—and told her what he wanted. If she was satisfied with the transaction, her customer received next day a correspondingly cordial hearing from the Grand Marshal. Even so this glove-shop cannot have proved a sufficient source of income, for Madame Burkov took steps to supplement it by introducing into her house gambling for high stakes. Her clients were members of Russian society, and the diplomatic world and their actress friends. One evening Schlözer took me there but Bismarck advised me afterwards not to go again. He also took the opportunity of telling me that German merchants in St Petersburg had refused to deliver to Madame Burkov except against cash payment valuable commodities they had procured from abroad at her request, whereupon Madame Burkov had driven up to their door with Count Adlerberg to compel them to deliver.

[1] Karl, Baron von Werther. Prussian Minister in St Petersburg, 1854–9, in Vienna, 1859–66, 1866–9; Ambassador of the North German Federation in Paris, 1869–70; German Ambassador in Constantinople, 1874–7.

The Grand Marshal was himself not over-particular about meeting his financial obligations, and thus came into conflict with Bismarck. Adlerberg had sent to Prussia for a number of labourers and artisans but had then failed to stand by the terms agreed upon. The people sought help from our Legation. Bismarck first tried to set things right through official channels. When he met with no success he went direct to the Tsar and in this way the trouble was smoothed out. It was quite obvious to me that Adlerberg had not forgotten this rebuff when I watched him talking to Bismarck one evening at a reception given by the French Ambassador. Bismarck was discoursing amiably to him, but the old man stood there hardly listening and looking distinctly bored and ill-humoured. Ten minutes later I saw Adlerberg talking to the Third Secretary of the French Embassy, his expression transformed to one of cheerful affability. Even a novice like myself could tell that Bismarck had made an enemy of Adlerberg. But such was Bismarck's standing with the Tsar that he could afford to ignore any hostility he aroused.

The Second Secretary, Herr von Schlözer, proved indispensable in the dispatch of the great mass of reclamations and other non-political work. The First Secretary, Prince Georg Croy,[1] was Bismarck's own choice, an unfortunate one as it turned out, because as Attaché in Paris and Secretary in Naples he had been unable to acquire the technical routine necessary to the First Secretary in St Petersburg. Schlözer, on the other hand, had spent seven years as an official in the non-political division of the Foreign Ministry, and so had a thorough grasp of technicalities; indeed he brought to non-political matters, which he had worked at for years, a greater interest than he did to politics, which Bismarck regarded as his province in any case. But without Schlözer to ease the burden he would hardly have found time for politics. Bismarck frankly acknowledged this to me, but without disguising the fact that Schlözer sometimes tried his patience. [...]

Realizing that he needed Schlözer, Bismarck showed greater forbearance than he received, for Schlözer was constantly complaining behind his chief's back, constantly criticizing his lack of conformity with the way of life proper to career diplomats. Schlözer became an admirer of Bismarck after the event. I should

[1] First Secretary in St Petersburg, 1859–62.

be surprised if his numerous letters, which must surely be published sooner or later, did not show that *until after Sadowa*
Bismarck's policy was a complete mystery to him. One evening
after Bismarck had been dictating to me before and after dinner,
I went out into the street and there met Schlözer. 'And how is
Otto?' he asked. I replied, 'At the moment he's reading the
newspapers with a map spread out on his desk.' 'Oh yes, the silly
chap's busy remodelling the map of Europe.'

A year or so later, when I was in Berlin from the end of 1862
until the spring of 1863, to take the examination for the Diplomatic Service, I met Schlözer again. He had not been appointed
First Secretary in St Petersburg as he had hoped, but had been
summoned to Berlin to work temporarily in the Foreign Ministry.
The impact of his personal disappointment may well have rendered his criticism of the Minister-President even more biting
than before. I can still see the spot, between the corner of the
Wilhelmstrasse and the Brandenburger Tor, where he said to me
on 1 April 1863, 'When God made Otto he made April fools of
us all. I'll admit that Otto is an effective parliamentary debater,
but in his knowledge of politics he is not to be compared with men
like Gneist,[1] Twesten,[2] and Virchow.[3] Otto has no enthusiasm
for Schleswig-Holstein. Otto just hasn't got the right touch and,
what's more Otto is a liar.' [...]

Politically Schlözer remained a racy raconteur to the end of his
life. Bismarck once said to me in our St Petersburg days: 'Thun[4]
(the Austrian Minister) knows what he's doing when he invites
Schlözer so often.' Then followed some remark about the way
good wine would loosen Schlözer's tongue.

From 1863 to about 1869 I lost sight of Schlözer. In the sum-

---

[1] Rudolf von Gneist. Jurist; Member of the Prussian Chamber of Deputies,
1858–93; Member of the Reichstag, 1868–84. During the Prussian Ministry's
conflict with the Diet, he sided with the liberal opposition; later he joined the
National Liberals.

[2] Karl Twesten. Municipal Court Judge; from 1861 Member of the Prussian
Chamber of Deputies; one of the leaders of the Progressives; in 1866 co-founder
of the National Liberal Party; from 1867 Member of the Reichstag.

[3] Rudolf Virchow. Professor and Director of the Pathological Institute in Berlin;
from 1862 Member of the Prussian Chamber of Deputies; one of the founders and
leaders of the Progressives; Member of the Reichstag, 1880–93.

[4] Friedrich, Count von Thun-Hohenstein. Austrian Minister to the Federal
Diet in Frankfurt, 1850–2; Minister Extraordinary in Berlin, 1852–7; from December 1859 Minister in St Petersburg.

mer of 1861 when he was Chargé d'Affaires, he wrote a stirring dispatch on the Sino-Russian Treaty of Amur[1] which he hoped would create a great effect in Berlin. But Bismarck, who had read this report in the Foreign Ministry, told me later: 'If a *Geheimrat* reads that sort of thing he will say to himself, "the man's cracked".' Bismarck had put me on to Schlözer to learn the necessary official jargon and I had absorbed the various expressions and connecting phrases so familiar to Schlözer as an experienced official, such as 'with reference to', 'in pursuance of', 'shortly...furthermore...in conclusion'. But I did not always win Bismarck's approval. I can still remember his reproof: 'This sort of style "furthermore he pulled up his nether garments and in conclusion buttoned them"— seems to me too verbose; it could be more concisely put.' [...]

Our Military Attaché was Colonel von Loen,[2] quite useless as a soldier but convinced he was an accomplished courtier because he paid compliments right and left, sometimes with unfortunate effect. Wishing to say something about dreamy eyes to La Grua, the singer, a big-boned woman with a moustache but with lovely eyes, he expressed himself like this: '*Madame, vos yeux me font toujours bâiller.*' At this she turned round and asked someone: '*Qui est-ce que ce nigaud-là?*'

On another occasion the Junoesque figure of a certain lady was being discussed. '*Oui*', said Loen, '*je voudrais être son Holopherne.*' Loen's kindness was purely verbal. I never heard of him lifting a finger for anyone. '*C'est un égoïste fieffé*', Bismarck once said to me.

Of the two secretaries at the Legation I much preferred Croy as an acquaintance and so I relied on him for the necessary training in the elements of official routine. But after a few days of this Frau von Bismarck told me her husband had sat up the evening before until midnight correcting my drafts, which technically had all been quite useless. She said I ought to be guided more by Schlözer because Croy, knowing nothing himself, was incapable of teaching anyone else.

So I turned to Schlözer and found him, despite his unattractive personality, a useful instructor in office routine, which was very extensive before the establishment of a consulate *de carrière*.

[1] The Treaties of Aigun, 1857, and Peking, 1860.
[2] Leopold, Baron von Loen. Prussian Military Attaché in St Petersburg, 1858–65.

My arrival in St Petersburg coincided with a period of political thaw. The removal of the rigid oppression of Tsar Nicholas released in the educated and semi-educated classes of Russian society a great surge of liberal enthusiasm and produced a crop of insults to the dead Tsar's memory. His statue had to be protected by an Imperial Guardsman because it had been defaced and covered with satirical verse. I was staggered at the expressions used in my presence by Horse-Guards officers and staff cavalry captains still in their twenties. I was to remember them many years later on hearing this remark from a man very familiar with Russian conditions: 'There are no royalists or conservatives in Russia. The institution of the Tsars stands in a democracy about as securely as an obelisk set in butter.'

The winter and spring of 1861 saw a period of lively political agitation in the university towns of St Petersburg, Charkov and Warsaw. [...] The St Petersburg students staged demonstrations and riots which had to be quelled by the military though without the use of fire-arms. One day a captain von Erckert in the Moscow regiment (he later became a Lieutenant-General), who often dined with Bismarck, told how a captain of the *Preobrachenski* regiment had been ostracized (nowadays we should say 'boycotted') by his comrades for ordering his company to use the butt ends of their rifles against the students. Erckert was a man of cool and sober judgement and I have no doubt of the accuracy of his account. It came to my mind again this summer, forty-five years after the incident described, when I read that a battalion of the *Preobrachenski* regiment had been degraded because of its unreliability.

In its early stages the 1861 agitation was academic and liberal in tone and expressed sympathy with the Poles. The Russian Government also met the Poles half-way. The Grand Duke Constantine[1] was sent to Warsaw as governor and the Polish margrave Wielopolski[2] appointed to work with him as head of the civil administration. But the Polish Action Party demanded the restoration of the Polish Empire as it had existed before 1772 and opened hostilities by means of armed mobs and summary

---

[1] Brother of Alexander II. Governor of Poland, 1862–3.

[2] Alexander Wielopolski hoped by a policy of collaboration with the Tsarist régime to regain for Poland her constitutional status of 1815.

executions. Thus the liberal element was allowed by the Poles, and consequently by the Russians, to be overshadowed by the national element. The Grand Duke Constantine and Wielopolski, the representatives of the policy of reconciliation, disappeared from the scene after the Poles had made attempts on their lives, and were replaced by a military administration. Meanwhile Katkov[1] had launched his powerful Russian nationalist press campaign.

I will only mention one personal recollection of that period. When Wielopolski came to St Petersburg to report to the Tsar immediately after his appointment he had a long conference with Bismarck. Bismarck had pointed out that the demand of the Polish Action Party for the restoration of Poland as it was before 1772 gave rise to territorial claims which neither Russia nor Prussia was prepared to meet. Wielopolski allayed his fears by saying that the claims of the really influential Polish groups were very moderate, and that, for example, they would not demand ports like Danzig or Elbing; in fact the prospect of that happening was very remote. Bismarck recounted the essentials of the conversation immediately afterwards, and I believe that Wielopolski's remark was engraved in his memory. [...]

Apart from one or two great receptions in the winter palace there was in my day no contact between the younger diplomats and the Court. We never received invitations from the Grand Dukes. The presentations were very tedious. Instead of arising naturally out of some Court reception as they do elsewhere they were arranged singly by each Grand Duke or Grand Duchess, who had an especial fondness for requiring one's presence in the middle of the day. We had to drop what we were doing, put on our uniforms and go and answer the usual questions in company with a handful of other secretaries or attachés. 'How long have you been here?' 'Do you know Russia at all?' 'Where were you before?' and so on. Even an interesting topic becomes monotonous through repetition. Once, when the Grand Duchess Michael (Princess of Baden by birth), a small, dark, good-looking lady, asked me, 'How long have you been in Russia?' I decided to introduce a slight variation and replied: 'Six weeks, your Imperial Highness, but I can only count three of them because the

---

[1] Michael Katkov. Russian publicist; ardent nationalist and champion of absolutism.

other three weeks I was ill.' A few days later Frankenstein,[1] an Austrian, told me that after the presentation the Grand Duchess had said she thought my reply impertinent because she had not been inquiring after my health. If, as I rather suspect, Frankenstein had hoped to annoy me, he achieved the opposite effect. Since then I have often had success with this psychologically interesting Court anecdote, which lent colour to the rumours that the entourage of her Imperial Highness had a far from easy time. In later years particularly, when the Grand Duke Michael was governor at Tiflis, the noble lady's difficult temperament was apparently often a force to be reckoned with in the more restricted Court circle. The view is generally held in Russia that the effect of Russian conditions on the German character is to develop it along much harsher lines than the more pliable Russian temperament.

I had arrived in St Petersburg after the German and before the Russian New Year celebrations. Shortly after my arrival I was presented at the New Year reception.

I cannot say that the Russian Court appeared to me impressive, at least so far as the masculine half of the company was concerned. The army of Court officials with their fat paunches and pasty, puffy faces without a moustache (which was forbidden) looked like a set of eunuchs. The ladies, in contrast, wearing their *kokochniks*, looked splendid. The Tsar was hardly an imposing figure with those bulging eyes of his. The Tsarina looked pale, ill, faded and joyless with not a trace of the radiant beauty she once possessed. [...]

My position did not bring me much into contact with the royal family. There was also an incident which contributed to my being ignored. I may as well mention it here even though it took place later, also at a reception. The Tsar and Tsarina were spending an evening with the diplomatic corps. Next to Bismarck stood the Swedish Minister Wedel-Harlsberg. The Tsarina was conversing with him and the Tsar was talking to Bismarck. Because of my office, I was standing behind Bismarck, so that I could not help overhearing the Tsarina asking the Swede, ' *Comment se porte votre femme?* ' Wedel was too embarrassed to reply. His wife, after a marriage which he himself had rendered an unhappy one, had died some months before and the announcement had been sent to

---

[1] Karl, Baron von Frankenstein. Second Secretary in the Austrian Legation in St Petersburg.

2-2

the Court and the diplomatic corps. *'Comment se porte votre femme?'* the Tsarina repeated. *'Elle est morte, Madame.'* Her Majesty, realizing how great was her *gaffe*, retrieved the situation as well as she could and inquired after his wife's last moments and the cause of her death, but both of them felt extremely uncomfortable.

As we were leaving I told Bismarck and Schlözer what I had heard.

A week or so later the Tsarina sought out Bismarck at another Court function and said: 'I thought you were too good a friend of mine to repeat any stupid remarks I may make.' He replied, 'I hardly venture to follow your Majesty.' 'But of course you do', she said. 'I mean that foolish remark of mine to Wedel. Baroness Meyendorff[1] tells me you have been repeating it.' He replied, 'Then Frau von Meyendorff has told another of her falsehoods. To begin with I did not overhear what passed. I had it from an attaché with very good ears, who was standing close by. But so far as I know he never visits the Baroness.'

When Bismarck told me of this I remarked, 'Well, I suppose it may be part of my duties always to be the scapegoat. I'm sure the Meyendorffs had the tale from Schlözer, who often goes to see them, but the Tsarina will go on thinking I am the culprit.'

'What a mistaken view of things you have', said Bismarck. 'A young man like you is fortunate if the royal family so much as notices his existence.'

I never saw the advantage, for from that day neither the Tsar nor the Tsarina ever spoke to me.

I experienced nothing else interesting enough to be recorded, because a young beginner like me had no social intercourse with people of note. I should just like to mention that, at a dinner given by Baron Stieglitz, Bismarck introduced me to the former Imperial Chancellor Count Nesselrode.[2] It was his diplomacy which had led to the Crimean War. He was born some eighty years before on board an English ship on the Tagus, and baptized according to the rites of the Church of England, to which he remained faithful all his life. A tiny little man, whose figure, head, and thin old man's voice came back to my mind in 1871 when I had occasion to

---

[1] Baroness von Meyendorff, *née* Countess Buol. Wife of the Russian diplomat, Baron Peter von Meyendorff.

[2] Karl Robert, Count von Nesselrode. Russian Chancellor, 1844–56.

observe and listen to Thiers.[1] Bismarck jokingly introduced me as a 'diplomat of the future', to which Nesselrode replied, 'In the future there will be neither diplomacy nor diplomats.' Nesselrode never lived to see how little his remark applied to Bismarck's career. He died a few months later and the funeral took place in the English chapel. Before he died he received a visit from the Tsar, an honour bestowed only on the highest dignitaries. Such visits, coming as they do only after the doctors have given up a case as hopeless, are said so to alarm the patient that they sometimes hasten his end. After coming out of the dying man's room the Tsar exchanged a few words with his son, Dmitri or Dim Nesselrode. Although well advanced in years he was generally regarded, even in St Petersburg, as a ne'er-do-well. The fact that not even his father's powerful protection had succeeded in procuring him a place tells strongly against the son. When the Tsar had gone Dim told an acquaintance who had called for news of his father: 'I was in a cold sweat lest the Tsar should wish to go into my room. Little X from the ballet is sitting there helping me to while away the hours of my father's illness.'

Nesselrode died, so far as I remember, early in 1862. From about that time Bismarck began to be bombarded with Russian attentions, so that even an ingenuous creature like myself could not help thinking that something extraordinary had happened or was about to happen. I imagine that the Russian Minister in Berlin[2] had reported that Bismarck had been designated as future Minister-President. The uninitiated, like myself, only knew that he was shortly to become the German Minister in Paris and that Count Goltz,[3] the Minister in Constantinople, would be his successor in St Petersburg. Goltz arrived soon after. But Bismarck's departure was delayed for four or six weeks because of complications which had arisen in Berlin. The resulting situation was most unpleasant for the two rival statesmen—as they certainly were at that period. The new Minister was completely overshadowed by

---

[1] Louis Adolphe Thiers. Chief of the Executive Power of the French Republic, 1871; President of the Republic, 1871–3.

[2] Andreas, Baron von Budberg. Minister in Berlin, 1851–6, in Vienna, 1856–8, in Berlin, 1858–62.

[3] Robert, Count von der Goltz. Prussian Minister in Athens, 1857–9, in Constantinople, 1859–62, in St Petersburg, 1862–3; Minister, then Ambassador in Paris, 1863–9.

his predecessor, who was regarded by the Russian Court as the coming man. Goltz had a small suite at the Legation where he took all his meals, after which he would have long discussions with Bismarck.[1] As I listened I had the impression that there were few questions on which they agreed. Count Goltz was the typical energetic *Landrat*, commonplace in appearance, self-possessed and yet awkward in society. He had a loud voice and in particular a very penetrating laugh which later in the Court circles of the Empress Eugénie earned him the nickname of '*La-joie-fait-peur*'. With qualities such as these he cut a poor figure beside Bismarck. The one thing they had in common apart from their self-assurance was the fact that neither of them had started his career as a diplomat. Goltz had risen in seven years or so from being a journalist and junior judge to the position of Minister in St Petersburg. Manteuffel[2] had made Goltz Minister in Athens because he was the best and most ruthless writer of the Old Liberal or *Wochenblatt* Party. Bismarck was fond of relating how Goltz visited him in Frankfurt one day while still a free agent, just to inveigh against everything and everybody. As he left, Goltz had to cross the courtyard, where an extremely fierce watch-dog barked furiously at him. Bismarck, still under the influence of their conversation, called down from the window: 'Goltz, don't bite my dog!'

In Athens, where there was nothing to do, Goltz developed an attitude of respectful adoration towards Queen Amalia, just as he did later on in Paris towards the Empress Eugénie. Irreverent attachés maintained that Goltz regarded it as one of his diplomatic duties to become a distant adorer of the first lady of whatever country he was in. This frame of mind influenced his political judgement too. Thus he imagined everything in Greece was perfect, and specifically sent a report to the effect that King Otto's position was very secure. In 1859[3] Baron Werthern-Beuchlingen,[4] who was later Minister in Munich for many years, was sent to

---

[1] In his 1898 memoirs Holstein writes: 'Immediately after my arrival in St Petersburg Bismarck had expressed the view that keeping a diary was incompatible with diplomatic discretion. I obeyed this hint and now I regret it, particularly because of the conversations Bismarck and Goltz used to have after meals round the fire.'

[2] Otto, Baron von Manteuffel. Prussian Foreign Minister and Minister-President, 1850–8.   [3] Should be 1860.

[4] Georg, Baron von Werthern-Beuchlingen. Prussian Minister in Athens from January 1860–2, in Munich, 1867–88.

Athens; he reported that the attitude of the Greeks towards King Otto was very far from loyal and that the King's position was extremely precarious. Goltz, whom these reports reached in the form of circular dispatches, took it almost as a personal affront that Werthern should assess the situation in Athens differently from his predecessor. Nor did Goltz attempt to restrain his criticisms; Werthern's political blindness was a theme I heard him constantly reverting to in the spring of 1862. However, in October of the same year the Greeks rid themselves of their King quite bloodlessly and painlessly, as if he were a tooth that had worked loose; they simply turned him out. So Werthern was proved right. It is common knowledge that from 1863 to 1866, during Count Goltz's term as Ambassador in Paris, he found himself constantly at variance with Bismarck over every question under discussion. I was unaware of these disagreements at the time, but I did hear from a member of the Paris Embassy that in those days Goltz said repeatedly: 'The man is wrecking my German programme.'

In later years Bismarck told me that the Empress Eugénie was perfectly well aware of the influence she wielded over the German [sic] Ambassador, and that she treated him with coolness or with friendliness according to the political requirements of the moment. This never failed of its effect.

In 1863 both the Polish and the Danish questions became acute. French, English and Austrian diplomacy supported Poland, while Bismarck remained resolutely on the side of Russia. Goltz would have liked to cast the Emperor Napoleon in the role of mediator, but Bismarck stood out against this, so the diplomatic campaign launched by the Cabinets of London, Vienna and Paris ended in victory for Russia.

As regards the Danish question, Goltz was of the opinion that Prussia ought to side with the Federal Diet in support of the claims of the Duke of Augustenburg,[1] while Bismarck would hear nothing either of the Federal Diet or the Duke, but adhered to his plan that any steps he took against Denmark should be dependent on Austrian co-operation.

Goltz's plans were neither new nor original, conditioned as they were by outside influences, whereas Bismarck went his own

[1] Friedrich, Duke of Augustenburg. Pretender to the Duchies of Schleswig and Holstein.

way—indeed for years he was in almost complete isolation. At that time I was hardly in a position to form my own opinion of Bismarck's policy, but I considered him a man of extraordinary abilities and with the blind faith of youth I felt sure he would make everything come right in the end. I was more or less alone in that view. Even the majority of the Conservatives had their own plans which they thought superior to Bismarck's. Thus when I was in Paris in January 1864 a Westphalian landowner, who had taken part in the 1849 campaign in Baden with the eighth Uhlan regiment, said to me: 'Now we're actually mobilizing. What sort of a policy do you call that? Of course Napoleon will take a hand to make sure he gets something. We should have armed the people of Schleswig-Holstein and then sat back and watched the fun. That was the right thing to do.'

In extenuation of such a remark by a man who was by no means a fool I must point out that the French were in those days firmly convinced that no frontier changes could be made in Europe without France's wishes being taken into consideration. Individual Frenchmen liked discussing this question with us Prussians and did so in the most friendly manner. They asserted that a discussion of outstanding differences between France and Prussia certainly need not lead to war, but that the east and north-east French frontier fixed at the Congress of Vienna was unnatural and must be adjusted at the earliest opportunity.

It was fortunate for Bismarck that his real significance, like that of the Prussian army, was completely unappreciated both inside and outside Germany. Not until 1866 did the world realize the truth about these two mainsprings of German greatness.

I shall deal later with foreign evaluations of the Prussian army. A characteristic example of the opinion held of Bismarck at this period is the advice given him by the Empress Eugénie when he took leave of her to become Minister-President in Berlin: if in the future he should be faced with knotty parliamentary problems, he was to consult Rouher,[1] for he was a man of immense resource (*l'homme aux expédients*). These words of the Empress have not, I think, been revealed before. I have them on the joint testimony of two men on the staff of our Paris Legation in 1862.

[1] Eugène Rouher. Minister of State and main Governmental speaker in the Corps Législatif, 1863–9.

CHAPTER II

THE WAR AGAINST DENMARK
1864[1]

Holstein assigned to Prussian headquarters. Bismarck and Wrangel. Clermont-Tonnerre: his views on the Prussian and Austrian armies. Loë as Military Attaché in Paris. Status of France and Prussia in England.

IN February 1864 I was sent to assist Minister-Resident Wagner,[2] who was to accompany the headquarters of the allied armies. The Austrians sent the Minister Count Revertera.

On the eve of our departure Bismarck sent for Wagner to give him final oral instructions. I waited downstairs in the Foreign Ministry. When Wagner came down he said in some excitement: 'The Minister-President told me: "I thought it over for a long time before advising His Majesty to march his troops into the Duchies. But now Prussia has entered the territory she must stay there even if it means another war."'

Our headquarters were at Flensburg. I arrived there far from well. The transition from the height of the Brazilian summer[3] to the icy winter of North Schleswig had been too sudden for my throat. I was obliged to go carefully for a day or two and was unable to accompany Wagner when he went to report to the Field-Marshal.[4] He returned in very low spirits. This is how he described the scene: the Field-Marshal had received him surrounded by the royal princes and the whole of his vast military staff. When Wagner presented himself the Field-Marshal replied: 'Tomorrow we transfer our headquarters to Hadersleben, but you are to stay here—you diplomats are out of place in military headquarters. But you can write to me, my boy.' And with that Wagner was dismissed.

---

[1] The chapter-division and the chapter-heading are the editors'. See Appendix I.

[2] Emil von Wagner. Minister-Resident in Mexico.

[3] Holstein had been Secretary in the Legation in Rio de Janeiro from June to November 1863.

[4] Friedrich von Wrangel. Commander-in-Chief of the Prussian and Austrian forces in the war against Denmark, 1864.

I said to him: 'In my opinion, Herr von Wagner, your duty is to remain with the headquarters to which the King assigned you, so long as they don't post a sentry at your door to prevent your getting out.'

Herr von Wagner did not agree—he thought he would put himself in an impossible position if he disregarded the Field-Marshal's order. He dispatched an attenuated version of events to Berlin but agreed to my writing privately to someone in the Foreign Ministry[1] to describe what had really happened. Next morning the headquarters moved north, but Wagner and I remained behind, I for my part very glad to recuperate.

This was the time when the conflict between Bismarck and Wrangel was at its height. From a military point of view, Wrangel saw no reason why the Prussian contingent should not march on Jutland. The Austrians had received orders to remain in Schleswig for the present. This only strengthened Bismarck's political objections to an isolated Prussian advance on Jutland. There had in consequence been a protracted disagreement between the Minister-President and the Field-Marshal. Finally the latter—just at the time when Wagner reported—had written or telegraphed to the King: 'All diplomats should be hanged.' This imitation of the Blücher manner was unsuccessful. The King had a sufficiently clear grasp of the situation to side with Bismarck. Wagner and I learned of the turn of events from a telegram which ran something like this: 'His Majesty is astonished that you have not remained with headquarters, to which he assigned you. You will proceed there immediately. Field-Marshal receiving direct instructions from His Majesty.' These direct instructions were in fact a sharp reprimand.

Wagner was very taken aback. He prepared himself for an atrocious reception. I, too, felt rather depressed, for this decision had come too soon. I should have been very glad of a few more days to recover. But we set off, and during the journey Wagner reflected on the best way of parrying the inevitable explosion of the Field-Marshal's fury.

When we reached Hadersleben I went to bed while Wagner went to see the Field-Marshal. He came back radiant. 'The Field-Marshal's a charming man. I didn't see *this* side of him the

---

[1] Probably Limburg-Stirum. Cf. diary entry of 25 January 1884 (*Diaries*).

first time. He came straight up to me and said: "Well, my boy, and where have you been all this time? I shan't let you run away again!"' The royal reproof had worked. Henceforth all was harmony.

I should like to insert here a remark Prince Bismarck made to me one day in the 'seventies: 'The way a man appears to other people vitally affects his position in society. Old Wrangel, for instance, is a most cultured and intelligent man with a great fund of learning. Yet he behaves like a clown, and is taken for one. In contrast, Eberhard Stolberg, who is not very intelligent and is a complete ignoramus, does know how to handle people and has in consequence been able to achieve a good position wherever he went.'

Count Eberhard Stolberg, a former cavalry officer, came into prominence chiefly as a result of his successful command of the *Johanniter* in the Danish War. Finally he attained the goal of his efforts and desires. He became Head of the administration for the province of Silesia. Opinion differed on his performance there, and Prince Bismarck's criticism may well have been an echo of judgements formed of him in Silesia.

I was not in a position to form my own view of the Count's administration of Silesia, but during the Danish War I was able to see with my own eyes the admirable functioning of the *Johanniter*, which he had organized.

The most interesting figure in the entire headquarters was, I thought, the French Military Attaché, Major Count Clermont-Tonnerre. He had been through the war in Italy as the Emperor's aide-de-camp. I learned later that he had lost this position as a result of malicious gossip. An unfavourable comment supposedly made by his wife, a Latour du Pin, about certain people at the Imperial Court, was the alleged cause of his being exiled to Berlin. A likeable man who made no secret of the fact that he was there to observe. In my view these observations went far towards confirming the Emperor Napoleon in his opinion that of the two great Powers Austria was a much more formidable military force than Prussia. The Austrians had sent only their crack troops to Schleswig, and their commanders sought for results in reckless onslaughts, '*Raufen*' as the Austrians say. In the encounter at Oeversee on 6 February the Austrians lost five hundred men quite unnecessarily, according to Prussian critics, because they simply charged straight ahead without any manœuvring. General Gablentz[1] required the same procedure of the cavalry, in spite of the quickset hedges which rendered cavalry movement practically impossible. One day Gablentz asked the commander of the Hussar Regiment—Colonel Nostitz I believe—'Well and how are things going?' He replied: 'It's pretty difficult, your Excellency.' 'Difficult, is it?' Within a week the regiment had a new Commander, Colonel Count Pejacevic—thirty-three years old, I was told—the same who later lost an arm in the war in Bohemia. This served as an example to the entire corps, and showed clearly what was expected. The Austrians behaved as if they felt the eyes of the whole of Europe were on them. Their recklessness and dash made a most favourable impression on the onlooker. Clermont-Tonnerre admired them and compared their spirited attack with the caution displayed by the Prussians, who preferred flanking tactics rather than throwing away human lives. One day Clermont-Tonnerre had been watching a minor encounter at Veile, during which the Prussian flanking column had taken hours to work its way round. Meanwhile the General Staff, who were looking on, felt bored. When the flanking column did go into action the Danes beat a hasty retreat; there was not one dramatic moment. Later I was told by Clermont-Tonnerre: 'The flanking movement was executed rather slowly. Your troops are good and obedient; they do as they are told. But the Austrians, ah, *they* have one of the best armies in the world! It took us all our time to beat them. I can still remember how on the evening of the Battle of Magenta[2] the Emperor was sitting with his staff in the Church at Buffalora. We all felt rather depressed, and the most we dared hope was that the French army would hold its positions. Quite late one of MacMahon's[3] adjutants came and announced his successful advance. Since then, as I can see more clearly every day, the Austrians have learnt a lot from us.' What pleased him most, as I have said, was the reckless attack of the Austrians.

He also criticized the bearing of the Prussian officers on the battlefield. He told me repeatedly: 'The way your officers expose

[1] Ludwig, Baron von Gablentz. Commander of the Austrian troops during the war in Schleswig-Holstein.

[2] 4 June 1859.

[3] Marie Edmé de MacMahon. Marshal of France; President of the French Republic, 1873–9.

themselves during the fighting, not merely by always placing themselves at the head of their troops, but also by remaining standing when their men are lying flat, shows that your army has not waged a major war since the introduction of precision weapons. The rule in the French army is that no officer shall expose himself without good cause. Your officers are still out for personal exploits. After a six or seven months' war you'll scarcely have any officers left.' Similarly the needle-gun won only his qualified approval. 'It may do very well for your soldiers who are so calm and obedient. It does not suit the French temperament. Our troops would very soon use up all their ammunition. Moreover the needle-gun has a range of only 500 metres or so, but our Minié gun has a range of 800 metres. Thus for a distance of some 300 metres we could spread disorder among your attacking columns, whereas you would still not be able to touch us.'

Clermont-Tonnerre also regarded the Austrian artillery as superior to the Prussian. He claimed that the French artillery was of quite outstanding quality. He spoke particularly, and enthusiastically, of an eight- or twelve-pounder that was so light that it only needed four horses to pull it.

When writing to Paris Clermont-Tonnerre probably expressed himself with even greater freedom than to me, representing as a fact the superiority of the Austrian army over the Prussian army. In so doing he undoubtedly influenced Napoleon's political attitude from 1864 until Sadowa. If he had not been convinced of Austria's greatly superior strength, Napoleon would hardly have undertaken to remain neutral in the event of an Austro-Prussian war, as he did at his meeting with Bismarck at Biarritz in 1865,[1] and he would certainly have prevented the alliance between Prussia and Italy.

After my return from America in 1867[2] I heard Bismarck relate more than once that when the royal train was due to leave for Reichenberg on 30 June 1866, he watched with some excitement to see if Clermont-Tonnerre, whose presence he desired in case he wished to get in touch with Paris, would appear.

But at the last moment Clermont-Tonnerre begged to be

[1] See Bismarck, *Die gesammelten Werke*, vol. v, no. 190, pp. 307–11.
[2] From December 1865 to April 1867 Holstein served as Attaché in the Prussian Legation in Washington. He returned to Germany in June 1867.

excused. Bismarck's comment on the incident was: 'The Emperor Napoleon disliked the idea that the representative of the French army might be involved in a great Prussian rout.'

The feeling that France had only just—and at great risk— succeeded in bringing her war with Austria to a fairly successful conclusion persisted not only with the Emperor Napoleon but also in the minds of many other Frenchmen.

Austria, supported by the sympathies of the non-Prussian Governments in Germany, which had been restrained with difficulty from participating in the war in Italy, appeared a greater danger than did an isolated Prussia. Clermont-Tonnerre used to justify the Peace of Villafranca by the following argument: France had attained her war aims—'*Nous avons doublé l'épaisseur du matelas qui nous sépare de l'Autriche.*'

I was surprised to see from the *Reminiscences* of Field-Marshal Baron von Loë[1] (p. 89) that the French Minister of War Count Randon[2] had informed him as early as mid-June that Count Clermont-Tonnerre would not be taking part in the campaign. The Emperor Napoleon had withheld his consent because he had also withheld it from the Military Attaché in Vienna, Colonel Merlin.

It appears doubtful whether Lieutenant-Colonel von Loë (as he was then) reported to Berlin what the Minister for War had said (p. 90). For he goes on to describe how on 30 June when the royal train was about to leave for Reichenberg Clermont-Tonnerre's name was called, but he was nowhere to be found.

Prince Bismarck was dissatisfied with Lieutenant-Colonel von Loë because he had deserted his post in Paris in order to take part in the war as aide-de-camp in the Imperial retinue. He was particularly displeased because after Sadowa von Loë had disregarded the urgent requests of Count Goltz and of Bismarck himself by remaining with headquarters instead of returning to Paris. In 1867 after my return from America I was one of a small company who heard the Federal Chancellor (as he then was) relate that he had spoken to Lieutenant-Colonel von Loë more or less in these

---

[1] Walther, Baron von Loë. Prussian Military Attaché in Paris, 1852–3, 1863–6; Colonel of the Regiment of the King's Hussars, 1870; from 1879 Adjutant-General to Wilhelm I; from 1884 General in command of the 8th Army Corps; later Field-Marshal. Holstein is referring to von Loë's *Erinnerungen aus meinem Berufsleben 1849 bis 1867* (Stuttgart and Leipzig, 1906).

[2] Jacques Louis, Count Randon. French Minister of War, 1851, 1859–67.

words: 'As Military Attaché in Paris you are my subordinate, and it is as your superior that I am issuing this reprimand, because you absented yourself unnecessarily from your post where you were urgently needed.' His words are clearly imprinted on my memory. Military Attachés have always striven to make themselves completely independent of any political control. It is obvious that such independence is harmful to political interests; the observations of these Military Attachés are of immediate significance for the direction of political as well as military affairs. Bismarck blamed Loë for the fact that the full extent of French unpreparedness was not realized at the crucial moment, that is during the peace negotiations at Prussian headquarters. Goltz had given a too favourable impression of the French position, said Bismarck. It was only after his Military Attaché returned to Paris that he learned how ill-prepared for war the French had been.

The reader familiar with these facts is struck by the painstaking exactness with which the Field-Marshal, throughout his narrative, mentions all the dispatches containing reports of the French unpreparedness for war. It is of course possible that the General Staff failed to acquaint the Minister-President with the contents of these dispatches. Again, there seems to the initiated an air of apology about the Field-Marshal's account of his departure from Paris to join the royal headquarters, and also about the motives he adduces. On page 112 he openly states that first Goltz and then Bismarck had urgently requested him to return, but in vain.

When I was in London[1] (1864 and 1865) I was left in no doubt of the immense prestige France enjoyed abroad. The Italian Minister, Marquis D'Azeglio, always referred to the French Ambassador, Prince de la Tour d'Auvergne, simply as l'*Ambassadeur*—to the intense annoyance of the others, particularly Count Bernstorff.[2] But I only mention this as a joke. Even so it was plain from every diplomatic conversation that the Emperor Napoleon's decision on any question was always awaited as being the one that counted.

We Prussians were thoroughly detested in England at this

[1] On 6 May 1864 Holstein was temporarily assigned to the Prussian Legation in London. In August 1865 he went on leave to the United States, where he was subsequently given an official post (see p. 29 n. 2).

[2] Albrecht von Bernstorff. Prussian Minister in London, 1854–61; Foreign Minister, 1861–2; Ambassador in London, 1862–73.

period. The Prince of Wales's attitude was hostile. I well remember the correct but frigid manner in which he acknowledged Count Bernstorff's greeting at the Court ball which took place the day Alsen was captured. But the English were not particularly well-disposed towards the French either. In 1865 the French horse *Gladiateur* won the Derby. After the races the coach carrying the Counsellor of the Embassy, the Marquis de Cadore, whose footman was wearing the French cockade, was mobbed by an angry crowd who pelted it with all kinds of missiles and shouted insults. Palmerston[1] who was then Prime Minister had, despite the Crimean War, retained for France all the mistrust of his youth. Thus he had supported the Mexican Expedition—only to back out at the last minute. During the Danish War Napoleon let it be known that he would be prepared to support any aggressive action against Prussia, provided he obtained an extension of the Rhine frontier. This put an end to Palmerston's warlike desires. When he informed the Commons of the failure of the Danish Conference,[2] it was in a speech full of virtuous indignation but devoid of any militant note. The Prince of Wales who had been listening from the Peers' Gallery, then left the House with the single word 'bosh'. At about this time the Prince is said to have proposed at a dinner of a regiment of the Guards his notorious toast, 'To the confusion of Germany'. The German Federation, which constituted the 'Germany' of that day, had participated in the Danish Conference and had been represented by the Saxon Minister Count Beust.[3] The Prince of Wales showed the Count his dislike quite openly, whereas in the presence of the Prussian Ambassador this sentiment had to be somewhat toned down. The Prince treated Count Beust with the utmost contempt, which he felt more keenly because previously, when Minister in London, he had been on the most intimate terms with the royal family.

The Duke of Augustenburg's cause was represented at the Conference by the Hanseatic Minister, Herr Rudolf Schleiden.

[1] Henry John Temple, Viscount Palmerston. British Prime Minister, 1855–8, 1859–65.

[2] The London Conference, 25 April to 25 June 1864. Summoned to settle the Schleswig-Holstein Danish Question.

[3] Friedrich Ferdinand, Count von Beust. Saxon Minister-Resident in London, 1846–8; Minister in Berlin, 1848–9; Foreign Minister, 1849–66; Austrian Foreign Minister, October 1866–71; from 1867, Chancellor; Ambassador in London, 1871–8, in Paris 1878–82.

He had first turned his attention to the Hansa Towns in 1849 when the Duchies came once more under Danish rule. A pleasant man but an inveterate particularist, of whom there were many before 1866. One evening I was going downstairs with him after some rout or other when he was asked the usual question: 'Whose carriage shall I call, Sir?' Schleiden replied in a shocking English accent: 'The Hanseatic Minister's carriage.' Immediately a stentorian voice could be heard outside calling: 'The Asiatic Minister's carriage!' which provoked a general outburst of tittering among the waiting footmen. Schleiden blushed furiously. I was really sorry for him, but at the same time I could not help feeling how absurd these petty states must appear to the foreigner.

CHAPTER III

PRELIMINARIES AND OUTBREAK OF THE FRANCO-PRUSSIAN WAR:
1867–1870[1]

France and Prussia's military victories. The Luxembourg crisis. Belgian mistrust of France. Attitude of Denmark. The Rouher documents. Hohenlohe and the attitude of Bavaria. The Hohenzollern candidature. Attitude of the Emperor Napoleon and Bismarck to the war. Outbreak of war. Holstein's Italian mission.

I CAN recall very little of interest drawn from my own experience during the period from August 1865 to the outbreak of war in 1870.

In any case I was in the United States until June 1867.

French reaction to the Prussian military victories was revealed to me through a remark made by the French Minister,[2] the Marquis de Montholon. During a discussion of the additional territory Prussia had acquired as a result of the war and the treaties of Nikolsburg and Prague the Minister said quietly and deliberately: '*Mais je ne vois pas ce qu'il y a pour la France dans tout cela.*' He took it for granted that France must ultimately reap some advantage.

But the opportunity had been lost when Napoleon in answer to the Italians' inquiry advised them to fight with Prussia. If Austria had been able to hold in reserve Italy and France in addition to her German allies, the outlook for Prussia would have been very uncertain. But by the time France felt the 'pangs of patriotism' after Sadowa, it was too late. France could do nothing alone. There was a shortage of troops, and the arsenals stood empty. A revolt in Algeria was only very partially to blame; the main cause was the Mexican Expedition. [...]

The French defeat in Mexico gave rise a few months later to

---

[1] The chapter-division and the chapter-heading are the editors'. See Appendix I.
[2] In Washington.

a cruel slogan at the Paris Exhibition: *Quel est le plus grand exposant? C'est l'Empereur, parce qu'il a exposé la France.*

Napoleon had hoped to restore French prestige by the acquisition of Luxembourg. But as soon as he realized that, contrary to his expectations, Prussia would not cede Luxembourg of her own free will he agreed to the well-known compromise[1] which came under heavy criticism at the time, both in France and in Prussia. Bleichröder,[2] the banker, told me how once, at some social gathering, Moltke[3] pointed to Bismarck and said: 'The extra blood which must be spilt one day is on that man's head.'

From the purely military standpoint and so far as the French army is concerned, Moltke was certainly right. I heard it said in many quarters that the French army had felt demoralized on account of its muzzle-loader gun, whereas the *chassepot* was superior to the needle-gun. In many other respects, too, the French army of 1870 was better equipped than in 1867. But from the political point of view Bismarck was undoubtedly right in securing a postponement of the decision. From what I heard from the Chancellor and his entourage on my return from America in June 1867, I assume that Bismarck was strongly influenced by the knowledge that Hanover was still in the throes of internal unrest and that in the event of war there would be an outbreak of 'murder and violence'. I remember how in 1870 when the Guelph faction became active he spoke with quite extraordinary abhorrence of the possibility of civil war, which inflicts far deeper wounds than does a regular war.

During King Wilhelm's stay in Paris in the summer of 1867 (as I learned later from Wesdehlen)[4] he was attended by the well-known Colonel Stoffel.[5] The French had arranged as part of the King's programme a visit to Offenbach's operetta *The Grand Duchess of Gérolstein*. During dinner Stoffel, who was sitting next to Wesdehlen, began: '*Plairait-il au Roi d'aller voir* La Grande Duchesse de Gérolstein *ce soir?*' The King ignored this, so Stoffel

[1] The Treaty of London, 9 September 1867. Prussia renounced her right to maintain a garrison in the fort of the town of Luxembourg. The Grand Duchy seceded from the German Confederation. Its neutrality and independence were guaranteed by the Powers.

[2] Gerson Bleichröder. Head of the Berlin banking house of that name.

[3] Helmuth, Count von Moltke. Chief of the Prussian General Staff, 1858–88.

[4] Ludwig, Count von Wesdehlen. First Secretary in the Prussian Legation in Florence and in Rome from 1868; in the Embassy in Paris, 1873–80.

[5] Military Attaché in the French Legation in Berlin.

repeated his question rather more loudly, and then again. He then turned to Wesdehlen with the remark: '*Décidément le Roi ne se soucie pas d'aller voir* La Grande Duchesse.' '*Peut-être bien*', replied Wesdehlen, and there the matter rested. Something else had to be devised for the King to do. The King saw in this operetta a caricature of conditions in Germany—as in fact it was. All other persons of royal rank, including the Germans, rushed to hear Offenbach's work before anything else whenever they were in Paris.

On his return from Paris the King paid a visit to Brussels. Keudell[1] told me later that he was repeatedly questioned by Belgians about the possibility of Prussia's handing over Belgium to France by way of compensation. Keudell's reply was that it was superfluous to discuss possibilities that might have existed in the past. As for the future, there was now no possibility of our ceding Belgium to France.

Then, in 1867, the suspicion felt by Belgium—and not Belgium alone—was directed mainly against France. Today, forty years later, that same suspicion is directed solely against Germany. The cause must not be sought in Germany's deeds but rather in German speeches and demonstrations. It was not necessary thus to render our position more difficult and to endanger the peace.

During the winter of 1867–8 I spent some time in Copenhagen as Chargé d'Affaires. The most interesting thing I recall from this period is a passage from a dispatch written by Minister von Heydebrand.[2] Before his departure he had quite a long discussion with the Foreign Minister, Count Beck-Frijs[3] on the subject of North Schleswig, whose future had been left undecided by Article V of the Peace of Prague.[4] Herr von Heydebrand then wrote that the Danish Minister had convinced him that Denmark would rather accept nothing at all than accept a trifle.

By this time all Europe was expecting a Franco-German war. When it finally broke out the French Minister in Munich, the

[1] Robert von Keudell. In charge of the Personnel Division in the Foreign Ministry, 1863–72; Minister in Constantinople, 1872–3, in Rome, 1873–87 (Ambassador from 1876).

[2] Georg von Heydebrand und der Lasa. Prussian Minister in Copenhagen.

[3] Juel Vind Frijs, Count of Frijsenborg. Danish Minister-President and Foreign Minister, 1865–70.

[4] The Peace of Prague, 23 August 1866, which ended the war between Prussia and Austria. Article V provided that North Schleswig should fall to Denmark if the population, by free plebiscite, should decide in favour of belonging to Denmark.

Duc de Cadore, arrived in Copenhagen and tried to enlist Danish support. When the Danes replied that it was a most grave decision because everything was at stake, Cadore is said to have retorted: 'Well, and what's that? Everything you have got left is *si peu de chose.*' The duke, a former naval officer, was well known for his bluntness. Such a reply was quite in character. I was told later that its effect was to alarm the Danes and strengthen them in their intention of remaining neutral.

It was also the Duc de Cadore who in the autumn of 1866 after his first consultation with the newly appointed Bavarian Minister-President, Prince Hohenlohe,[1] wrote the dispatch whose contents became known to the Prussian Government four years later, and which afterwards became public. During the war there were found in the country house at Cerçay (I think it was) belonging to the former French Minister Rouher great piles of documents relating to foreign affairs, which had presumably come into his possession when he was the principal speaker for the Government. The fact that Rouher had kept these documents points either to inefficient working of the administrative machine, or to the possibility that even when President of the Senate he had remained in direct contact with the Foreign Ministry. At any rate these documents were confiscated. While several of us were looking through them, I came across a book of dispatches containing extracts from the reports of French representatives in Germany during 1866. They showed that in the autumn of that year the French Foreign Ministry had asked for reports on the probable attitude of the central and southern German governments in the event of a Franco-Prussian war. The Minister in Darmstadt had been given a straight answer by Dalwigk,[2] which left no doubt of that statesman's hostility to Prussia and sympathies for the Confederation of the Rhine—which were in any case very well known. The head of the Frankfurt house of Rothschild[3] had expressed himself with greater reserve to the French representative there, but had emphasized that the immediate cause of war, the avowed war aim, and the

---

[1] Chlodwig, Prince zu Hohenlohe-Schillingsfürst. Bavarian Minister-President, 1866–70; German Ambassador in Paris, 1874–85; Governor of Alsace-Lorraine, 1885–94; Chancellor of the German Reich, 1894–1900.

[2] Reinhard, Baron von Dalwigk zu Lichtenfels. President of the Ministry of State in the Grand-Duchy of Hesse; Foreign Minister and Minister of the Interior.

[3] Meyer Karl, Baron von Rothschild.

wording of the declaration of war would substantially influence the attitude the German cabinets would adopt.

But Prince Hohenlohe had told the Duc de Cadore plainly that if neutrality were impossible, then Bavaria would support Prussia in any event, whatever the immediate cause of war or the declared war aim. The Minister appended to his report of this conversation the following remark: 'Prince von Hohenlohe's replies have shown me that if the Tuileries (I remembered this way of referring to the Head of the State because it was new to me) have not given up the idea of making an ally of the King of Bavaria, then he had better be prevailed on in good time to take another Minister-President.'

Some years later I learned from Prince Hohenlohe himself, who in the meantime had become German Ambassador in Paris, that this advice had been taken to heart in the Tuileries. About the beginning of 1870 Cardinal Hohenlohe[1] had informed his brother in Munich that the Holy See had been requested by Paris to bring all its influence to bear in order to get rid of the Bavarian Minister-President. At the same time allusion had been made to the possibility of a Franco-Prussian war in the near future. The Vatican was the more willing to meet this request, in that Prince Chlodwig had made himself highly unpopular during the Vatican Council.[2] He had advocated, though unsuccessfully, a policy of defending the episcopal power against the autocratic tendencies of the Jesuits. And so in early February the Prince was obliged by the votes of the clerical Right in both Chambers of the Bavarian Parliament to resign. This reminds me how one day in 1874 or 1875, when his son-in-law's father, Count Schönborn-Wiesentheid, was dining with him, the Prince with that gentle smile of his said to me: 'He was President of the Upper Chamber at the time of my downfall and had a good share in bringing it about.'

Prince Hohenlohe also used to tell how, a few months later—I think in April 1870—when the Crown Prince of Prussia expressed to him his regret upon his resignation, he replied that he regretted it also on account of the accompanying circumstances. For if his information was correct, his removal constituted one of the preliminary measures for a French attack. He said that the Crown Prince referred to this conversation in later years.

[1] Gustav Adolf, Prince zu Hohenlohe-Schillingsfürst.
[2] The Oecumenical Council of 1869–70.

From the spring of 1868 up to the outbreak of war I had left the Diplomatic Service[1] but I learned by chance various details about the initial phases of the Franco-German conflict. In the early summer of that year I spent most of my time in Bonn as the guest of Major Baron Max Schreckenstein,[2] who was confined to bed by a severe ankle injury and remained bedridden for the whole of the war. The unfortunate man, who died over thirty years ago, lives in my memory as one of the most versatile and witty conversationalists I have ever come across. One day he asked me all kinds of questions—most of which I could not answer—about Spain, its army, its finances and its people. He gradually came to the decision to take me entirely into his confidence, for after all I still belonged to the diplomatic world and was only on leave. His brother, who was at the court of Prince Anton von Hohenzollern,[3] had given him the fullest information about the Spanish candidature. As a result I learned all kinds of intimate details about the Hohenzollern candidature. When Prim[4] had offered the throne to the hereditary prince, his father had at once informed Prince Bismarck, who then sent Bucher and Versen[5] to Spain to see how the land lay.[6] Meanwhile Prince Karl Anton, who rather prided himself on his connection with the Bonapartes and set great store on maintaining good relations with them, had set discreet inquiries on foot in Paris. His agent was a Mme Cornu, a former governess or companion who enjoyed the confidence both of the princely branch of the Hohenzollerns and of the French imperial family. Mme Cornu had informed the Emperor Napoleon of Prim's offer, and the Emperor had received the news sympathetically. More than that I cannot now remember, nor can I say whether he gave his consent or merely nodded and smiled, but I am perfectly certain that Mme Cornu noticed not the slightest trace of any misgivings or opposition; there was nothing that might have been a warning to the candidate for the throne. How-

---

[1] Holstein had taken leave to participate in a venture to provide a mechanical towing system for river and canal transport.

[2] Major of the King's Hussars; then Commander of the 7th Uhlans.

[3] A distant relative of the King of Prussia, and father of Prince Leopold von Hohenzollern-Sigmaringen, to whom the Spanish throne had been offered.

[4] Juan, Count Prim. Spanish Prime Minister, 1868–71.

[5] Max von Versen. Prussian Major.

[6] Shortly after 4 April 1870. See Bismarck, *Die gesammelten Werke*, vol. vi b, no. 1548, pp. 314–15.

ever, only a few weeks after I had been told all this, the Duc de Gramont[1] made his provocative speech in the Chamber of Deputies and Prince Karl Anton vainly strove to avert war by a renunciation of his son's claims. The demand for a guarantee with which the French replied to the Hohenzollern withdrawal made war inevitable.

My impression of the respective attitudes of Bismarck and the Emperor Napoleon to the war question is this. Bismarck handled the Hohenzollern candidature rather as one waves a lighted match over a gas tap to see whether it is turned on. The Emperor was free to make the candidature of the prince seem acceptable or unacceptable to the French, depending on whether he treated the prince as a Catholic and a relative, or whether he attached decisive importance—which in fact occurred—to the name Hohenzollern.

Gramont's provocative speech of 4 [sic] July showed, in Bismarck's opinion, that France had decided on war, since Prussia could not possibly tolerate such language. So from then on Bismarck took a hand in things, by shortening the Ems telegram, etc. From July onward Bismarck wanted war, but Napoleon had wanted it before then. The slightest hint to Mme Cornu would have been enough to make Prince Karl Anton, and thus his son, withdraw the candidature at once. The fact that the Emperor did not drop any such hint would of itself be sufficient proof of his bad faith without the further evidence provided by the diplomatic moves resulting in the downfall of Prince Hohenlohe, which the French Minister in Munich three years earlier had called a necessary prelude to a Franco-Prussian War. The Emperor was a kind-hearted man with a dislike of bloodshed, and in addition he held a high opinion of the capacity of the Prussian army after 1866. But since Sadowa and even more since the Mexican fiasco the Napoleonic star had been on the decline. Since the last plebiscite[2]

[1] Antoine Alfred Agénor de Gramont, Duc de Guiche. French Foreign Minister. The 'provocative speech' of 6 July 1870 was delivered after news had leaked out that Prince Leopold would accept the Spanish offer if he were elected by a large majority in the Cortes. Gramont threatened war if Prussia did not withdraw the Hohenzollern candidature.

[2] The plebiscite of 8 May 1870, was concerned with the question whether the nation approved of the changes in the constitution introduced since 1860, and would ratify the 'Senatus Consultum' of 20 April 1870. The result of the plebiscite was 7,358,786 'Yes' against 1,571,939 'No'. The great number of 'No' votes was regarded by many as a defeat for the Government.

particularly, when even a section of the army, e.g. the regiment in the Caserne du Château d'Eau in Paris, had openly voted against the Empire, the Emperor had been gradually forced into a position in which he regarded even a major war as the lesser evil.

On my arrival in Berlin as a result of Gramont's speech and the Berlin demonstrations on 8 July to which it gave rise, everything seemed calm on the surface, but Colonel Stiehle[1] and other General Staff officers I spoke to thought that war could hardly be avoided this time. Stiehle also told me he had found Moltke on the sofa with a novel of Sir Walter Scott's in his hand. When the Colonel passed some remark about such reading-matter at such a moment, the General placidly replied: 'Why not? Everything's ready. We've only got to press the button.'

Count Bismarck's return from Varzin more or less coincided with the news of the withdrawal of the Hohenzollern candidature. This made the Chancellor look very sombre. 'Gramont's speech really put the fat in the fire. Nothing can be done about it now.'

The French deprived this renunciation of its effect by demanding a formal guarantee that the Hohenzollern candidature would not be renewed. Bismarck for his part brought the matter to a decision when he gave an edge to Abeken's Ems telegram by shortening it. I called on the Chancellor one evening after he had completed this task. 'Have you read the latest "*Wolff*"[2] [report] yet?' he asked with immense satisfaction.

When the King arrived on the 15th a council was held at the temporary Potsdam station almost opposite the 'Karlsbad'. The King, the Crown Prince, Bismarck, Moltke, and Roon[3] were present. The King wanted only partial mobilization at first but the Crown Prince said: 'No, total mobilization from the start.' As he left the room the Crown Prince said to the people waiting outside, 'War and mobilization'.

The following day I dined with the Chancellor. A few of his sons'[4] friends were there and one or two others I cannot remember. I was next to the Chancellor. When we had sat down he counted the guests—'Thirteen'. He then muttered to himself: 'On occa-

---

[1] Gustav von Stiehle. Chief of Staff to Prince Friedrich Karl, 1870.

[2] The name of a German news agency.

[3] Albrecht, Count von Roon. Prussian Minister for War, 1859–73; Prussian Minister-President, 1872–73.

[4] Herbert and Wilhelm von Bismarck.

sions like this there are usually thirteen.' But the superstition was proved wrong. All thirteen came back safely, though two, Herbert[1] and Count Matuschka, were wounded.

A few days later Keudell came to see me in the Tiergarten Hotel early one morning when I was still in bed, and asked me whether I was prepared to undertake a mission to Italy. An unknown man whose name now escapes me[2] had written from there and offered to organize a volunteer corps for attacks either on Nice or Rome, where there was a French garrison. I was to have a look at the man, examine what forces he could muster, and form an opinion of what might be done to hamper the Italian Government in its intended co-operation with France. I was to have a certain sum of money at my disposal in case it should be necessary. Bismarck felt a certain mistrust of the Prussian Minister in Florence, Count Brassier de St Simon, on account of his French origin; this was the reason for my mission. To get the Count out of the way for a time, Bismarck recalled him to Berlin for consultation.

Railway traffic throughout Germany was disorganized by troop movements so I travelled via Görlitz, Reichenberg and Vienna. In Italy, not far from Florence, I saw at a railway junction a regiment making for the north-west frontier.

I found that Wesdehlen was Chargé d'Affaires in Florence and asked him to put me in touch with some of the leading figures of the radical opposition. I wished to discover from them the state of affairs and the political atmosphere before meeting my volunteer corps man. Wesdehlen, who disliked mixing with anti-government elements, told me the only person he knew in opposition circles was a Doctor Guastalla, who would be able to give me further introductions. Through him I made the acquaintance of Crispi[3] and a Garibaldian, General Fabrizi. They both confirmed

[1] Herbert, Count von Bismarck. From 15 January 1874, in the Foreign Ministry; attached to several Legations, but principally employed as private secretary to his father; First Secretary in the German Embassy in London, November 1882–4; Acting First Secretary in St Petersburg, January 1884; Minister at the Hague, 11 May 1884–5; Under State Secretary in the Foreign Ministry, 10 May 1885–6; State Secretary, 1 May 1886–90; Prussian Minister of State, 1888–90.

[2] Angelo de Angeli.

[3] Francesco Crispi. Italian lawyer and politician; collaborator of Cavour and Garibaldi; from 1861 Deputy for Palermo (radical Left); President of the Chamber, 1876; Minister of the Interior in the Depretis Cabinet, 1877–8; Minister-President, 1887–91, 1893–6.

what I knew already, namely that the opposition and in fact all the Italians were bitterly hostile to the Emperor Napoleon for refusing to allow them to occupy Rome. The opposition had already sent sharply worded messages to the King, who was known to be very much in favour of supporting the Emperor Napoleon.

I asked Crispi whether, in view of the animosity towards France so widely felt in Italy, one might expect marches of volunteer corps against Nice or Rome. He replied: 'I hope not; it would be highly undesirable for the opposition. A lawless act of that kind would compromise us in the eyes of the Government and the country, and weaken our whole position. On the other hand such an incident might even be rather welcome to the Government.' After that my course was quite clear. When this volunteer corps man arrived and assured me nothing could be simpler than to launch a powerful diversion against Rome which would immobilize the French troops there, I replied that it would be at the same time an act of hostility against the Holy See, and therefore I could certainly not entertain the idea. He then said that a march on Nice would be if anything easier to arrange. Since I had by this time formed the opinion that the fellow was an agent of either the Italian or the French Government, I told him I had instructions not to commit myself to anything that might make the already difficult position of the neutral Italian Government still more difficult. I then sent him this formula in writing so that I could finally be rid of him. I had been aware for some time that the Italian Government had had me under police observation. I continued to be followed until I crossed the frontier again at Ala.

While I was staying at the Albergo della Pace—as the only guest of the season—the well-known Count Vitzthum,[1] roving diplomat for Count Beust, was staying at another hotel and striving to persuade the Italians to attack immediately. Austria, he explained, was prevented by Russia's unfriendly attitude from joining them in the field at once, but would do so as soon as the winter prevented a Russian attack. To counteract this Austrian move, my friends, Crispi and colleagues, made it clear to the Ministers and also to the King that they would oppose by every possible means any government that made itself the vassal of

[1] Friedrich, Count Vitzthum von Eckstädt. Austrian Minister in Brussels, 1868–72.

Napoleonic policy. Crispi's newspaper, the *Indipendenza*, I think, carried threatening paragraphs which he wrote in my presence.

The Italian policy of the Second Empire had earned it Crispi's deepest hatred, but for England he felt a lively sympathy and gratitude. He had played a leading part in organizing Garibaldi's Sicilian expedition, but the expedition would have failed at the outset but for some English warships which on the day of the landing interposed themselves between Garibaldi's vessels and a Neapolitan squadron, thus preventing it from going into action. [...]

I regarded my mission to Florence as accomplished once I had acquired the certainty that the opposition would exert itself to the utmost to prevent Italy from renouncing her neutrality. I suggested to Crispi that he might let a member of his Party—Cucchi,[1] who later became Under-Secretary of State—travel back with me for direct oral consultation with Count Bismarck. Cucchi was to leave a day early and wait for me at Rosenheim. I realized the practical good sense of our splitting up when (as I said above) I noticed I was shadowed by a detective as far as the Italian frontier.

My mission was successful but lost all practical significance through our victories, which opened up for the Italians the way to Rome.

But I must just tell one more story about this man with his volunteer corps, whose overtures had occasioned my journey.

When I was attached to the Paris Embassy in 1871 I had a letter from this fellow in which he said he had taken a job on the French Northern Railway in order to earn his living, but that he hated the French as much as ever, and placed himself at my disposal in case there was anything I wanted to find out. There was no doubt I was dealing with an agent of the French police. It would have been greatly to their advantage to learn from the type of questions I put the things we were anxious to investigate. I did not reply.

On my way home, during a halt at Brenner station on 5 August, the station-master came up to my compartment to inform me of the telegram announcing the victory at Weissenburg. As I travelled through Bavaria I saw the railway coaches—mainly

[1] Francesco Cucchi. Italian Deputy.

goods wagons—which had taken the troops to the frontier; they were decorated with greenery and bore the legend: 'Express goods for Paris.'

In Mainz I met Count Bismarck and made my report. As the royal headquarters was about to move off, the Chancellor took me to the station in his carriage. He said he could not let me travel with him because of Cucchi, and told me to follow with Cucchi in the next train as far as Homburg (in the Palatinate). However, he was not to be called Cucchi but some other name for security reasons. The Chancellor suggested some ballet dancer's name, possibly Gasporini, I forget. (Cucchi agreed to this ballet dancer's name, though with very bad grace.) Then, as the train pulled out, I stood and saw the King standing alone at the long window of the royal coach. The old man looked grave, noble and impressive. He gazed calmly at the handful of people who uttered not a sound, and for the most part did not even greet him.

I had heard ever since my childhood that the population of Mainz was disloyal; their behaviour at that historic moment justified their bad reputation. [...]

On my arrival in Homburg I was met by Otto Dönhoff,[1] a member of Prince Karl's[2] retinue. He almost fell over himself in his eagerness to know where I had been. I learnt at the same time that during his last few days in Berlin, when no news of me came through (I did not telegraph until I had seen how the land lay), Bismarck had said I had probably been killed. I answered evasively, but it was no good. Prince Karl, who was perpetually bored and always eager for news, at once asked me to tea. 'Now, where have you been?' 'Your Royal Highness, I really don't know, but Count Bismarck probably does.' 'This mystification is ridiculous. Why, it's common knowledge where you've been.' (He had not the least idea.) 'Yes, your Royal Highness, but for slaves to the service like us a matter remains secret as long as those are our instructions.' The Prince spoke jokingly about 'a corporal and two men to have this man arrested,' and then went on to make quite pleasant tea-time conversation, but he never forgave me. Later, when we were at Versailles for several months, he entirely ignored me.

[1] Prince Karl's Master of the Horse.
[2] Karl, Prince of Prussia. Brother of Wilhelm I.

Cucchi still did not manage to have a detailed discussion with Count Bismarck in Homburg, so we accompanied headquarters to Saarbrücken in a Foreign Ministry carriage.

Before leaving Homburg I had had an opportunity of watching some Saxon battalions march past the King. The infantry, particularly a battalion of chasseurs, gave a lusty and rousing 'Hurrah'. The Horse-Guards gave their 'Hurrah' as if they were in a drawing room and the regimental officers, nobility from the Saxon Court with a sprinkling of Guelphs, hardly raised their sword-hilts as high as their faces. This difference in bearing was most striking—as indeed it was intended to be.

From Saarbrücken I went with Cucchi and a few acquaintances to visit the battlefield at Spichern. He, as a former Garibaldian who had been taken prisoner at Monte Rotondo, took a keen interest in the traces of the French defeat—knapsacks, weapons—and took away some worthless trifle as a souvenir. Later he had a long talk with Count Bismarck, although the subject discussed, the co-operation of Italy and France, was now hardly topical after the French defeats at Wörth and Spichern. Their conversation took place during a walk. Cucchi told me later he had no idea that Bismarck, a civilian, was so popular with the troops.

Cucchi then returned to Italy and I to Berlin, because headquarters had no room for me on the march.[1] [...]

[1] The accuracy of Holstein's report of his Italian mission is borne out by documents contained in the Foreign Ministry's files. The essential passages from these documents are published in Bismarck, *Die gesammelten Werke*, vol. vi b, nos. 1707, 1717, 1719, pp. 421, 430–1, 432.

CHAPTER IV

THE CONCLUSION OF PEACE: 1871[1]

Karl von Bismarck-Bohlen. Life in the Villa Jessé. Delbrück and Bismarck. Abeken and Bucher. Moritz Busch. Abeken and Keudell. Bucher. Wagener. Keudell. Hatzfeldt: his early relations with Bismarck. Recollections of the war with France. Favre sues for peace. Bismarck and the German generals. Conditions in France. Holstein attached to Fabrice's staff; in Rouen; in Soisy. The Commune. Thiers.

FRAU VON ARNIM-KRÖCHLENDORFF,[2] when her brother became Minister-President, felt it was her duty to instruct her sister-in-law in the social graces. She was aided and abetted in this by Count Karl Bismarck-Bohlen. He was not without talent but bone idle. Too indolent to remain an officer, too worldly to endure life on his estate, he went the rounds of the spas in summer, and in winter drifted about Berlin or other big cities. He would often say: 'I don't like walking but I'd rather walk a couple of miles than write one page.' He thought this very witty, took particular pleasure in sharply paradoxical statements and boasted of his own heartlessness. It was, however, a mistake to think this was affected. He really *was* heartless. His cousin, the Minister-President, used him as an envoy to deliver oral messages, and would possibly have made even more out of him, if he had shown any willingness to work. But that was just what was lacking, and in addition Count Karl Bismarck was soon at odds with Frau von Bismarck. The joint effort made by him and Frau von Arnim to reform Johanna Bismarck was a complete failure. Whether her husband would have succeeded in a similar attempt will always remain an open question, for he never tried. She for her part could claim with some justification that if her husband saw nothing to criticize then it was no affair of the rest

[1] At this point Holstein had made a break in the text. The chapter-heading is the editors'. See Appendix I.
[2] Malwine von Arnim-Kröchlendorff, *née* von Bismarck. Sister of Otto von Bismarck.

of the family. Frau von Bismarck's manners were eccentric, as she well knew, but she shared her husband's fixed resolve to make other people adapt themselves to her in their social contacts, instead of vice versa. Her sister-in-law and her cousin failed to appreciate the strength of this determination to go her own way when they embarked on their campaign of reform. There were violent scenes and Frau von Bismarck would complain to her husband, who defended her right to behave as she pleased. He had learned to accept his wife as she was, and expected everyone else who had dealings with her to do the same.

As a result of these quarrels Karl Bismarck (as he was generally known) left in a huff. When war came in 1866 the Minister-President recalled him and appointed him Commandant at his headquarters. He was also entrusted with the safeguarding of the Minister-President's person, which was indeed a responsible task in that period of disturbance and attempted assassinations. Working under Karl Bismarck was the renowned and infamous Stieber.[1] He was quoted as saying once 'The chaps at the top must be kept worried about something,' and so he was always bent on making his reports as interesting as possible. These two, Stieber and Karl Bismarck, were cut out for each other. Karl Bismarck's suspicious, crabbed, malicious nature found its fullest scope in this type of activity. Stieber's reports often enabled him to appear interesting to his eminent cousin without any effort on his part. I can well imagine that in the conditions prevailing from 1866 until after the Franco-Prussian War, the period during which he was in office, he ruined many a man's life without proof or even probability that such a course was necessary. I remember one such case. During the early months of the Franco-Prussian War our Foreign Ministry received instructions inspired by Karl Bismarck from Bismarck's headquarters in the field, to direct the attention of the chief of police[2] to a 'suspect' Frenchman, a language teacher. Opinion in the Foreign Ministry was that the chief of police was expected to banish this Frenchman from the country. Luckily for the latter I was asked to discuss the matter with Herr von Wurmb. He was a good-natured man who adhered to the principle of 'live and let live' so far as he could. He took this

[1] Dr Stieber. *Geheimer Regierungsrat*; Head of the Prussian security police.
[2] W. L. von Wurmb. Chief of the Berlin police.

communication from headquarters to be a hint to deport the Frenchman but remarked that the man had naturally been under close observation for some time, without the slightest ground for suspicion being discovered. Then followed one or two comments on Stieber's methods.

In these circumstances I was most strongly opposed to the expulsion of this Frenchman without further ceremony, and promised to obtain a statement to this effect from the Under State Secretary, von Thile.[1] I had no difficulty about this. I returned to Wurmb fully empowered to inform him of the opinion of the Under State Secretary that if police observation had brought nothing suspicious to light, then the assumption underlying the Chancellor's order was false. Wurmb replied: 'Very well, I won't deport him. But, take it from me, we shall get no thanks. I know my Chancellor.'

Incidentally, I never heard that Wurmb suffered any unpleasantness because of this. And I cannot entirely agree with Wurmb's final remark. The Chancellor was suspicious and pitiless, and sometimes took action on the strength of mere probability. But he did not delight in cruelty for its own sake like Karl Bismarck or, in later life, Herbert. I must just mention here that in September 1872 I was substituting for Bucher and arrived at Varzin on the very day Herbert had ridden an old horse lame—it was formerly one of Prince Putbus's hunters. Prince Bismarck, who took care of his horses, was most displeased and said just one thing which has stuck in my memory: 'Herbert is a tormentor both of man and beast.'

But to return to Karl Bismarck. He was kept on as Commandant at headquarters, i.e. Court Chamberlain to the Chancellor, during the Franco-Prussian War. I would regard as his outstanding achievement in this capacity the fact that on 16 July he sent to Huster, the *restaurateur*, to find out which was the most capable of his young chefs liable to military service. Karl Bismarck then requisitioned the man indicated by Huster to be chef at Bismarck's headquarters. His cooking was good, but rich and heavy. It was far too solid for anyone doing sedentary work all day. When I went

[1] Karl Hermann von Thile. Prussian Minister to the Holy See, 1855–7, in Vienna, 1857–9; Under State Secretary in the Foreign Ministry, 1862–70; State Secretary, 1870–2.

to Versailles I soon realized that the two meals provided—one at 11.30 and one at 5.30 I think—were too much for my constitution, so I always had one course brought to my rooms near the Villa Jessé, and naturally finished much earlier than the main party. In this way I was already sitting working when the others came back from their meal.

In the big office where, except for Karl Bismarck and the Press chief, Dr Moritz Busch,[1] the entire Foreign Ministry staff did its work—and towards the end there were more than twenty of them —the atmosphere was dreadful. In an attempt to improve it a small pane had been smashed at the top of one of the windows on Bucher's instructions. But our admirable Head of the Chancery, Wollmann, who sat nearest the window, complained of the draught and had thick brown paper stuck over the broken pane. The next day I went into the room as usual before the main table had risen. A minute later Bucher appeared, hurried over to the window, drew his sword and jabbed it through the brown paper in several places. Then he returned his sword to its corner, said to me, 'In the course of the day so and so many cubic feet of air come in and out through those slits', sat down near me and at once fell fast asleep, or so it seemed. He had a habit of sitting there for hours with his eyes closed when there was no work on hand, but rumour had it that he could hear even the faintest whisper in the room. On this particular day Bucher had hardly sat down when the office staff came pouring in after their meal, noisy and boisterous as usual at that time of day. I went into the adjoining room where the Chancellor was sitting round the fire with his Foreign Ministry staff and some guests. When I returned after some time I saw Wollmann clasping the top of his head and looking suspiciously at his window. 'There's a draught in here, that's certain. Where's it coming from?' He never found out. Bucher sat quite still, dead to the world.

It was at this period that I came to admire Delbrück's[2] iron constitution. He spent several weeks in Versailles, and ate regularly two large meals each day; he was particularly fond of really unwholesome foods (stuffed pigs' trotters with truffle sauce was

[1] Moritz Busch. Political writer; joint editor of the *Grenzbote*; in the German Foreign Ministry, 1870–3.

[2] Rudolf von Delbrück. President of the Federal Chancellery and of the subsequent Reich Chancellery, 1867–76; Prussian Minister of State, 1868–76.

his favourite dish) helped down with a generous amount of wine, but he remained cool and phlegmatic with the same unruffled approach to his work. Whenever I heard him engaged in discussion, lucid but uninspiring, completely devoid of Bismarck's gripping, lively eloquence, I was reminded of something Savigny[1] said to me in August while he was on temporary duty in the Foreign Ministry at Thile's request: 'The strength of Delbrück's position', Savigny said, 'is that he is only interested in the things that Bismarck finds boring.'

Detailed work was Delbrück's strong point, whereas Bismarck could only find patience for it in cases of paramount importance.

Delbrück with his unvarying equanimity was an exception. The sedentary life we led, the heavy eating and drinking, coupled at times with extreme nervous tension, gradually made themselves felt.

Abeken and one of the clerks died soon after the war, both from heart trouble. The Chancellor, who bore the full weight of responsibility, suffered most from this nervous strain, which would show in some of his remarks at table and afterwards. Once, when a most efficient clerk brought him the wrong document at first, he rounded on him with 'If there is a repetition of this muddle, you will be sent packing by the next coach.'

Once during a meal he was running through all the French frontier fortresses when he came to a standstill, so I supplied two names. I immediately got my share: 'May I ask you not to interrupt, or I shall lose the thread.'

What the Chancellor said about the Queen and the Crown Princess, who were reported to be scheming to prevent the bombardment of Paris, is better not repeated. His views are well enough known.

Our stay in Versailles was particularly fraying to our nerves because of the high room temperature the Chancellor insisted on. One day he complained bitterly of the cold. 'The office staff apparently does not wish me to come downstairs.' We looked at the thermometer; it was between 16 and 17 degrees. When the

---

[1] Karl Friedrich von Savigny. Prussian Diplomat; Minister to the Federal Diet in Frankfurt, 1864–6; in 1866 he became an opponent of Bismarck, with whom he had collaborated hitherto; from 1867 Member of the Prussian Chamber of Deputies; from 1868 Member of the Reichstag; from 1871 one of the leaders of the Centre Party; his wish to retire from the service of the state was not granted until July 1871.

Chancellor unbuttoned his military greatcoat you could see it was lined with doeskin, but he only undid it when the temperature was at least 18 degrees Réaumur with a huge fire burning in the grate.

Most of the table-talk was provided by the Chancellor and his guests, one or two of whom were regularly invited, but nearly always just for lunch. Hatzfeldt[1] would also take part in the conversation, because in the Chancellor's eyes he enjoyed the highest social standing. The other members of the staff usually remained silent.

The Chancellor did not afford Abeken the outward status to which his great ability should have entitled him. Bismarck, who always set store by externals, was offended at the way Abeken, who cut such a sorry figure, could never be deterred from riding on horseback on great occasions. And so the little man had to put up with cutting remarks from his chief, which were all the more scornful when Abeken was not present. [...]

Abeken was well liked by the King and his entourage, whereas Bucher, because of his former refusal to pay taxes,[2] was completely ignored. From the very first day of Bucher's return the King never refused the Minister-President—later the Chancellor—anything he wanted for him, but he himself never spoke a single word to Bucher. The evening of Favre's[3] first visit to negotiate terms of surrender, the King, or rather the Kaiser, came to call on the Chancellor. After their conversation His Majesty came down to the room where the Foreign Ministry officials sat and spoke to one or two of them, but did not even look at Bucher. I think Bismarck regarded Bucher's low status at Court as an advantage, because he knew that Bucher knew it was Bismarck alone who kept him on.

Because of this Prince Bismarck regarded him as his tool, and used him to carry out all kinds of strictly confidential and personal

---

[1] Paul, Count von Hatzfeldt-Wildenburg. Attaché in Paris, 1862–6; Secretary of the Legation at the Hague, 1866–8; *Vortragender Rat* in the Foreign Ministry, from 1868; on Bismarck's personal Foreign Ministry staff, 1870–1; head of the French Section in the Foreign Ministry, 1872–4; Minister in Madrid, 1874–8; Ambassador in Constantinople, 1879–81; State Secretary in the Foreign Ministry, 1881–5; Ambassador in London, 1885–1901.

[2] In 1850 Bucher was condemned to fifteen months' imprisonment for his share in the resolution passed by the Prussian National Assembly in November 1848, whereby it refused to pay taxes already voted, as a counter-measure to the proposed transfer of the Assembly from Berlin to Brandenburg.

[3] Jules Favre. French lawyer and politician; member of the provisional French Government and peace negotiator.

business which, though not exactly in the domain of diplomacy, was connected with it. He only found fault with Bucher or criticized him to other people when he considered Bucher had not done a specific job properly. Bismarck never made Bucher's personality and idiosyncrasies the subject of general merriment, as he so often did with Abeken, even after the latter's death. For instance the lively interest Abeken took in events was coupled with the desire to experience them as fully as possible. And so during the 1870 campaign—I forget what happened in 1866—he insisted on having a horse provided for him and sometimes rode in the royal suite. Prince Bismarck, who was as vain as he was tall, was annoyed to think that this misshapen creature was a member of *his* staff, which explains why he was the first to make cruel jokes about Abeken's appearance. One of his favourite stories told how during a battle—I think Sedan—he suddenly heard above the thunder of the cannon a strange piercing croak, which made him say to himself: 'How on earth can an old woman have got on to the battlefield?' Lo and behold, it was Abeken. Or Prince Bismarck would tell how Abeken went to Olmütz[1] and came back having changed his views completely and become a supporter of the treaty. The best thing Prince Bismarck said of him ran something like this: 'Abeken's drafts contain a lot of useless verbiage, but you do find all you need in them. You need only cut to produce a good dispatch.' Which is as good as saying that Abeken had some ideas of his own, whether he got them from the files, from books, or out of his own head. The Chancellor never accused Abeken of 'insufficient knowledge of the files'.

One of the things that annoyed Bucher most was the way Abeken, as 'specialist for high policy', took over every matter the moment it became important. After Abeken's death, it is true, part of this work went to Bucher, but the post of chief drafting officer (Bismarck's expression) went not to Bucher but Radowitz,[2]

---

[1] To avert the war that threatened in November 1850 between Prussia and Austria, Friedrich Wilhelm IV commissioned Otto von Manteuffel to negotiate with Austria. By the Punctuation of Olmütz of 29 November 1850, Prussia renounced her claims to the leadership of Germany within the Prussian (Erfurt) Union and recognized the existing Federal Diet in Frankfurt, which was substantially controlled by Austria.

[2] Joseph Maria von Radowitz. Secretary of the Legation in Paris, 1865–6, 1866–7, in Munich, 1867–9; Consul-General in Bucharest, 1870–1; Chargé d'Affaires in Constantinople, 1871–2; *Vortragender Rat* in the Foreign Ministry, 1872–4;

and later on I often heard Prince Bismarck refer to the post of chief drafting officer as Radowitz's post even while Bucher was still in the service. Obviously the Prince thought the latter unsuited for this work. He said of Radowitz: 'What he writes is not particularly good, but he does get something done, he's a speed merchant.' Bucher did not possess this faculty for rapid work. When he knew what he had to say he wrote competently, in a concise and sometimes arid style, but I never saw him produce any great quantity of work, nothing comparable to Abeken. I can still see Abeken as he came downstairs from his conference with Bismarck on really busy days. He would hurry over to his seat with quick short steps, sometimes impatiently dip his pen in the ink even before creasing his paper, put his pen in his mouth, crease his paper, and then he was off, without hesitation or interruption. He had not the advantage of knowing shorthand and being able to reproduce verbatim all Bismarck said, but he made up for this by an easy style and, I am convinced, by his intellectual ability which in matters of high policy was far superior to Bucher's.

It is no reproach to say that Abeken wrote quite differently before and after Olmütz. The responsible *Vortragender Rat* has so far not been invented; the Minister alone bears all responsibility. The *Vortragender Rat* who knows his place and does his job well is not concerned with the direction of policy, but must justify the policy framed by his Minister with the most valid arguments available. It is clear from Bismarck's own observations on the two men that Abeken was much better fitted for this task than Bucher. I am of course only thinking of what Bismarck said during his active career as Minister. The opinions he expressed later during his Coriolanus or *Zukunft* phase, must be disregarded in any objective assessment of people and things.

And while we are on the subject of political *volte-faces*, what is Abeken's attitude toward Olmütz compared to Bucher's refusal to pay taxes?

I was in direct contact with Abeken only during my months at Versailles, and I never formed the impression that he tried to make things difficult for anyone. [...]

Minister in Athens, 1874–82 (during which period he was frequently recalled to the Foreign Ministry); Ambassador in Constantinople, 1882–92, in Madrid, 1892–1908.

There was in the entire Foreign Ministry only one person from whom Bucher did not stand aloof, and with whom he struck up a lasting friendship—Moritz Busch, the writer. Whether he owed his appointment to Bucher's influence I cannot say, because I was not in the service at the time. But I could tell at Versailles that they were on friendly terms, whereas there was very little exchange of views between them and the rest of the Foreign Ministry staff. Busch was the only man who did not work with the rest of us, but up in his own room, and he rarely appeared down below except for meals. What struck me first of all was his extravagant, overdone admiration for the Chancellor—'to me he's like the Lord Jesus Christ' he would say constantly—and I also noticed an unusual coarseness of thought and language. I soon saw that in the one-sided feud between Bucher and Abeken—one-sided because Abeken did nothing but irritate Bucher by his mere existence—Busch was entirely on Bucher's side and referred disdainfully to Abeken as nothing but a pen-pusher and so forth. He used stronger terms as well. I had not much interest in all this and held strictly aloof from it, so that now I can only remember the broad outlines of what went on. We all knew, and of course so did Prince Bismarck, that Busch kept a diary used mainly for noting down every word of Bismarck's table-talk. I can still see Busch sitting some way away from Prince Bismarck and listening intently with his hand to his ear. When *Bismarck und seine Leute*[1] came out later on, everyone who had heard the original conversations thought that all Bismarck's delicate shafts of wit had been omitted. Only his more caustic remarks remained and even they had often been blunted. It was like Seidlitz powder without the fizz. Prince Bismarck was the first to feel this, not out of good nature, but out of an author's wounded vanity.

After the war Moritz Busch was removed from his post because Keudell recommended Professor Ägidi[2] to the Chancellor as a specialist on [the] *Kulturkampf*. Ägidi's wife was a cousin of Keudell's. To Bucher this change was a source of great resentment. He attributed to Keudell personal motives, particularly the desire

---

[1] *Graf Bismarck und seine Leute während des Krieges mit Frankreich. Nach Tagebuchblättern*, 2 vols. (Leipzig, 1878).

[2] Ludwig Karl Ägidi. In charge of Press matters in the Foreign Ministry, 1871–7. Cf. Moritz Busch, *Bismarck. Some Secret Pages of his History* (London, 1898), vol. ii, p. 105.

for self-advertisement in the Press. When I arrived in Berlin in the spring of 1876, I found Bucher busily but secretly working to undermine Ägidi's position—an attempt which gradually succeeded.

Moritz Busch, who had been denied the coveted title of *Legationsrat*—which was immediately given to Ägidi—still kept in touch with the Chancellor after he left his post, and often visited him in the country. I once met him at Varzin, probably in the autumn of 1872. He was quite one of the family. Prince Bismarck would often talk with him and go out for drives with him, and it was not difficult to tell that Bismarck had his plans concerning Busch, just as he had concerning Bucher. The latter told me once or twice in the 'seventies that Prince Bismarck had said to him: 'Now, when we've both left the service'—it was well known that Bismarck liked referring to this possibility, especially when he was dissatisfied with His Majesty—'you must come and stay with me in the country. Then we'll write our memoirs.'

Keudell and Abeken were on very good terms. Keudell was full of attentions to Abeken. Working together for months on end in one room as we did at Versailles, we were able to form a clearer picture of individual relationships and methods of work than in normal times. I had often noticed that whenever Keudell was given an assignment by the Chancellor that was at all out of the ordinary, he would call Abeken into the next room and would emerge after some time with pencilled notes from which he would then work. The rest of us gradually became convinced that whenever anything but a pure routine matter cropped up, Keudell was incapable of producing anything off his own bat. One day, shortly after Abeken's death,[1] Bismarck gave expression to this idea when he said: 'Now I know the secret of the Abeken-Keudell partnership. Up to now I couldn't understand it. But I can now see that since Abeken left us Keudell can no longer do anything.'

Prince Bismarck had a similar experience with Bucher a few years afterwards. I will come to that later. Until 1870 I had scarcely known Bucher. During the war, first in the Foreign Ministry, then at Bismarck's war headquarters, we were thrown together more. All I knew of him till then was that he had been one of those who refused to pay taxes, had fled to England and earned his living there for some years as a newspaper corre-

---

[1] Abeken died on 8 August 1872.

spondent and publicist. The *Nationalzeitung*, to which he contributed, had, he thought, underpaid him and, to use his expression, 'lied to his pocket', i.e. it had given out that his income was larger than it really was. He was inclined to be resentful by nature, and bore a deep grudge against Wolf and Zabel, the directors of the *Nationalzeitung*. How far this feeling was justified I am not competent to judge. During his stay in England Bucher looked about for other sources of income. His *Parlamentarismus wie er ist*[1] was widely read in the 'fifties. I read it as a student, but of course without understanding the practical application of the questions discussed. Bucher was also private secretary for some time to a politician called Urquhart,[2] who was quite prominent at that period. The latter devoted great industry and a good deal of his wife's fortune to obtaining material with which to attack Russia's Eastern policy; he then published it in the *Portfolio*, a collection of several volumes. Bucher was sent to Constantinople with the task of finding concrete evidence against Russia. He described his journey in quite an attractive book,[3] but failed to produce anything for his employer who dismissed him as a result. Amongst those who knew Bucher there can be no two opinions on his unsuitability for the role of practising diplomat. With his stunted body, his abnormally ugly face and unhealthy complexion, he had that partly timid, partly embittered reserve of people who have lost heart because they are social failures. This was combined with a strong inclination towards the opposite sex, which, under the circumstances, must have caused him many hours of misery. I was able to guess at the life he lived in London from a little story he told me one day at Versailles, almost by way of an excuse. We had gone for an hour's walk before our meal. I had resolved not to speak before Bucher did. However, he said nothing, so we walked along in silence. When we arrived back at the Villa Jessé without having exchanged a single word, I made some remark to draw his attention to the fact. 'Yes', said Bucher, 'it's hard to break free from long-standing habits. My habit of silence dates from my stay in England. I can still remember how, one evening when I'd come

[1] (Berlin, 1855.)

[2] David Urquhart. British writer; Secretary of the Embassy in Constantinople, 1835–7; after his recall he attacked the Eastern policy of Palmerston, whom he accused of Russian sympathies; Member of Parliament, 1847–52.

[3] Lothar Bucher, *Bilder aus der Fremde*; vol I, *Unterwegs* (Berlin, 1862).

home and was going upstairs, I decided to call down to the maid who tidied up my room. I suddenly discovered I had lost my voice. I was too hoarse to speak. I had felt a tickle in my throat but had no idea I was hoarse, because I'd had no occasion to say a single word all day long.'

After he was reinstated, the 'man who had refused to pay taxes' continued to stand rather aloof from the other officials, particularly in the Foreign Service. The effect of a hard life, as I have observed in other people besides Bucher, is to warp the character. This was very noticeable in his case. There was nothing remarkable in his continuing to detest his former enemies. But he would sometimes say the most surprisingly harsh things even about people—outside official circles—who had shown him great kindness year in year out.

It so happened that during our last weeks at Versailles, in the big office in the Villa Jessé, I sat between Bucher and Wagener.[1] The man who refused to pay taxes and the founder of the *Kreuzzeitung*[2] addressed each other in monosyllables. Bucher confided to me that when he was obliged to flee in the winter of 1848 it was Wagener who caused a warrant for his arrest to be sent out over the telegraph. Bucher's escape was entirely due to the fact that the telegraph system was not working properly that day.

From 1864 Bucher held the office of *Vortragender Rat* in the Foreign Ministry. On my return to Berlin in 1867 he was there. He was useful to Bismarck because he was the only lawyer in the Political Division, because of his knowledge about conditions in England, and perhaps also because of his connection with one or two of the London exiles, though most of them regarded him as suspect after his reinstatement. He had kept in touch with Franz Pulszky, whom he used, as I learned subsequently, as intermediary in the negotiations over the Hungarian Legion[3] in 1866. I was in America in 1866.

[1] Hermann Wagener. Leader of the Conservatives in the Prussian Chamber of Deputies; Member of the North German Reichstag; *Vortragender Rat* in the Ministry of State.

[2] A conservative daily paper.

[3] In June 1866 Bismarck opened negotiations with General Georg Klapka, one of the leaders of the Hungarian Revolution of 1848–9, with a view to forming a Hungarian Legion composed of emigrants and deserters to fight against Austria. At that time Pulszky was in Italy. Cf. Franz Pulszky, *Meine Zeit, mein Leben* (Pressburg and Leipzig, 1882), vol. IV, p. 253.

Bucher had a particular hatred of the Emperor Napoleon and the Pope. Bismarck originally regarded the Catholic Church as one of the forces of order. Some time between 1867 and 1870 I once heard him say: 'The Jesuit Order is a solid organization. Under certain circumstances it would be a force you could count on.' I remembered this saying because it so very much astonished me. Bismarck acted in accordance with this view when, at the time of the Vatican Council, he refused to follow Prince Hohenlohe's proposal to support the bishops in their traditional role of opposition to the Papal absolutism aimed at by the Jesuits. It was not until the newly formed Centre Party in the first German Reichstag elected Windthorst[1] and Savigny as its leaders that I noticed traces of suspicion in Bismarck. Windthorst could be described without exaggeration as an enemy of the Reich, and Savigny had been on very bad terms with Bismarck personally since 1866. Because Savigny had been such a success as Minister to the Federal Diet in 1866, Bismarck had picked him out for the post later occupied by Delbrück. But the break came when Savigny claimed the right of direct access to the King. Bismarck refused this, and Savigny relinquished the post. On the outbreak of the Franco-Prussian War Thile appointed Savigny temporarily to the staff of the Foreign Ministry, but Bismarck objected to this arrangement and after a short time Savigny again took his departure. From what little I heard at Versailles and later about domestic affairs I came to the conclusion that if the Centre Party had elected one of the Reichenspergers[2] or Mallinkrodt[3] as party leader, there would have been no *Kulturkampf*. The Chancellor saw in the choice of Windthorst and Savigny the signs of a threatening attitude and took up the challenge. Bucher welcomed the *Kulturkampf* with undisguised satisfaction. Once when I wrote to him from Paris, round about 1875, and asked how long he thought the *Kulturkampf* should go on, he replied laconically: until a German National Catholic Church had been established.

When I returned to Berlin in the spring of 1876, I found that Bismarck had had enough of the *Kulturkampf*, whereas Bucher,

[1] Ludwig Windthorst. Minister of Justice in Hanover, 1851–3, 1862–5; from 1867 Member of the Reichstag.

[2] August and Peter Reichensperger. Co-founders and for many years leading members of the Centre Party in the Reichstag.

[3] Hermann von Mallinkrodt. Member of the Reichstag from 1867.

the Foreign Ministry official responsible for ecclesiastical affairs, was still busily agitating. But he had little opportunity to do so because the State Secretary, von Bülow,[1] reported to the Chancellor and then passed on his instructions to the Foreign Ministry officials. Bucher had his share like everyone else, and was furious because he was denied direct access to Bismarck. He maintained that he could tell merely from Bismarck's appearance and intonation how he was expected to write his draft, and without these signs he could not convey the right shades of meaning.

On the other hand Herbert told me his father had said Bucher's style depended on his shorthand notes. When he used to report in person to Bismarck, all he did was to take down everything the Chancellor said. Now that was no longer possible, Bucher's style had changed.

Despite all their external differences Bucher in some respects resembled Marschall.[2] Marschall, too, was taciturn, not always by accident, in fact when he was State Secretary he could allow his thoughts and attention to wander when it suited him. Both men, Bucher and Marschall, had their first experience of high policy quite late in life, after they were forty-five; neither of them evolved any independent views on policy, but they both possessed a variety of useful knowledge of ecclesiastical, legal and (particularly Marschall) economic affairs, as well as the treatment of the Press. Finally, neither of them had any initiative. In Marschall's case this was inherent in his character; Bucher, after the failure of that first bold revolutionary escapade, had been confirmed in his natural tendencies by bitter experience.

This characteristic of Bucher's explains why he could not maintain the position he had held with Bismarck under subsequent State Secretaries. At the height of his powers, that is until the advent of Schweninger,[3] Bismarck did not need any stimulus or complement in the domain of high policy, and it was only exceptionally that he drew on the knowledge or the memory of the

[1] Bernhard Ernst von Bülow. Minister to the Federal Diet in Frankfurt for Holstein and Lauenburg, 1851–62; Minister of State in Mecklenburg-Strelitz, 1862–8; Minister representing Mecklenburg-Strelitz in Berlin, 1868–73; State Secretary in the German Foreign Ministry, 1873–9.

[2] Adolf Hermann Marschall, Baron von Bieberstein. Minister representing Baden in Berlin, 1883–90; State Secretary in the German Foreign Ministry 1890–7; Ambassador in Constantinople, 1897–1912.

[3] Dr Ernst Schweninger. Prince Bismarck's doctor from 1881.

responsible official. But Bucher's knowledge in other fields often enabled him to make himself most useful to Prince Bismarck, for example during their long stays in the country, by telling of his earlier experiences as a rural magistrate. But the demands made on the officials by the new men to hold office as State Secretary, Bülow, Hohenlohe,[1] Stirum,[2] Hatzfeldt, proved quite different.

Bülow was a man of great gifts with an immense capacity for work, and with a life of hard work behind him. A frigid personality, with unvaryingly impeccable manners, who probably allowed no one outside his family to be really close to him. But at the same time he did his utmost to be unfailingly just, and when he had enough scope, energetic too. He was thoroughly well-informed on legal matters, particularly in the field of constitutional law and economics, and had made his mark at Frankfurt as a skilful diplomat, but he did not feel at home with Bismarck's foreign policy. It now fell to the responsible *Räte* in the Political Division, in keeping with their title of *Vortragende*, to initiate their new chief. The one man who failed to do that was Bucher. I gathered from his conversation—though in 1873 and 1874 I was only in Berlin for short periods—that he was annoyed because Bülow now stood between him and direct contact with the Chancellor. He regarded the whole business as a plot and refused to realize that Bismarck, now his main life's work was done, had merely wished to ease his burden. Sometimes he expressed the idea that, once the new State Secretary had committed a real blunder, Bismarck would realize just what was the effect of this innovation. But I do not regard this as the main factor, which was rather Bucher's lack of any overall view. Bucher was incapable of summing up a diplomatic situation, of picking out events in the past which—subject to the principles governing contemporary policy—could serve as points of departure for future policy. All the time I knew Bucher, I never heard him express any opinion on the political situation, except once in 1877 or 1878 when we were walking along the Charlottenburger Chaussee. His views surprised me so much that I can

---

[1] In 1880 Hohenlohe was interim Head of the Foreign Ministry.

[2] Friedrich Wilhelm, Count zu Limburg-Stirum. Prussian Minister in Weimar, 1875–80; interim Head of the Foreign Ministry, 1880–1; in 1881 he was given indefinite leave of absence; Member of the Prussian Chamber of Deputies, 1871–1905 (from 1893 leader of the German Conservative Party); Member of the Reichstag, 1893–1906.

still remember what he said. He summed up the Eastern Question by saying it would be a mistake to help the Bulgarians, because the Greeks were a more interesting people who had rendered far greater services to civilization and were therefore more deserving of assistance. This was the opinion of a scholar, not a politician, to whom Bulgaria and Greece were no more than cards to be played at the suitable moment. But no matter whether Bucher held defensible views on foreign policy or whether, as I rather suspect, he had only instinctive desires which he was unwilling or unable to express, he was not the man to offer guidance to his newly appointed chief. And so a coolness sprang up between him and Bülow, which on Bucher's side gradually developed into an intense hatred. A contributory circumstance was that Bülow was one of the many people eager to end the *Kulturkampf*.

After the death of the State Secretary in the autumn of 1879 and before the new appointment, the responsible Foreign Ministry officials once more had direct access to the Chancellor, but Bucher cannot have been so successful as before. The reason may have been that both he and Prince Bismarck were older and more settled in their ways. Once—Bucher told me this himself—when Bucher in silence handed Bismarck the document to be dealt with and settled down to write, Bismarck told him that a thorough study of the files by the official concerned should precede any report; he, Bismarck, could not carry all the files in his head. Afterwards the Prince told Herbert who happened to be in Berlin, that if all the officials were like Bucher and expected him to dictate their dispatches word for word, then it would be simpler to call on the services of a clerk. (Bismarck mentioned Mechler,[1] the Head of the Chancellery staff.)

The friction between the two men, who after all had worked together for many years, may also spring from the fact that in matters of ecclesiastical policy, which were constantly being discussed, they took opposite sides. Bismarck, who in the autumn of 1879 had held discussions at Gastein with Jacobini,[2] the Papal Nuncio, desired the end of the *Kulturkampf*, Bucher did not. At

---

[1] Gustav Emil Mechler. In the Foreign Ministry, 1870–86; temporary Head of the Chancellor's Secretariat 1886–9; Head of the Central Bureau of the Foreign Ministry, 1889–1920.

[2] Ludovico Jacobini. Papal Nuncio in Vienna, 1874–80; Cardinal-State Secretary from the end of 1880.

that period direct communications passed between the Kaiser and the Pope; Bucher's task was to draft them according to the Chancellor's instructions, and I translated them into French. Things did not always go smoothly. Bucher thought he understood French better than he actually did. He had coined the formula that he 'did not want to sacrifice the contents to the style', that is, he required his sentences to be translated literally. I protested, because with such a method quite impossible German expressions would have crept into the text. My relations with Bucher became more strained mainly because I was gradually called on to do the more responsible work. But they markedly deteriorated after the following incident. In October or November 1880[1] Bucher came and told me there was some question of resuming relations with the Vatican: whom should he suggest to the Chancellor to carry out preliminary negotiations in Rome? He had thought of Stumm.[2] I replied that I thought Stumm unsuitable, first because of his personality and second because some years previously it had fallen to him as Chargé d'Affaires ('*Il tenente* Stumm' he was called in the Vatican newspapers) to break off relations. The Vatican would be unfavourably prejudiced against him even before he arrived. I said it was a happy chance that Busch[3] (the Under State Secretary designate in the Foreign Ministry) was on leave just at that moment and was touring round Italy. He seemed to me the most suitable man for these negotiations. Bucher obviously disliked this proposal intensely. Not that he and Busch were on bad terms —on the contrary. But it was in keeping with Bucher's views that he should prefer someone unsuitable. He replied curtly that he had no idea where Busch was at the moment, anyhow we could hardly spoil his little bit of leave. Then he went to make his report to Bismarck. Immediately afterwards the Chancellor sent for me.

---

[1] Should read 1881. Busch was already Under State Secretary at the time of these negotiations.

[2] Ferdinand, Baron von Stumm. First Secretary in the Embassy in St Petersburg, 1878–81, in London 1881–3; Prussian Minister in Darmstadt 1883–5; Minister in Copenhagen, 1885–7; Minister, later Ambassador, in Madrid, 1887–92.

[3] Dr Klemens August Busch. Dragoman in Constantinople, 1861–72; Consul in St Petersburg, 1872–4; temporarily attached to the Political Division of the Foreign Ministry, 1874–9; Consul-General in Budapest, 1879–80; temporary Head of the Political Division in the Foreign Ministry, 1880–1; Under State Secretary, March 1881–5; Minister in Bucharest, 1885–8, in Stockholm, 1888–92, in Berne, 1892–5.

He began by talking of other things, then he said: 'Bucher's been suggesting for these negotiations with the Pope all kinds of people who don't appeal to me. Have you anyone in mind?' I suggested Busch, giving my reasons briefly, and the interview ended. Half an hour later Bucher came back and said Bismarck had just instructed him to have Busch summoned to Rome by our Embassy there, so that he could take charge of the negotiations with the Curia. I told Bucher I had put forward Busch's name when Bismarck asked me. Bucher went off in a bad temper and behaved differently towards me ever after. He was the less disposed to forgive me my part in the settlement of the *Kulturkampf* because Busch, my nominee, met with success in his undertaking.[1]

Bucher's aversion to the peace negotiations with the Curia may also have affected the quality of his work. I have already mentioned that Prince Bismarck had criticized it. I also learned at about this time—perhaps from Herbert, I do not remember—that Bismarck intended to entrust certain tasks to *Wirklicher Geheimer Oberregierungsrat* Hahn instead of Bucher. Hahn, editor of the *Provinzialkorrespondenz*, had also published a book on Bismarck,[2] and was without the slightest doubt an outstanding writer and stylist. Schlözer, too, who loved to affect an air of mystery and thus often gave things away, told me one day that Bucher was past his best, and that he, Schlözer, had already been told the name of his successor. The plan had to be dropped because Hahn's health broke down as a result of overwork, and in 1882 he had to retire altogether. But in any case, I am sure it was only a question of lightening Bucher's burden, possibly by relieving him of his work on ecclesiastical affairs, and not of dismissing him. Bucher told me repeatedly during the 'seventies that Prince Bismarck had said he must come and live with him in the country when they had both left the service, and help him to put his memoirs in order. So Bismarck had no intention of breaking with Bucher.

Apart from Dr Moritz Busch, Bucher's only other close friend was the Minister Count Limburg-Stirum. An industrious man, but without any talent or sense of what was fitting, he had contrived

[1] Cf. diary entry of 10 February 1882 (*Diaries*); Busch's letter of 9 December 1881 (*Correspondence*).

[2] *Fürst Bismarck. Sein politisches Leben und Wirken urkundlich in Thatsachen und des Fürsten eigenen Kundgebungen dargestellt*, 5 vols. (Berlin, 1878–91); vol. v by Dr C. Wippermann.

between 1876 and 1880, when Minister in Weimar, to make his position in society impossible, even though he was a Count, was wealthy, and was Prussia's representative. To escape persecution by anonymous letters and notices in the papers, he relinquished his post in 1879 or 1880 and obtained leave of absence, either for a short time or indefinitely. After this unpromising beginning it seemed doubtful if he would be given office again; he owed his recall mainly to Bucher's influence. In September 1880 Prince Hohenlohe, who was acting as temporary State Secretary during the interval between Bülow's death and Hatzfeldt's assumption of office, asked for a month's leave. Prince Bismarck declared that Busch, whose post as Under State Secretary would not be established before the following spring, could not deputize for the State Secretary since he was only a second-class *Rat*, and so some Minister must be called in during Hohenlohe's leave. To the astonishment of the Ministry staff, and, as it was generally assumed, at Bucher's instigation, Bismarck's choice fell on Stirum. Busch gave no sign of being annoyed, but he requested several months' leave for health reasons and went to Italy.

Stirum had no idea what his official duties entailed and his friend Bucher, who shunned any responsibility like poison, refused to give him advice. In the Political Division this task therefore fell to me. It was the first time I was given any sort of discretionary work. Of course all the more important decisions emanated from Varzin; the Ministry only had to make suggestions or carry out orders. Just at this time a conference was sitting in Constantinople to carry out the adjustment of the Greco-Turkish frontier, which the Congress of Berlin had expressed as a *vœu*, so we had plenty of work. Stirum's temporary period of office was prolonged because Hohenlohe caught typhus and never resumed his functions in Berlin, and Hatzfeldt could not yet leave Constantinople. At Christmas Herbert Bismarck wrote to Stirum from Friedrichsruh to say that the Chancellor wished to invite him there for the holidays, and to ask to be prepared to stay for a few days, because one day would not be long enough for Prince Bismarck to say all the pleasant things he had in mind.

Stirum went there and came back very pleased with life; his one regret was that his parrot, which had been left in the office, had starved or frozen to death.

In the New Year Busch returned from Italy and resumed his work as acting Under State Secretary. To avoid any unpleasantness with Busch I told Stirum that I should give up my role of adviser, and that he must look to the Under State Secretary in future. I may say that we did not gain the impression that the direction of affairs was now uniform or consistent. Then a few months later I had a letter from Herbert Bismarck[1] to say that his father desired me to write and tell Hatzfeldt that he must come at once, because Stirum could not be kept on any longer. Naturally I carried out this order and also showed Bucher Herbert's letter. I could tell by the change in Stirum's manner that Bucher had said something to him.

Bucher was most annoyed. He may have hoped that Stirum would eventually fill competently the position of State Secretary; at any rate he had a particular dislike of Hatzfeldt as his superior. At a small dinner-party given by some of the Foreign Ministry officials to Count Stirum, Bucher made a speech which began with the words: 'The future comes on hesitant foot.' He meant Hatzfeldt.

Stirum himself expected to be appointed Ambassador in Constantinople to succeed Hatzfeldt, and made no secret of cherishing this hope. But the Chancellor would not hear of it. Instead, Herbert instructed me on behalf of his father to sound Stirum about accepting the post of Minister at the Hague. Stirum declined it; he even seemed insulted.

Hatzfeldt and Bucher did not get on well. Hatzfeldt would say: 'People talk about Bucher's shrewd judgement. But I've known him now for a number of years and am still waiting to hear him express and develop one single idea of his own on politics.' [...]

Bucher's strong point—and his value to Bismarck—lay in his knowledge of legal matters, particularly constitutional and international law, and of modern diplomatic history. During one of the final sessions of the Congress Waddington[2] raised the point that Greece needed an extension of her frontiers if she was to be viable, and that the Congress should formulate a 'wish' (vœu) to this effect, but the proposal was discouragingly received. Beaconsfield,[3]

---

[1] Not found.

[2] William Henry Waddington. French Foreign Minister, 1877–9; plenipotentiary at the Congress of Berlin.

[3] Benjamin Disraeli, Earl of Beaconsfield. British Prime Minister 1874–80; first British plenipotentiary at the Congress of Berlin.

whose sympathies lay with Turkey, said coldly: 'Greece is a young state and when you're young you *can afford to wait*.'[1] And with that the session closed. When I met Bucher later he said: 'There must be a precedent. The Congress of Vienna or some other Congress must have formulated a *vœu*. I'll just go and look up one or two Congress protocols.' A few hours later he returned having discovered his precedent. I cannot remember whether I told Bismarck of Bucher's find over a meal, or whether I asked Herbert to inform him. Prince Bismarck asked to see the document and then, on the strength of this precedent, supported the French proposal. The Greeks owe their frontier extension of 1881 mainly to those two opposites, Bucher and Hatzfeldt. Bucher had provided the basis for the Congress's *vœu*, but it was Hatzfeldt who prevailed on the Sultan to comply. But for the confidence Hatzfeldt inspired in the Sultan the conference of 1881, which was to put into effect the 'wish' of the Berlin Congress, would have yielded no result. The diplomatic world expected a fiasco, and the news that the Sultan had given way on Hatzfeldt's advice came as a surprise. I well remember that the British Ambassador, Lord Ampthill,[2] wrote a note that day—I think to Busch—which began with the words: 'Bravo, Hatzfeldt'.[3] Perhaps he said 'Bravo' with his tongue in his cheek because it was a diplomatic victory for Germany, and in any case Ampthill did not like Hatzfeldt. The two men were very different. Not until later, when Hatzfeldt's office of State Secretary brought them constantly together, did this difference really stand out. Ampthill worked hard both on important and on trifling matters, but Hatzfeldt was only interested in broad issues. Whenever Ampthill came along to Hatzfeldt with something he thought trivial, he would put on a bored expression and say: 'Would you mind taking it to Busch, he knows all about it.' Ampthill, a man with extremely pleasant manners but with considerable self-esteem—as indeed was Hatzfeldt—never failed to take offence. When Ampthill died in 1884, Courcel[4] said to me: 'The odd thing about Ampthill was that, in other respects a serious-

---

[1] In English in the original.
[2] Odo Russell, first Lord Ampthill. British Ambassador in Berlin, 1871–84.
[3] See Wolfgang Windelband, *Bismarck und die europäischen Grossmächte 1879–85* (Essen, 1940), p. 216.
[4] Alphonse, Baron de Courcel. French Ambassador in Berlin, 1882–6, in London, 1894–8.

minded man, he could always be counted on whenever there was a chance of playing a trick on Hatzfeldt (*de faire une niche à H.*).'

But to return to Bucher. He made no secret of the fact that Hatzfeldt, who outshone him both socially and intellectually, was unacceptable to him as a superior, and so he made life as difficult for him as possible. Hatzfeldt bore all this with patience, calmly overlooked the fact that Bucher never called on him in the Villa, and very rarely altered anything in Bucher's drafts.

When Herbert Bismarck took over the direction of the Foreign Ministry in the spring of 1885, first as Under State Secretary, he and Bucher soon quarrelled. Herbert Bismarck, presumably to show who was master, took the first opportunity of going right through one of Bucher's drafts and correcting it to an extent he had rarely experienced even from Prince Bismarck himself. Bucher, furious, declared in the Central Bureau that he would not put up with such foul treatment and demanded his release. This was granted, but Prince Bismarck smoothed him down by various means, such as an annual pension allowance of 2000 marks from the *Welfenfond*.[1] He also remained constantly in touch with him and invited him to stay in the country.

This is how I would briefly sum up Bucher's character: he was so reticent with his views on the handling of foreign affairs that there seemed some ground for the opinion held, for instance, by Hatzfeldt, that apart from the *Kulturkampf* Bucher usually formed no independent opinion at all. On the other hand he liked to display his solid factual knowledge, and whenever the opportunity offered he made his superiority felt. Schlözer, in his stylish but superficial way, once called the Archbishop of Cologne the 'Primate of Prussia' in a report written from Rome. Bucher immediately drew up an unpleasantly dry dispatch in which Schlözer was informed that this title did not exist, and why. Since both men were on good terms, the proper way of correcting the error would have been by personal letter. But one must admit Schlözer had the reputation for taking things easy. It was said in particular by people who were in a position to judge that he had never read the

---

[1] A fund created by the Prussian Government out of the fortune of King George V of Hanover, who had sided with Austria in 1866, subsequently refused to accept Prussian suzerainty, and was exiled. The fund did not come under the control of the Prussian Finance Minister or the Chamber of Deputies, and could be conveniently used for special purposes.

May Laws.[1] Nor is it an exaggeration to say that, especially towards the end of his period of office in Rome, his reports were almost exclusively concerned with explaining why he had been unable to perform satisfactorily a commission entrusted to him. That is why Herbert wished to get rid of Schlözer in 1889, but could not make his father agree; he said he had 'really got used to the old fogey'.

Among the people Bismarck summoned to Versailles was *Geheimrat* Wagener, founder of the *Kreuzzeitung*. He had begun his career as a solicitor somewhere in Pomerania, had then been very active in the Conservative Party, and later—whether through Bismarck or at an earlier period, I cannot say—he had entered the civil service. I often heard it said that Bismarck would have liked to make him Under State Secretary in the Ministry of State, but the King would not hear of it, because Wagener, in his usual acid, biting manner, had attacked the Princess of Prussia[2] in the *Kreuzzeitung*. That was many years before, but had never been forgotten. The King simply ignored the existence of Wagener, as of Wagener's old enemy, Bucher. The Conservatives, to whom Wagener had rendered great service, now thought him not conservative enough, and levelled all kinds of criticism at him. Of this I cannot judge. But during the weeks we sat working next to each other, I became firmly convinced that Wagener was a man of great gifts. Even so one occasionally glimpsed a streak of lighthearted cruelty, as in the following incident.

A certain Prince Friedrich zu Sayn-Wittgenstein, a man of evil reputation, had been cashiered because of debts, and had then earned himself the worst possible name amongst the German colony in China. He had finally returned to the army and, as Captain with the 2nd Dragoon Guards, had ridden a successful attack at Mars la Tour on 16 August. Though I knew nothing about it at the time, he had been the occasion of a discussion between the Chancellor and Wagener. It must be explained that shortly before the army left Berlin, the Prince had married his mistress, a member of the Lilienthal family of ballet dancers— naturally without his family's consent. His younger brother had

---

[1] The May Laws of 1873, directed against the Catholic Church in Prussia at the time of the *Kulturkampf*.

[2] The title of Wilhelm I's wife, before his accession to the throne of Prussia.

previously married one of the Lilienthal sisters. Prince Friedrich Wittgenstein's marriage was invalid because he had not obtained consent. On the outbreak of war a number of such marriages had been contracted without waiting to obtain consent; otherwise there was no objection to them. In official quarters there was every intention to treat these marriages as valid, though technically they were not. This was the more necessary because many of these young husbands were already dead and their widows with child. But Prince Friedrich Wittgenstein's stepmother saw the matter in a different light. She was by birth a Princess Bariatinsky, had gone over to Catholicism, and was friendly with Queen Augusta. It was to her that the Princess turned, with a plea that her stepson's marriage might be declared invalid because he had failed to obtain consent. The Queen had passed on this request to the proper quarter, with presumably no idea of its full import. For obviously such a request could only be met by a decree that was generally binding, whereby all the marriages entered into without consent at the outbreak of war would expressly be declared invalid, instead of being formally recognized after the event.

This affair had come from Berlin to be submitted to the Kaiser, and it depended on the way Bismarck put the case and the decision the Kaiser made, whether widows and orphans of those who had died defending their country would live in honour or dishonour. Wagener, as *Rat* in the Ministry of State, was put in charge of the affair. One day Bismarck came into our office—a very rare occurrence—went up to Wagener and began to talk about this affair. Since I sat next to him I heard everything. Wagener was for declaring the marriages invalid, pointed out the undesirable situation that would result if, at every general mobilization, the law of consent were automatically suspended, and so on. Wagener spoke with a bold assurance, even contradicting the Chancellor. I felt a certain admiration for his behaviour although, so far as the facts were concerned, I agreed absolutely with the Chancellor. He curtly and decisively dismissed Wagener's objections, stressing the claims of humanity and pointing out that the honourable name of a number of widows and orphans was at stake; he ordered the report to the Kaiser to be drafted along those lines. And that is how the question was settled.

Princess Friedrich Wittgenstein, *née* Lilienthal, was then persuaded by means of a payment of thirty or forty thousand gulden to obtain a divorce, and subsequently married a theatre director called Ullmann. Doubtless the dowager Princess Wittgenstein had wanted to save this sum. In this affair Wagener took the line of formal correctness, and showed he was not exactly tender-hearted.

Wagener came to a sad end. During the *Gründerzeit*[1] that followed the war he had invested in a scheme for the construction of a branch line in Pomerania. Of course this line has now been working for years, but at that time the company went bankrupt when the great crash came in 1873. Wagener was held fully responsible for a sum which far exceeded his modest fortune. At the same time he was attacked by Lasker[2] in the Parliament as a *Gründer*,[3] and Delbrück made no attempt to save him. Prince Bismarck went to visit Wagener at the time, but did not judge it advisable to advocate retaining him in the service. So Wagener resigned, but the creditors levied a distress on his pension. I had it from a reliable source that during his last years Wagener barely kept body and soul together, and lived by copying and similar work. This piece of ill-usage also served to pay off an old score, but I will mention no names, because much of what I was told may well be exaggerated.

Karl Bismarck also came to a sad end. The Chancellor did nothing for him, and Delbrück refused to make him a *Vortragender Rat*. Soon after the war Karl Bismarck left the service, lived for the most part in Venice, and finally committed suicide.

I got to know Herr von Keudell when he came to St Petersburg in 1861 or 1862, on the Bismarcks' invitation. He was a musical acquaintance of Frau von Bismarck's, and it is mainly to her that he owes his career. Frau von Bismarck told me, shortly after her husband had become Minister-President, that he needed an *homme*

---

[1] The term applied to the period of rapid expansion of business activity and speculation following on the Franco-Prussian War.

[2] Eduard Lasker. Member of the Prussian Chamber of Deputies, 1865–79; Member of the Reichstag, 1867–83; until 1866 he belonged to the Progressives; then founder and leader of the Left wing of the National Liberal Party; in 1880 he left the National Liberal Party and joined the so-called Secessionists in 1881. In 1883 he retired from parliamentary life. Died in New York on 5 January 1884.

[3] Lasker's attack was directed against the railway concessions which Wagener and other *Gründer* had obtained from the State.

de confiance for secret transactions and that she had recommended Keudell. I could tell from the way she spoke that Bismarck had received the suggestion with no great enthusiasm and was still undecided. But when I returned from Brazil in 1864, I found Keudell installed in charge of the Personnel Department. Pleasant, taciturn, insincere, his outstanding musical talent did not prevent him from being selfish and unreliable as a friend. He shared with Bucher, from whom he differed so widely in other respects, the habit of silence. Both men held their tongues in the hope of enhancing their prestige; they felt, justifiably enough, particularly in the case of Keudell, that it paid them better to leave people in uncertainty about their opinions. In this way, namely by a prudent silence, Keudell had succeeded in earning and maintaining the reputation between 1864 and 1870 of being Bismarck's closest confidant and collaborator. I thought so too, until working together in the same room at Versailles enlightened me. Bismarck had in fact taken him on at his wife's request and would soon have got rid of him but for the certainty that his wife Johanna would have been deeply hurt. For Keudell used to play and sing to her, and arranged all kinds of musical entertainments besides. This was the only kind of social life the Princess valued; she regarded all her other social obligations as mere duty.

Keudell was ambitious. The discrepancy between his ability and his aspirations had an unfortunate effect on his behaviour towards his colleagues. The Chancellor must have treated him really badly at times, as I could tell from Keudell's own accounts in which he spoke of Prince Bismarck's morbid irritability. I could mention many instances of Keudell's letting down his colleagues. I will give just one example, and relate the incident which led to the break between Bismarck and the Under State Secretary von Thile.[1]

Thile, formerly Minister to the Holy See, was an elderly, very wealthy man with no children, who had been saddened by the loss of his only son. He worked to pass the time, without ambition, and was therefore not afraid to make it known that on occasion he disagreed with Bismarck. The position of Under State Secretary was not a pleasant one. The *Vortragende Räte* in the Political Division received their instructions direct from Bismarck. Then, admittedly, the drafts were placed before the Under State Secretary,

---

[1] Thile was State Secretary when the break took place.

but, because he had not been present when the instructions were given he was ignorant of the chief's intentions. Thus it was quite possible for Bismarck to cross out a correction made by the Under State Secretary and to restore the original version by the *Vortragender Rat*. Bismarck told me himself that this happened once or twice, and that since then Thile merely appended his initials without altering a word. Bismarck regarded this as unwarrantably touchy. And I often had the impression that a good deal of Thile's criticisms had come to his ears, thus creating a state of chronic irritation which would flare up at the first opportunity. This opportunity occurred in the autumn of 1872, when the Emperors of Russia and Austria were both in Berlin. One day when manœuvres were in progress, Kaiser Wilhelm sent a message to Bismarck saying he wished to confer the Order of the Black Eagle on the two Ambassadors Károlyi[1] and Oubril,[2] and intended to do so after the review, before dinner; he therefore asked for the insignia to be sent to the castle at once. As the Chancellor was also watching the manœuvres, the message was passed on to Thile, who discussed it with Keudell, who was in charge of the Personnel Department, and then dispatched the two decorations as he had been ordered to do. He would hardly have made such a decision had he known how strongly Bismarck disliked Oubril. But Thile lived in a world of his own, did his work and took little notice—perhaps too little—of his chief's moods. Oubril was of French origin, had French sympathies and moreover, being a Catholic, was regarded by Bismarck as secretly in league with the Centre Party. Bismarck supposed that Gorchakov had planted this unattractive personage in Berlin to force through the appointment of Michael Gorchakov[3] as Ambassador. Bismarck once [told] me—I cannot remember whether it was in 1872, that is before the meeting of the three Emperors, or in 1873—that when Gorchakov was discussing the question of ambassadors with him, he said: '*Dites un mot et mon fils sera ambassadeur.*' But Bismarck was not at all disposed to make this concession, and so the quarrel over Oubril dragged on for years. Bismarck also conceived a grudge against Alexander II because he had emphatically refused to transfer Oubril, even though

[1] Alois, Count Károlyi. Austro-Hungarian Ambassador in Berlin, 1871–8.
[2] Paul von Oubril. Russian Ambassador in Berlin, 1871–80.
[3] Michael, Prince Gorchakov. Son of Prince Alexander Gorchakov. Secretary in the Russian Embassy in Berlin, 1868–72.

Bismarck had requested it in person. It may be that this incident, like Gorchakov's request, occurred after 1872, but in fact Bismarck was already at daggers drawn with Oubril in the autumn of 1872, and no one knew that better than Keudell, who spent his evenings in the Bismarcks' drawing-room. Nothing could have been easier for Keudell than to advise the Under State Secretary to send for the insignia, but to delay their dispatch until he had reported to the Chancellor immediately after his return. They could still, if Bismarck agreed, have reached the palace in good time before the guests sat down to dinner. But Keudell said nothing of the kind and let the Under State Secretary go straight to his doom. For when Bismarck heard later from Keudell that Oubril, whose stay in Berlin was intended to be made as unpleasant as possible, had received the highest honour attainable without his being consulted, he flew into a rage. And with good cause. For the conferring of this order was an important political act. Of course Bismarck might have told himself that the old Kaiser, who left him a pretty free hand in politics, had wished to show his independence in front of his two fellow-emperors. But I doubt whether Bismarck thought this, for indulgence towards human weaknesses was not one of his qualities. At any rate Keudell came up to Thile the following morning and said to him (as I well remember from Thile's account): 'I've been wondering all night long whether to repeat to you what the Chancellor said about you yesterday. But I've come to the conclusion that it's impossible.'

Naturally Thile handed in his resignation at once, because Keudell's words obliged him to assume the worst. Prince Bismarck summoned Balan[1] to take his place. I was told in the Foreign Ministry, during a few days' leave in Berlin just after completing my four weeks' duty at Varzin, that Keudell had seemed 'thunderstruck' at the news of Balan's appointment, for he had hoped for it himself. I did not meet Keudell during those days, but I thought his behaviour towards Thile justified such a suspicion. But in any case Keudell's hopes, assuming they existed, were based on false premises, for by that time he had already ruined his chances professionally so far as the Chancellor was concerned.

Keudell next turned his attentions to the Legation in Constan-

---

[1] Hermann von Balan. Minister in Brussels, 1868–74; acting State Secretary in the Foreign Ministry, 1872–3.

tinople. The titular holder of the post was the ailing Count Hein-rich Keyserling,[1] a close friend of Keudell's. He had just married a Countess Anrep and was on the point of resuming his duties after rather a long period of sick leave, when he was informed that in view of his health a successor had been appointed, none other than his friend Keudell. Needless to say Keyserling was far from pleased. 'I know I couldn't take part in a gymnastic competition, but my health would have been quite equal to the duties of Mini-ster in Constantinople.' I can well remember his saying this.

On my return to Berlin in the autumn of 1873 I learned that Keudell, who was on leave in Berlin at the same time, was not doing very well in Constantinople. There was one particular *faux pas* the Chancellor reproached him for, and it was doubtful whether he would be kept on. But no, things turned out differently. King Victor Emmanuel, after a period of surly hesitation, had finally decided to visit Berlin. His whole behaviour and in particular his frank confession: '*Sire, à un moment j'ai été bien près de vous faire la guerre*', had left a favourable impression behind, and my good old friend Launay[2] seized on this moment to further a long-cherished desire, the raising of the Legation to an Embassy. As a preliminary step in this direction Launay, on instructions from his Government, asked for Keudell to be transferred to Rome, where the post of German Minister had just become vacant. Keudell had managed to maintain his prestige as Bismarck's 'right-hand man', and Launay imagined it would be child's play for a man like him to raise both Legations into Embassies. Bismarck agreed to the transfer requested by the Italian Govern-ment, but when he entered the drawing-room later on he said: 'Just imagine, the Italians are asking to have Keudell as Minister. Well, if they want the blockhead they're welcome to him.' Within a year Launay's wish to become Ambassador was fulfilled. The Italian Government proposed the change, which was unhesi-tatingly granted in Berlin.

I can recall nothing, either good or bad, of Keudell's diplomatic achievements during his period in Rome, 1873–86. He enter-tained pleasantly the many German residents with whom he was

---

[1] Heinrich, Count von Keyserling-Rautenburg. Minister in Constantinople from October 1869.

[2] Eduard, Count di Launay. Sardinian Minister, then Italian Minister and Am-bassador in Berlin, 1856–92.

very popular, and played the piano with Queen Margarita. But in 1886 fate caught up with him. At that time Robilant[1] was the Italian Foreign Minister, and preliminary *pourparlers* were in progress between Rome and Berlin on the renewal of the Triple Alliance concluded in 1883.[2] One day in spring or summer Bismarck asked me: 'Isn't there any reply yet from Rome to our latest statement on the Triple Alliance? It's taking a very long time.' I confirmed that there had as yet been no response from Rome and asked whether I should drop a hint to Launay. 'No', said the Chancellor, 'I refuse to make two consecutive moves. We'll wait.' Herbert had fallen seriously ill at the end of April 1886 and did not return until autumn. Shortly after his return, perhaps in October, he sent for me and said: 'Launay has just called and asked whether there was any reply to the overtures Count Robilant made to Keudell in spring about extending the Triple Alliance. I told him:"I've not the faintest idea, I was not here at the time!" What actually is the position?' I explained that no such reply had arrived from Italy. 'Well', said Herbert, 'perhaps Keudell told my father something when he was in Varzin recently. I'll find out.' But nothing was known at Varzin either. So now Keudell was asked what had happened. His answer was plaintive and subdued. Count Robilant had indeed said something to him about the Triple Alliance in the early summer. But immediately afterwards, that very afternoon in fact, the Ambassador had left Rome because of a threatened typhus epidemic and had gone to Lake Maggiore. As a result the entire affair had slipped his memory.[3]

At the same time that Keudell's report arrived, Launay came to

[1] Nicolis, Count di Robilant. Italian Minister and Ambassador in Vienna, 1871–85; Foreign Minister in the Depretis Cabinet, 1885–7.

[2] Should read '1882'.

[3] Holstein's chronology in this paragraph is inaccurate. Launay asked Count von Bismarck on 25 September 1886, whether Herr von Keudell had sent in a report on a very interesting conversation he had had with Count Robilant before going on leave. He, Launay, could not allude to the matter until it was mentioned to him. By order of the Chancellor, Keudell was asked by a dispatch of 30 September whether Count Robilant in his last interview with him before he went on leave had made any statements necessitating a reply from Berlin; in Keudell's report of the interview of 5 August (cf. *Grosse Politik*, vol. IV, no. 822, pp. 184–6) there was no evidence of this. Keudell replied on 5 October that Count Robilant had not touched on the question of the renewal of the Triple Alliance in that conversation. Keudell's answer cited above by Holstein has not been found in the files of the German Foreign Ministry.

see me and said he had received a letter from Robilant which, as one of Keudell's friends, he found extremely embarrassing. In the letter which Launay then read out to me it was stated that Keudell, *qui avait complètement perdu la boule*, had confessed to the Minister that his last communication concerning the Triple Alliance had not been passed on but forgotten.[1] Count Robilant was known to be a nervy, touchy individual. One of his hands had been shot away at Novara, and this mutilation had affected his whole personality. As Ambassador in Vienna he had earned himself the nickname in society of *l'honneur de l'Italie*, because his susceptibility had led him to use this expression more often than seemed necessary. And so the effect on him of Keudell's confession can be imagined. Robilant had been very uneasy over Bismarck's inexplicable silence, and now it turned out that the Ambassador had entirely ignored his communication. No wonder the letter concluded with instructions to Launay to see that an Ambassador was sent to Rome with whom the Foreign Minister could discuss serious matters (*choses sérieuses*). That was the end of Keudell's career.

I suggested as his successor Count Solms[2] (Madrid) who just previously had shown courage and dignity in his handling of the Caroline Islands question[3] in Spain.

Paul Hatzfeldt's acquaintance with Bismarck dates from the Chancellor's earliest Frankfurt years. It is well known that the Hatzfeldts' home background was deplorable. Mother and father each went their separate ways. To remove his only sister, who later became Countess Nesselrode, from this unhealthy home atmosphere, Paul Hatzfeldt carried her off and took her to a boarding-school in Austria run by nuns. At the instigation either of the father or the mother, Bismarck was instructed by telegram to conduct a search for the fugitives and, if possible, to arrest them. Up to now Bismarck's opinion of Paul Hatzfeldt, who was said to have taken part in a street riot in 1848 when only sixteen, could hardly have been worse. He revised it, however, when the young fugitive appeared before the Minister, explained the situation and asked for his support. Instead of having the

---

[1] There is nothing about Launay's complaint to Holstein in the files of the German Foreign Ministry.

[2] Eberhard, Count zu Solms-Sonnenwalde. Minister in Madrid, 1878–87; Ambassador in Rome, 1887–93.

[3] See diary entry for 23 August 1885 (*Diaries*).

young people arrested, Bismarck helped them on their way. I think
the memory of that first meeting predisposed Bismarck favourably
towards Hatzfeldt. They next met ten years later in Paris, where
Hatzfeldt was a junior Secretary. Then in 1867 or 1868 Hatzfeldt
took the immense step from Secretary at the Hague to *Vortragender Rat* in the Political Division. Bismarck gave as the reason
for the appointment that he needed someone with a complete
mastery of French. Bismarck added that he preferred Hatzfeldt's
style to Wesdehlen's, although the latter had learnt French as his
mother tongue. (Wesdehlen's father was called Petitpierre; he
was a native of Neuchâtel who, when private secretary to the
Prussian Minister Count Waldburg Truchsess in Turin, married
one of his daughters. As a result he became Count Wesdehlen.
The Minister's two other daughters both married, one the Attaché
Count Dohna Schlobitten and the other a Count Robilant. She
was the mother of the Italian Foreign Minister mentioned in
these memoirs.) Hatzfeldt was received in the Wilhelmstrasse
with no great enthusiasm. This was certainly true of Bucher and
Keudell. Whenever work was assigned it was so arranged that he
hardly got any. He did not exactly run after work either, but went
on leave as often as he could, which provoked still more spiteful
remarks from his envious colleagues. This situation persisted up
to the beginning of the 1870 campaign. Bismarck took with him
three officials of the Political Division, Abeken, Keudell, and Hatzfeldt, and also Busch, the journalist. Hatzfeldt was the only one
of the four who knew French well, and since the war was fought
in France there were plenty of occasions when Hatzfeldt's linguis-
tic knowledge was indispensable. Almost as useful to Bismarck
was the information Hatzfeldt had acquired about various people
during his several years in Paris.

Hatzfeldt really came into his own when the peace negotiations
began. I too, working under him, was given a vast amount of
work. Sometimes it took considerable self-control not to lose
one's temper when people who seemed to imagine they were good
linguists tried to force one to introduce into a difficult phrase some
French words they thought particularly suitable.

As I look back on that period I still keep remembering isolated
events which have nothing to do with Hatzfeldt, but which I mention here so that they will not be left out.

I can see in front of me the door of a house bearing the legend in chalk: 'Billet for one President of the Reichstag and two Deputies.' That was when the deputation to the Kaiser arrived.

And then I can hear Bismarck's angry outburst on the evening of 18 January,[1] when he spoke of the tactless sermon preached by the pastor Rogge (Countess Roon's brother). He had chosen a text which ran: 'Come hither, ye Princes' (or is it Kings?) 'and be chastised.' Certainly a happy choice. Bismarck said: 'I've said to myself more than once, why can't I get at this parson? Every speech from the throne has first to be considered word by word, yet this parson can say just what comes into his head.'

In lighter vein, by contrast, was Bismarck's tale of how vain young Schwarzburg[2] (nicknamed 'Prince of Arcadia') addressed the assembled royal personages with the words: 'Greetings to you, fellow vassals.'

On 19 January, when the last big sortie from Paris was in progress, I was sent with a message to General Blumenthal.[3] On my way I met the Crown Prince, who with a numerous staff was going to the aqueduct at Marly, where he hoped to obtain a front-seat view of the battle. Only Blumenthal had stayed behind in Les Ombrages (the Crown Prince's villa), because from there, the receiving centre for all the military telegrams, he could if necessary take action. The rest of the staff on the aqueduct were mere onlookers. The General was wearing a grey house-coat that came down to his knees, spoke as if he had a cold, and slowly paced the room with his hands behind his back. When I had delivered my message and received an answer Blumenthal added: 'You can also tell the Chancellor that the first assault has been repulsed. Of course the French are capable of attacking again several times, two or three days running. But they'll get a good beating every time. That I can guarantee.' I was impressed by the General's calm self-assurance, for the roar of the cannon and the rattle of the machine-guns sounded quite near, and when I returned to the Villa Jessé where Bismarck lived, I found Karl Bismarck superintending the packing-up and loading of the archives. He had given the orders for this, not the Chancellor.

[1] The day of Wilhelm I's coronation as German Kaiser at Versailles.
[2] Georg Albert, Prince von Schwarzburg-Rudolstadt, 1869–90.
[3] Leonhard, Count von Blumenthal. Prussian General; Chief of the Crown Prince's staff, 1866 and 1870; later Field-Marshal.

A few days later we were sitting at lunch when Captain (now Field-Marshal) von Hahnke,[1] sent by the Crown Prince, appeared and announced: 'Favre, the Minister, is waiting at our advance post.' Immediately Leverström,[2] the famous Black Rider, was sent out as escort alongside Bismarck's landau, which went to meet the Minister and his entourage. Favre was accompanied by his son-in-law, a landscape painter,[3] also by a young soldier and the American Consul-General, Read. While Bismarck went up to his study with Favre, the rest of us had to make conversation, no easy task. Read in particular obviously had the impression that every word he said gave something away, so he maintained almost complete silence. The soldier, a M. Hérisson, looked on the lighter side. He said it was no unusual sight in the streets of Paris suddenly to see a dog come round a corner in alarm, ears flying in the wind, pursued by one or two elegant gentlemen who wanted to roast him for dinner. He also said there would in future be two sorts of Frenchmen, *ceux qui ont mangé du rat et ceux qui n'en ont pas mangé.* The first type would be distinguished by a particular air of pride.

The painter, Favre's son-in-law, was downcast and silent. When after a very long time Favre finally came downstairs, his son-in-law softly asked him a question while Bismarck was talking to the others. Favre, without saying a word, merely raised his eyes to heaven for a moment with a look I shall never forget. He had an expressive face and in intonation and bearing, like so many French lawyers, he tended to be dramatic. But at that moment his expression of horror was meant in bitter earnest. Bismarck had informed him of the peace terms.

I will say nothing of the negotiations of that period, because they have long since been known in every detail.

I was struck by the perhaps intentional failure to grasp the situation, or the apparent lack of sense, shown daily by the Paris Press. Whereas Favre had telegraphed to Bordeaux that Paris was capitulating because food supplies had run out, the majority of the Paris dailies wrote as though the capitulation was an act of cowardice on the part of the Government, which must be opposed

---

[1] Wilhelm von Hahnke. Head of the Imperial Military Cabinet, 1888–1901.
[2] The Foreign Ministry's dispatch-rider.
[3] Martinez del Rio.

by every possible means. Even after Mont Valérien and the other forts had been occupied by our troops, Paris continued to behave like an unruly child that imagines its screams will extort indulgence or summon help. The Government was accused of cowardice and treachery, and the most desperate resistance was called for, which under existing conditions could mean only one thing— street-fighting. One day I had to escort a French general—de Valdan, I think—on a visit to General von Moltke. Valdan was in charge of the military part of the armistice and demarcation-line negotiations. As we went along the Frenchman spoke openly of the ferment in Paris. There were elements, he said, which wanted disorder and conflict, '*mais ils trouveront à qui parler*'.

With such a state of affairs it was an act of inspired political wisdom for Bismarck to insist on departing from the stereotyped military procedure, which always regards the occupation of the enemy capital as the indispensable stamp of complete victory. Our General Staff vigorously supported this latter view. The French, both civil and military, declared that for the whole of Paris to be occupied by the German army without a struggle was inconceivable, and that the French authorities faced the turbulent passions of the populace with no effective means of curbing them.

When Bismarck asked what street-fighting in Paris might cost us, Moltke told him we should lose not less than a thousand men, possibly more. At this Bismarck declared that our war aims had already been fully achieved without the occupation of Paris, and that he did not feel justified in sacrificing another thousand German soldiers. Moreover it was impossible to predict the possible effect of some slogan like 'Massacre of the Paris populace' on the European Powers, already in a state of nerves because of the long duration of the war and the German victories.

It was remarkable that even such an outstandingly intelligent man as Colonel Verdy[1] entirely failed to appreciate this logic. Towards the end of February I called on him with a message and found him in his office, even though everyone else was dining at the Hôtel des Réservoirs. He said he could not eat anything, he had felt so keenly Bismarck's refusal to grant the army the reward of victory, namely the entry into Paris.

[1] Julius von Verdy du Vernois. Section Chief in the General Staff, 1870–1; War Minister, 1889–90.

The differences between Bismarck and the General Staff had sprung up immediately after the battle of Sedan. At that time a council of war was held at which Bismarck suggested that an imaginary line be drawn between Sedan and Belfort, behind which the German armies should be drawn up to await the French attack. Moltke and the other generals said they were in favour of offensive tactics and the King shared this view; the results proved them right. Since then Bismarck's presence was never requested at a council of war. He felt this very much, but one can understand that professional soldiers were not prepared to let a civilian in uniform teach them their own job. And I must say myself that on psychological grounds I think the attacking method the more suitable against the French. If we had remained on the defensive the war would have lasted longer, France would have had time to train her recruits, and the French armies would have been tougher opponents after training for six months than for six weeks. The question whether our war aim—the defeat of the enemy—could be better attained by defensive or offensive strategy was a purely military one. But by the end of February 1871 the enemy *was* defeated and our war aims were achieved. Now political considerations were the determining factor and Bismarck was right in being unwilling to risk difficulties with other Powers for the sake of a triumphant entry into Paris. During my subsequent five years' stay in Paris I was told several times, not by the French (they were too patriotic and tactful to say such a thing to a German), but by Francophile foreign diplomats and journalists: 'If you had temporarily occupied Paris in March 1871 and restored order, the Commune would never have happened.' That I can well believe. The people of Paris, armed and trained for months, still convinced that Europe could not for ever leave Paris in the lurch, would have directed their fury against the Germans. Would Gorchakov, Beust, Visconti Venosta,[1] to say nothing of the English, really have remained passively looking on while street-fighting raged in Paris for several days on the scale of the June days of 1848 and the struggles of the Commune in May 1871? No one is prepared to assert that categorically, and so no one can say that Bismarck was wrong in refusing to restore order in Paris for the French.

[1] Emilio, Marchese di Visconti Venosta. Italian Foreign Minister, 1863–4, 1866–7, 1869–76, 1896–8, 1899–1901.

When Bismarck left Versailles a few days after the ratification of the preliminary peace treaty, we already knew that Paris was in the grip of anarchy. The *garde-mobile* from the provinces, who had been through the siege of Paris, had been dismissed. As we drove from Versailles to Lagny we met a number of them trying to make their way on foot to their homes, which presumably were not far away. There remained behind in Paris the troops, demoralized by the military reverses and their contacts with the mob, and the Paris National Guard, by far the greater part of whom were revolutionaries. The leaders of the social revolution had no doubt that the time was ripe for an insurrection; the Government without prestige; the army still partly in German hands, and in any case disaffected after the defeat; and the 'people of Paris' armed and drilled for months, although this drill was not particularly serious. The battalions at Belleville even had a number of cannons they refused to give up. With the Government's attempt to have *les canons de Montmartre* seized, open conflict broke out. The military refused to open fire on the *Communards*. General Lecomte, who had in vain given the order 'Fire', was murdered, as was the commanding officer of the National Guard, General Clément Thomas.

I was obliged briefly to mention these events for the sake of a connected narrative. When I arrived in Rouen on 19 March to take up my post with General von Fabrice,[1] I learned that 18 March, notorious enough already, marked the beginning of a new revolutionary era.

Fabrice, the Saxon War Minister, had been Chief of the Saxon General Staff in 1866. There was no love lost between him and the Prussian generals, and all kinds of malicious comments passed between them in their written communications. I was struck by the consideration bordering on timidity which the Saxon general showed in his dealings with the French. For example, in our Rouen hotel, the name of which escapes me, we paid a very stiff price for dingy rooms. Even so, Fabrice was well suited to fill the complicated dual role of military-cum-civil governor of the occupied territories and of diplomatic representative of the Imperial Government. He had an outstanding gift for organization,

[1] Georg Alfred, Count von Fabrice. Head of the Saxon War Ministry after the 1866 war; during the armistice in the Franco-Prussian War, he remained behind in France as the Chancellor's representative, and was responsible for arranging the preliminary peace negotiations.

and was himself a very hard worker, but his particular flair was for the delegation of the extremely varied work in such a way that disagreements hardly ever arose among his heterogeneous staff. To facilitate relations with the 'Versailles Government', as it was called at the time and in subsequent years, a French soldier with diplomatic training, Lieutenant-Colonel Delahaye, had been attached to our staff. He had, as he told me one day, voted 'No' in the first plebiscite[1] (21 December 1851), and wrecked his career as a result. He was a likeable man, typical of the older school of Frenchman, and before the war had been Military Attaché in Florence. In the midst of German troops, attached to the occasionally irascible Fabrice, he discharged his functions with quiet dignity and self-control. I am led to conclude that this period left rather unpleasant memories behind from the fact that although we had been on the best of terms and I had made his professional life easier for him more than once, he never put in an appearance during my five-year stay in Paris later on.

In the middle of April Fabrice was instructed by the Chancellor to move his headquarters nearer to Paris. So we went to Soisy, near Enghien.

I can remember nothing of interest from this Rouen period. Jules Favre and Pouyer-Quertier, then Finance Minister, came separately to negotiate questions of detail in connection with the *libération du territoire* and the speedy return of French prisoners-of-war from Germany to Paris. Favre still striking tragic and dramatic attitudes, Pouyer-Quertier energetic, gay, light-hearted. A lasting impression was made on me by the sailors who had been summoned from Le Havre to Versailles to set a good example to the troops fighting the Commune. They passed through Rouen, a somewhat disorderly rabble. Most of the groups carried a tiny tricolour flag, and looked half timidly, half savagely at our East Prussians who watched indifferently as they marched by.

In Soisy we lived in the château of a French stockbroker. More than six months' use as a billet had taken toll of its contents, so that we first had to procure all kinds of necessities such as bedding, particularly blankets. The divisional staff of the Schoeler Division who were there before us had left behind a little dog which the French had christened '*Kaput*'. I ought to say that the word '*kaput*'

---

[1] The plebiscite gave Louis Napoleon the right to give France a new constitution.

had figured prominently in arguments between soldiers and house-holders over objects that had been broken or had disappeared.

The view of Paris from Montmorency or the Moulin d'Orge-mont was remarkable during this period. The north and north-east of Paris was still surrounded by German troops, but the *Versaillais* held the south-east, south and west. All was quiet along the German zone; you could see the northern region trains steaming into Paris crammed with foreign sightseers, English and American. In the area held by the *Versaillais* you could also see smoke rising, not from locomotives but from the cannons which were trained not merely on the forts occupied by the *Communards* but on isolated points in the city as well. A heavy fire was directed against the Arc de Triomphe, where the *Communards* had hauled up one or two guns. Directly below the Moulin d'Orgemont lay the Gennevilliers peninsula, which is formed by a bend in the Seine. Anyone wishing to go from Versailles to St Denis, i.e. to reach the northern railway line, had to use the route across Gennevilliers which at some points was exposed to fire from the guns stationed on the *enceinte*. The *Communards* greatly enjoyed firing an occasional shell just when a few carriages would be passing along the road. I did not notice any accidents, but this firing on travellers—the French Ministers also had to take the Gennevilliers route on their way to Frankfurt—provided the local colour of that period.

Shortly after we had changed our quarters a dispatch came from Berlin informing us that the English bishops had requested Prince Bismarck to intercede for the release of Cardinal Darboy[1], Arch-bishop of Paris, who had been taken prisoner by the *Communards*. Fabrice was therefore instructed to approach the leaders of the Commune. Fabrice put the affair in my hands and I discussed it with Dr Cahn, the Head of the Chancery of the Bavarian Legation who, on the staff of the Swiss Legation, had been through the first siege of Paris and was fully conversant with conditions there. Dr Cahn thought the War Minister, General Cluseret, was the man I wanted. He was powerful and sufficiently free from preju-dice to procure the Archbishop's release. So I instructed Dr Cahn to take the necessary steps and he fixed an interview in Fort Aubervilliers, I think for 25 April. Cluseret, an adjutant and Cahn drove up in an elegant coach, with coachman and footman in pike-

[1] Georges Darboy. Archbishop of Paris from 1863. He was shot on 27 May 1871.

grey livery. [I] learned later that the coach belonged to the last Imperial War Minister, Count Montauban de Palikao.

I waited for Cluseret in a little casement. Upon entering—blue tunic and black floppy hat, both American—he stopped dramatically in the doorway and addressed me with: '*Vous voyez, Monsieur, je ne suis pas aussi bandit que vous avez pu le croire.*' A forceful, shrewd face with a repellent but most resolute expression about the mouth and chin.

I began by informing him of my commission with regard to the Archbishop, adding that the German army had so far remained a neutral onlooker of the French civil war. This neutrality would be endangered if the Commune aroused the animosity of the civilized world by crime and excess. Cluseret replied that from the very first he had regarded the imprisonment of the Archbishop as pointless, in fact a political mistake, but his protests had been in vain. Now, with the instructions I had given him, he possessed the necessary backing and had no doubt he would succeed in obtaining the Archbishop's release.

We fixed a day during the following week for another meeting to discuss the outcome of Cluseret's negotiations with the Commune, and also the question of what should be done next about the Archbishop.

After we had disposed of the concrete question Cluseret, with true French eloquence, treated me to [a speech] of an hour and a half on his plan for the reorganization of France. All I can remember now is that he wanted to split France up into autonomous provinces on the American model.

Then we parted and Dr Cahn told me two days later they had had difficulty in re-entering Paris because the adjutant, who had been lavishly entertained in Aubervilliers by the officers of the 2nd Guards Regiment, had forgotten the password.

On the day when I was to have my second interview with Cluseret in the afternoon, Dr Cahn appeared at my bedside at half-past-six in the morning and informed me that Cluseret had been arrested overnight by order of old Delescluze,[1] who [was] the most influential member of the Commune.

[1] Louis Charles Delescluze. Exiled during the Second Empire, he returned to France after 4 September 1870; was elected to the National Assembly as representative of the Seine *Département*; Civil Delegate for the war; he led the struggle against the regular army and met his death on the barricades on 25 May 1871.

This step, as I only learned later from the American Legation in Paris, was completely justified, for Cluseret was about to betray the Commune to Thiers. The intermediary was an American of French origin from New Orleans, named Loubat [?]. The terms of the transaction were not yet agreed. Cluseret demanded a million dollars; Thiers, always economical, thought three million francs enough. There was also a difference of opinion over the most suitable method of carrying out the betrayal. Thiers demanded that one of the gates of Paris should be thrown open in the traditional manner. Cluseret called this a naive procedure. The right thing to do was to stage a sortie and to send word of it to Versailles in good time. It would then be up to the troops to force their way into the city together with the repulsed *Communards*. In this way the whole affair would occur quite simply and naturally. The plot had reached this stage when Delescluze got wind of it and put Cluseret where he could do no harm. This happened on 30 April.

Some weeks later—I think it was a Sunday—Fabrice, his staff and I were dining with the Crown Prince of Saxony, who had moved his headquarters to Montmorency. During the meal a telegram arrived from the Chancellor, whom we had informed the previous day that the extraterritoriality of the American Legation had been violated by the Paris National Guard. Bismarck's telegram ran: 'The American Minister, who had protected German interests, now deserves our protection.' Fabrice was to take suitable measures. After Fabrice had reached an understanding with the Crown Prince, I was sent home to draft a note to the Commune, requiring satisfaction to be made to the American. I demanded this 'within twenty-four hours', Fabrice cut down the time-limit to twelve hours. The note was delivered that very night by Herr von Puttkamer, one of General Pape's[1] adjutants, at the *Communards*' advance post.

Meanwhile news had come in from the German advance posts and also over the telegraph from Versailles that on the afternoon of the same day (Sunday), the Government troops had succeeded in forcing the *enceinte* and entering the city (a naval lieutenant named Trèves was in first) and that the street-fighting had begun. Under those circumstances we could hardly expect an answer to

[1] Alexander von Pape. Prussian General; Commander of the 1st Infantry Division during the war of 1870–1.

our ultimatum, and it was equally impossible in my opinion to hold the leaders of the Commune responsible now for any further developments.

But the very next morning, within the twelve hours, a note arrived from Pascal Grousset, the *Délégué aux Relations Extérieures*, to say that this excess by a handful of National Guards against the American Legation had made a painful impression on the Commune. Immediately news of the incident had been received, all possible steps had been taken to give satisfaction. The Minister had expressed himself satisfied. (This statement was later proved to be accurate.)

The style of Pascal Grousset's note, firmly written in his own hand, came up to every diplomatic requirement. The writer was probably in no doubt that the death struggle of the Commune had begun, and that his own life hung by a thread. And so this letter, which, like his handwriting, bore no trace of emotion, was well fitted to arouse sympathy for Pascal Grousset, the valiant Corsican. That is why I was glad to learn later that he had escaped the *poteau de Satory*, and had been deported to New Caledonia; but I was even more delighted to read in 1874 that he had succeeded in escaping.

But to return to Cluseret. Immediately after the street-fighting began the Commune decided to set him free and entrust him with the command of Montmartre; now he was to show his mettle. Of course, those of us who were outside Paris also heard of this, because we were kept informed of what went on in the city. The progress of the street-fighting was slow, so it was possible to tell in advance just when the attack on Montmartre, Cluseret's position, would take place. In order to watch this I went to an observation post overlooking the north-west side of the assault area, part of which was not built over. Montmartre, Belleville, La Chapelle formed the actual heart of the insurgents' territory, which led one to expect bitter fighting. So I was all the more surprised to see an assault column in close formation advancing up a slope without a single shot being fired by the enemy. Then, when the column had reached the top and disappeared between the houses, we heard only isolated shots, an indication that single *Communards* were being wiped out just where they were found. My observations, which only covered a restricted area, were later confirmed by the military reports which were unanimous in stating that Montmartre had been captured almost without a struggle. Cluseret had disappeared but turned up in Switzerland soon after. The suggestion was voiced to me later by the Americans that Cluseret, as commandant of Montmartre, had most probably negotiated with Versailles a second time to save his skin. But this sounded like pure supposition, whereas the earlier negotiations spoken of above (with Loubat [?] as go-between), were mentioned as a definite fact.

In connection with the Commune I should like to give here one of Thiers's sayings which has remained in my memory. Thiers, speaking of the Commune when he was still President of the Republic, said that a republican regime, because of its anonymity, was able to bear a greater responsibility than any monarch because the odium incurred by harsh measures was more widely spread. '*Ainsi moi, j'ai fait canarder trente mille hommes et personne ne m'en veut, tandis que Louis Philippe a gardé toute sa vie le nom de Boucher de la Rue Transnonain.*'

A further recollection of the Commune.

Auber, the composer, died in Paris on 13 May, aged nearly eighty.[1] On learning he was seriously ill, the Commune decided that the author of the *Dumb Girl of Portici*, which had given the signal for the Belgian Revolution on 25 August 1830, must be accorded a national—or communal—funeral. But Auber's family, who were dyed-in-the-wool bourgeois, thought this a horrifying idea. Since open resistance seemed futile and even dangerous, they kept his death secret. I presume it was meant as a joke when the news reached Soisy from Versailles that, in expectation of happier times, the corpse of the master had been laid on ice. Even so his funeral did not, to my knowledge, take place during the Commune.

A recollection of little Thiers. A man of restless activity. Was known to get up early, at five in the morning. Slept in the evening before supper from seven to eight. '*Le monde s'écroulerait qu'il dormirait tout de même de 7 à 8*' someone told me. Once, when I had been sent to him with an important message, I arrived at the Versailles *Préfecture* a few minutes after seven. The *huissier* whose duty it was to announce me, went in and then said: '*M. le Président dort.*' Thiers took this nap in an armchair. Then at eight I delivered my message and found him in excellent spirits.

[1] Should read 'nearly ninety'.

Thiers, incidentally, was a *bon vivant*. On his famous tour of 1870 during which he vainly summoned the European Courts to France's help, he was accompanied by his chef.

In his negotiations with Bismarck Thiers must have shown quite unusual ability, for Bismarck spoke of him in a different way from all other Frenchmen. Though I heard Bismarck make one or two innocent jokes about Thiers, I never heard him say anything really derogatory about him.

I heard him speak in public only once in the Chamber of Versailles. A thin old man's voice. But in the absolute silence that reigned one caught every word. He was speaking against the income tax and concluded with the words '*et enfin, c'est un impôt révolutionnaire*'. For Thiers was a representative of the *tiers état*, people of means, and not, like Miquel,[1] a Marxist.

Despite his thin little voice Thiers as an orator exercised a magic power over his public. One would have to have seen and heard what happened to understand how the Chamber elected in 1871, with its overwhelming proportion of royalists, pushed through a clause in the Constitution[2] forbidding the President of the Republic to engage in parliamentary activity. I doubt whether they would have succeeded in overthrowing Thiers had he himself been allowed to plead his cause before the Chamber.

[1] Dr Johannes Miquel (see p. 146, n. 2) who was known to have held Marxist views in his youth.

[2] Holstein refers to the law of 13 March 1873, regulating the relationship between the President and the Assembly.

CHAPTER V

RADOWITZ[1]

Bismarck's lack of self-control after 1871. His unique position as a political hero after three wars. No inclination for war in 1875. Radowitz's threats against France not inspired by Bismarck. Radowitz's earlier relations with Bismarck. Holstein's part in the Arnim affair. Radowitz and the Arnim affair. Radowitz and State Secretary von Bülow. The Radowitz family. Verdict on Radowitz.

WHEN I took leave of Bismarck in June 1863 before my departure for Brazil, he had me shown in while he was conferring with President von Gerlach,[2] said one or two kindly words to me, and then continued his conversation with Gerlach. As I went out I just caught Gerlach saying to Bismarck: 'You're a most promising young man, but...'. That is all I heard. These few words uttered by Gerlach with the placid self-assurance of the school-master came back to me later, when I read of the disputes between the two men. In 1863 Bismarck certainly needed the self-control he possessed at the outset of his political life in order to endure such a superior attitude. He put up with it from Gorchakov too. But after 1871 I never heard of one single example of his self-control. On the contrary I gradually formed the opinion that he sought the reward for his achievements in refusing to bow to anyone's will but his own, and in obliging everyone with whom he had official contacts to comply with his whims. If he had been a professional soldier he might well have gone to war more often. But he was sufficiently clear-sighted to realize what a unique event it was in the history of the world that after three victorious wars it was not a military commander but Bismarck, the civilian, who enjoyed the highest admiration both at home and abroad. The reason for this was quite natural:

[1] The chapter-heading is Holstein's. This part of the memoirs was written in 1907.
[2] Ernst Ludwig von Gerlach. President of the Magdeburg Court of Appeal 1844–74; joint founder of the Conservative Party in Prussia and of its organ, the *Kreuzzeitung*; one of the leaders of the extreme Right in the Prussian Chamber of Deputies; as a Legitimist he opposed the 1866 annexations; after 1871 he voted with the Centre Party as an 'unaffiliated member'.

during the Bismarckian period Prussian policy, or rather Prusso-German policy, was Bismarck's personal creation, whereas the military leadership was impersonal and anonymous. The political plans which had enabled the armies to win their victories originated, as everyone knew, with Bismarck alone. He had devised them, paved the way for them, forced them through. The contrary was known to be true of the conduct of these wars. Everyone knew that most of the work had been done by men in the second or even third rank in the hierachy like the three 'demi-gods' Verdy, Bronsart,[1] and Brandenstein.[2] The Kaiser's achievements were generally underestimated because of his distinguished reserve and modesty. The Crown Prince enjoyed the full measure of recognition he deserved, and to which his popularity as a liberal-minded man contributed. Prince Friedrich Karl,[3] judging by all I heard from perfectly trustworthy soldiers, was considerably over-estimated; the public had not realized to what extent his mental and physical powers had failed him during the Franco-Prussian War. Caprivi,[4] one of the Prince's intimates, admitted to me that his importance lay less in his leadership than in his training of the troops. But in any case people knew that the three leading army commanders had not really been leaders at all. And so it was that the figure of Bismarck towered far above the military junta. But another war might change all that, particularly if the aged Kaiser, as was to be expected, did not take part in the campaign, thus obliging his Chancellor also to remain behind in Berlin. This would have branded him afresh as a civilian, a stigma he had striven all his life to throw off. Bismarck was well aware of all this. He had acquired so much for the German Empire and for himself that he had no desire to embark on another game for high stakes. I heard him say: 'You know where a war begins but you never know where it ends.'

[1] Paul Bronsart von Schellendorf. Prussian General; member of the General Staff, 1861–78; War Minister, 1883–9.

[2] Karl von Brandenstein. Prussian Lieutenant-General; Section Chief at head-quarters in charge of the entire army railway system.

[3] Friedrich Karl, Prince of Prussia; son of Prince Karl, the brother of Friedrich Wilhelm IV and Wilhelm I. Commander of the 2nd Army during the war of 1870–1.

[4] Leo, Count von Caprivi. Chief of Staff of the 10th Army Corps, 1870–1; Section Chief in the War Ministry, 1871–83; Head of the Admiralty, 1883–8; General commanding the 10th Army Corps in Hanover, 1888–90; Chancellor of the German Reich, 1890–4; Prussian Minister-President, 1890–2.

I am firmly convinced that is why Bismarck had not the remotest intention of provoking a war with France in the spring of 1875.[1] He only wanted to intimidate the French and put an end to the insulting behaviour they had indulged in ever since the war.

I remember one such case in 1872. A Frenchman had killed a German soldier—from Saxony I think—sleeping out of doors, by smashing his skull with a stone. The murderer was brought before a French jury. The famous defence counsel Maître Lachaud had the effrontery to exclaim during his speech for the defence: 'Is there any one of us here who would not like to have killed a German too?' Thunderous applause and an acquittal. Not merely in this case, but one may say on every occasion that offered, the French made it clear that they regarded themselves in their defeat as beyond the law and in their dealings with Germany as exempt from many of the considerations normal to international relations. It was to intimidate the French that Konstantin Rössler,[2] in the spring of 1875, wrote on Bucher's instructions the now famous 'War-in-Sight' article. That could have been passed over, but the immoderate expressions used by Radowitz after a dinner-party at Schleinitz's at which Gontaut[3] was present, were not so easily forgotten. I think that on that occasion Radowitz really did use the language attributed to him by Gontaut in his memoirs *Ma Mission en Allemagne*.[4] Gontaut was regarded as a man of integrity; moreover, Radowitz's after-dinner outburst against him was described to me immediately afterwards almost exactly as it appears in Gontaut.

Under those circumstances the French might well feel uneasy, but Bismarck was not bent on war. I am not alone in noting that after the Franco-Prussian War Bismarck's immediate family, drunk with the power they had attained, indulged in an orgy of undisguised disdain and ill-treatment of others. Herbert said to me one day: 'I'm often amazed at what people will put up with.'

[1] Holstein discusses this point in greater detail in his comments on Bismarck's Russian policy (see Chapter VII).

[2] Konstantin Rössler. Prussian *Regierungsrat* and publicist.

[3] Anne Armand, Vicomte de Gontaut-Biron. French Ambassador in Berlin, 1873–7.

[4] André Dreux: *Dernières Années de l'Ambassade en Allemagne de M. de Gontaut-Biron*, 1874–77, *d'après ses notes et papiers diplomatiques* (Paris, 1907), pp. 90–6. The dinner party Holstein refers to was not given by Schleinitz but by the British Ambassador. See *Grosse Politik*, vol. I, no. 177, pp. 275–7.

The Chancellor, too, undoubtedly took pleasure in alarming people. The 'War-in-Sight' article was commissioned by Prince Bismarck as a means of spreading alarm. On the other hand I am equally certain that Radowitz's threats against Gontaut were his own idea. Even after Bismarck's retirement, when some question arose in connection with the Gontaut episode, he gave out that he would hardly have selected as a confidant a man like Radowitz whose tongue ran away with him after his second glass of wine.

In fact Radowitz at no period enjoyed Bismarck's confidence. The latter expressed in his conversations undisguised hatred and scorn of Radowitz's father;[1] he and Bunsen,[2] he declared, were the biggest liars he knew. Radowitz himself was aware of Bismarck's dislike of his father, but this only stirred him to greater efforts to curry favour with Bismarck. To that end he seized an opportunity which occurred at the end of the 1866 campaign—also after a dinner—of flattering Bismarck whilst sharply criticizing Goltz's policy. Goltz came to hear of this. Hitherto he had vied with Radowitz in violently censuring Bismarck's policy and had been most kind to Radowitz, who found Paris a strain on his purse; he had even given him board and lodging. When Radowitz returned to Paris after the campaign was over the Ambassador took him to task and gave him to understand that his transfer seemed indicated. Radowitz asked for his transfer in Berlin, and was sent to Munich, where he met his wife. She was related through her mother, Countess Schlippenbach, to the Lehndorff, Eulenburg and Dönhoff families, whom Count and Countess Bismarck held in particular regard. It was to this connection that Radowitz owed his rapid promotion to Consul-General in Bucharest. Judging by the way Countess Bismarck spoke of the affair I assume she had a hand in it. A few years later he went as Minister to Athens, but worked in the Foreign Ministry nearly all the time Bülow (senior) was State Secretary. During this period I heard Bismarck pass two comments on Radowitz: 'Radowitz is a speed merchant (*Raschmacher*),' and 'Radowitz is a pushing young Southern Slav'. About Christmas 1879, not long after the death of Bülow, the State

[1] Joseph Maria von Radowitz. Prussian General and statesman; intimate of Friedrich Wilhelm IV; Member of the National Assembly, 1848; Foreign Minister, 27 September–2 November 1850.

[2] Josias von Bunsen. Prussian Minister-Resident in Rome, 1827–38, in Berne, 1839–41; Minister in London, 1842–54.

Secretary, Bismarck was speaking of Radowitz one day at Varzin when we were alone together. He ended with the words: 'A complete scoundrel. If he ever thinks he's been badly treated he'll be a second Harry.'[1] I can still see him sitting on the edge of the chaise-longue twirling the tassels on his dressing-gown. I never found out the basis for this judgement, but I presume it was connected with the Arnim affair and that Radowitz had used this for blackmail.

When Arnim began to work in Paris for a Bourbon restoration, Bismarck decided to transfer him. I had myself recommended his transfer in two or three letters to Bucher,[2] for the sake of peace and quiet.[3] That is my real share in the Arnim affair. Arnim was to be transferred first to Rome and then to Constantinople. But Radowitz had his eye on Constantinople. From that moment he looked on Arnim as a rival to be got rid of at any price. He used the influence he wielded over the State Secretary, von Bülow, to intensify proceedings against Arnim and in particular to force matters to a trial. He also involved me in these machinations quite without my knowledge. In the spring of 1874 I was suddenly summoned to Berlin. On my arrival I found I was to express my opinion [of] Dr Guastalla,[4] whom I had met during my mission to Florence in 1870, and who now wanted to found a pro-German paper in Rome. But I was told by various people in Berlin: 'Oh, you've come because of the Arnim trial', which I could deny with a clear conscience. Later I became convinced that Radowitz had engineered my recall in connection with this insignificant Italian question so as to divert attention from himself to me in the Arnim case.[5] A few hours before my return to Paris he spoke to me of the

---

[1] Harry, Count von Arnim-Suckow. Minister, then Ambassador in Paris, 1871–4. The Imperial Government instituted criminal proceedings against Arnim for refusing to return some documents he had appropriated from the archives of the Paris Embassy. He was first condemned to three months' imprisonment for crimes against public order and then to nine months' for abstracting official documents. After his conviction Arnim fled to Switzerland, where he published the pamphlet *Pro Nihilo* (Zurich, 1876), in which he utilized his knowledge of official secrets to launch a virulent attack on Bismarck's policy. As a result he was condemned to five years' penal servitude for high treason, *lèse-majesté* and criminal libel of the Chancellor.

[2] See *Darstellung* [...] *Untersuchungssache wider* [...] *Arnim* [...], pp. 234, 238–40.

[3] At that time Holstein was Second Secretary in the Paris Embassy.

[4] See p. 42.

[5] Holstein arrived in Berlin on 10 May. The telegram summoning him was drafted by Bucher on Bismarck's instructions. (From the Foreign Ministry files.)

Arnim affair for the first time, and began by remarking: 'Well, the ball's been set rolling; now that Arnim has refused to surrender the documents there's no avoiding a trial.' I disagreed and gave my reasons. The main difference between us was that I took the view that the Kaiser himself should call on Arnim to surrender the documents, whereas Radowitz flatly rejected the suggestion and maintained that it was enough for the demand to come from Arnim's official superiors [i.e. the Foreign Ministry] and that the Kaiser must not be involved in the affair. I persisted in my view, supporting it with all the arguments I could, and then returned to Paris.

Quite apart from any objective reasons, I should have been opposed to the trial merely on selfish grounds. For it was obvious that it would mean nothing but unpleasantness for the Paris Embassy staff.

In later years Bucher told me as an official secret that the same day on which this conversation took place Radowitz wrote to him in Varzin to say he had been talking to me and that *I was in favour of the trial*. To take away any inclination I might have to pursue the matter Bucher said he would be unable to give evidence in this matter because it was official; he had destroyed Radowitz's letter, and the Chancellor would regard any revival of the Arnim affair as a lack of consideration towards himself.

Nevertheless I am sorry I did not go ahead no matter what the consequences, though it would doubtless have meant the end of my official career.

Radowitz for his part continued to give the impression of being completely unconcerned in the Arnim affair. The very day when Arnim was arrested in Nassenheide, Frau von Radowitz inquired whether she might visit Countess Arnim, but the request was refused.

I think there was some secret in the Arnim affair which enabled Radowitz to exert a certain pressure over the Bismarcks. In the late autumn of 1880, that is, about ten months after the Chancellor's derogatory remark about a 'second Harry', I was summoned to Friedrichsruh to receive a message for Prince Hohenlohe, but I soon realized that I was really there to express my opinion of a letter from the Chancellor to Radowitz which had been dispatched a few hours before I arrived. Herbert showed me the draft at once. The contents made it clear that Radowitz must have complained at not yet having been made an ambassador. In his reply the Chancellor apologized for the delay, gently admonished him to be patient and went on to speak of the prospects to which Radowitz's talent and achievements entitled him. In conclusion he even expressed the hope that Radowitz would not lose patience. I have never, either before or since, read any communication of Bismarck's which came anywhere near the tone of this.

'Well, what do you think of it?' asked Herbert. I replied in exactly these words: 'That's not a letter, it's a petition.' 'Tell that to the Chancellor.'

I did so. The Chancellor sent for me immediately afterwards and at once asked me whether I had read his letter to Radowitz. 'Yes.' What did I think of it? 'Your Highness, it's not a letter, it's a petition.' The Chancellor made no reply.

Herbert was instructed to telegraph to the Foreign Ministry and ask them to return the letter to the Chancellor. This was done. A few days later another letter from the Chancellor was forwarded to Radowitz via the Foreign Ministry, presumably saying the same as the first, but in more measured terms.[1]

Without some quite definite reason, without some specific fear, Bismarck would never have shown such deference to Radowitz. Radowitz probably possessed something in writing the publication of which could harm Prince Bismarck. This idea was also expressed in a remark Herbert made years later to Paul Hatzfeldt. In the autumn of 1889 the Kaiser, together with Herbert, went first to England and then through the Mediterranean to Constantinople, where Radowitz was Ambassador. When he was discussing the proposed trip to Constantinople Herbert said to Hatzfeldt: 'It's a pity His Majesty can't bear Radowitz and would much prefer to see him out of the way. That would be a great mistake because *Radowitz knows too much.*' That was Herbert's actual expression. Hatzfeldt, who had an excellent memory, repeated the conversation to me shortly afterwards. We agreed that this was probably a case of something more specifically personal than legitimate diplomatic secrets.

[1] Holstein probably means Bismarck's letter to Radowitz of 31 October 1880. Hajo Holborn, *Aufzeichnungen und Erinnerungen aus dem Leben des Botschafters Joseph Maria von Radowitz* (Berlin and Leipzig, 1925), vol. II, pp. 149–50.

Radowitz, as I may have mentioned, was State Secretary von Bülow's adviser on diplomatic affairs. Bülow, in other respects excellently fitted for his post, felt uncertain of himself in the domain of German high policy to which he had just come quite fresh. But Radowitz, from his earliest manhood, always appeared completely self-assured. In addition his fluent Slav eloquence gave him an advantage over the average North German, to whom is often applicable the expression which Alphonse Daudet devised to describe the German Swiss: *peuple à conversation difficile*. But the important factor for Bülow, the outsider, much more than for the Chancellor, was the power exercised in society by Frau von Radowitz's important family connections.

Radowitz himself was of Serbian origin. His grandfather came from Serbia with a company of light lancers (*Tovargis*, or some such name), enlisted in Prussia during the Seven Years War, and after the war settled in Brunswick as a wine-dealer. His son, an outstandingly handsome young man, became during the period of the Rhine Confederation an officer in the Westphalian army, later in the Prussian army, and married a Countess Voss with a reasonable fortune, who became a Catholic under his influence. He had come as far as this when he was informed by the Brunswick Court of Justice that the liquidation of the estate of the bankrupt wine dealer Radowitz, deceased, had finally yielded a balance of 13,000 thalers; the heir was to furnish proof of his identity. Radowitz curtly replied that he failed to understand the communication from the Brunswick Court. He had no connection with the bankrupt wine-dealer. I have often heard Prince Bismarck tell this story. He usually added: 'So Radowitz denied his own father out of vanity. He didn't need what his father left him, he had enough with his wife's money.'

This disdain for money shown by the later General von Radowitz was never shared by his son. He worked on the principle that his country owed him, not bread and meat, but oysters and champagne. Thus during the period he was employed in Berlin he managed to draw the salary for his post in Athens as well, so that the total was rather higher than the salary earned by the State Secretary, then only 36,000 marks.

Radowitz's official activities were not always free from pompous humbug, as the following typical incident shows. Radowitz, helped by the experienced orientalist Busch,[1] was in charge of Near Eastern affairs. In 1876, when I began my Berlin observations, the Near East was in a state of ferment. The Chancellor gave audience to no one but the State Secretary. He, like his son, the present Chancellor,[2] was gifted with an excellent memory. After the interview he sat down and wrote out very fast in a graceful but not easily legible hand each directive, point by point, in less than no time. The sheets relating to the Near East were handed to Radowitz. He took them with a solemn expression, shut himself in his room and simply copied out what the State Secretary had written. I am not exaggerating. It took me some time to hit on the truth. But it was impossible to be mistaken. Bülow's pencilled notes remained between the leaves of Radowitz's draft, and I have compared the two memoranda many a time.

In his dealings with his colleagues, and particularly with subordinates, Radowitz showed a rudeness most unusual in the diplomatic service. Because of a trifling error he frightened an old ciphering clerk, *Hofrat* Wihr, to such an extent that the man, who already had a weak heart, fell seriously ill. One day he instructed Secretary of Legation von Thielau[3] to take a sealed letter to Dr Fuchs, the director of the Wolff telegraph bureau. Thielau, rather surprised at this errand, asked at least to be given some idea of the contents of the letter in case Fuchs spoke to him about it. Radowitz refused, and they ended by having an unpleasant quarrel.

Radowitz later behaved with the same harsh brusqueness towards the Turks and made himself so increasingly unpopular that the Sultan finally decided to make a personal complaint. Using the services of a naval adviser, who wrote to the office of the Kaiser's Naval Cabinet, he informed Berlin that he, the Sultan, deeply regretted that he was making no headway in his relations with Germany. He was making every possible effort and did not think the fault lay with him; it must therefore lie with the German

[1] Klemens August Busch. See p. 63, n. 3.

[2] Bernhard, Count von Bülow, Prince from 1905. Secretary in the Paris Embassy, 1878–84, in St Petersburg, 1884–8; Minister in Bucharest, 1888–94; Ambassador in Rome (Quirinal), 1894–7; State Secretary in the Foreign Ministry, 1897–1900; Chancellor of the German Reich and Prussian Minister-President, 1900–9.

[3] Wilhelm Otto von Thielau. Secretary in the Madrid Legation, 1876–8; Consul-General in Sofia, 1878–81, in Budapest, 1881–3; Minister in Oldenburg, 1883–4, in Weimar, 1884–6.

Ambassador. The Naval Cabinet passed on the naval adviser's letter to the Foreign Ministry and Caprivi, then Chancellor, summoned Radowitz to Berlin.[1] This recall aroused joyful expectations in Radowitz. His wife told her acquaintances: 'He's going to be State Secretary. They've had enough of Marschall.' Caprivi told me that when Radowitz learnt the real reason for his journey he made his disappointment very obvious. In the Foreign Ministry he gave vent to his indignation at being summoned personally instead of being requested to make a written statement. The only information he vouchsafed was an assurance that he had always said and done the right thing, and that the Turks had always been in the wrong.

Scarcely had Radowitz returned to Constantinople than the Sultan instructed his Ambassador[2] in Berlin to say there was hardly anyone he liked so much as Herr von Radowitz.[3] But of course that could not alter the situation, nor was it meant to. About a year later Radowitz was transferred to Spain. There, as circumstances demanded, he led a quiet life. There were only occasional complaints from specialists who had been sent to Spain to negotiate commercial treaties that the Ambassador's brusque behaviour had made their task more difficult.

When Radowitz was summoned to Berlin in late autumn 1905 to be briefed for the Algeciras Conference,[4] there was some head-shaking in the Wilhelmstrasse over his odd behaviour. Someone said the Ambassador was no longer capable of reading and understanding a complete article in the *Kölnische Zeitung*. An American journalist who had spent a month at Algeciras came back with the story that the German delegate had caused the other first delegates an enormous amount of trouble because none of them had succeeded in eliciting from their German colleague a single clear-cut statement. It had been acknowledged on all sides that this

[1] The Sultan's communication was received in Berlin on 23 June 1891. Radowitz was called to Berlin on the following day. In a marginal comment Wilhelm II stigmatized the Sultan's communication as: 'Unparalleled cheek.' (From the Foreign Ministry files.) [2] Tewfik Pasha.

[3] There is nothing on the communication of the Turkish Ambassador in the files of the Foreign Ministry. Radowitz reported on 16 July 1891, that the Sultan had assured him of his complete confidence, and had sent the same information to Wilhelm II, who was in London. A copy of this directive to Rustem Pasha, the Turkish Ambassador in London, is in the files of the German Embassy in London.

[4] Radowitz was first delegate to the Algeciras Conference, 1906.

diplomat was quite unusually skilled in the art of concealing his ideas. But the doubt had gradually arisen, quite hesitantly at first, whether he had any definite ideas at all. And, said the American, they were still discussing this question when he left.

It is possible that Radowitz hoped by a great show of friendship to France to pave the way for the Ambassadorship in Paris. This was also asserted about Marschall during and after the Hague Conference[1] this year, perhaps with some justification also. But the main obstacle to a German success at Algeciras was less Radowitz's behaviour than that of the Kaiser.

[1] The second Hague Peace Conference, 1907.

CHAPTER VI

THE FRANCO-GERMAN RAPPROCHEMENT[1]

Gontaut-Biron's efforts to restore the House of Bourbon. The Kaiserin Augusta as his ally. The restoration of the Bourbons prevented by the Comte de Chambord's personality and by Bismarck. Italy, Tunisia, Albania. Bismarck helps France to acquire Tunisia. The Tonkin affair. Bismarck furthers a French settlement with China. Ferry overthrown for collaborating with Bismarck. Courcel's opinion. Holstein on the French character. Failure of the policy of reconciliation. Collaboration with France in China, 1895. French refusal to negotiate over the Portuguese colonies. France refuses to collaborate in China, 1900.

THE idea of a reconciliation with France is not new. It was born at about the time of the Peace of Frankfurt and during the last thirty-six years it has been exploited by French diplomacy at various periods, in various ways and with various results.

There was first the Vicomte de Gontaut-Biron, a man of integrity and a convinced royalist. He took great pains to spread the belief that the restoration of the French monarchy would mean the erection of a firm bulwark against revolution from within or from without. Talleyrand said the same thing at the Congress of Vienna, and was believed. But Europe had learned since then that the Bourbons had not proved a bulwark against internal revolution and, moreover, during their brief reign had pursued a most aggressive foreign policy. '*Si nous restions six mois de plus, la Belgique se donnait à nous*', writes the Prime Minister Prince de Polignac in his memoirs.[2] And it may also be assumed with a fair degree of certainty that during the last years of the reign of Charles X French diplomacy was bent on regaining the Rhine frontier by a general readjustment of European frontiers in the grand manner.

---

[1] This chapter continues the memoirs written by Holstein in 1906–7. The chapter-heading is Holstein's.

[2] Jules Auguste Armand, Prince de Polignac. French Prime Minister, 1829–July 1830. Holstein is referring to Polignac's *Etudes Historiques, Politiques et Morales* (Paris, 1845).

On the first occasion Prussia earned small thanks for her share in the restoration of the Bourbons. Hence it is understandable that Gontaut's theory was indifferently received by Bismarck. Meanwhile there existed in Berlin a group of people working for a Bourbon restoration, and at the head of this group was the Kaiserin Augusta. The late Minister von Friedberg[1] told me that the Kaiserin said to him one day: 'I regard myself as a *Sœur Grise*, whose duty it is at all times to care for those who feel insulted or wronged.' The Kaiserin actually did live up to this principle, in itself a noble one, and as a result found herself in constant opposition to government policy. The political opposition of the moment, for instance the Centre Party during the *Kulturkampf*, was treated by the Kaiserin as insulted and wronged. It was the same with France after the war. Moreover, the Kaiserin had been brought up to admire France and England, and so she was inclined to rate their culture and their individual citizens higher than those of her own country. Gontaut-Biron, though he looked like a *notaire de province*, impressed the Kaiserin because he was a Frenchman and a younger member of one of the most distinguished French families. He had no difficulty in winning the Kaiserin over to the view that a Bourbon restoration would be a good thing not only for France but also for Germany. Berlin's high society, particularly Catholic circles, shared the Kaiserin's views, and Count Arnim, our Ambassador, endeavoured to gain a hearing for them on the official level.

My own opinion, as was revealed during the Arnim trial,[2] was that the restoration of the monarchy would be dangerous. My conviction had been strengthened by the observation that certain of the Paris Embassies whose anti-German tendencies were known to me, were working for a restoration with every possible means. It was prevented partly by the attitude of Germany, but mainly by the Comte de Chambord[3] himself who, as Bismarck put it, preferred the truffle-filled existence of a pretender to the cares and perils of a sovereign's life. By proclaiming: '*Le fils de Henri IV ne saurait abandonner son drapeau*', he did in fact ruin the prospects of his candidature. President MacMahon, whose monarchical

[1] Heinrich von Friedberg. Prussian Minister of Justice, 1879–89.

[2] See *Darstellung* [...] *Untersuchungssache wider* [...] *Arnim*, p. 233.

[3] Henri Charles Marie Dieudonné, Comte de Chambord. Pretender to the French throne.

sympathies, like those of his bustling, moustached little wife, the daughter of the Duc de Castries, were never in doubt, said in 1873 after the Comte de Chambord's manifesto: 'Let the white flag be unfurled and the *chassepots* will go off of themselves.' It was supposed at the time that the Comtesse de Chambord, alarmed by people's references to the fate of Marie Antoinette, had forced her husband to take the course which led to the failure of his candidature.

As I have already said, I still believe that Prince Bismarck did right in helping to work against a restoration of the monarchy. But I should also like to mention that Crispi, the converted revolutionary, held a different view. In 1889, when he came to Berlin with King Umberto,[1] he told me: 'Prince Bismarck was wrong to allow the continuance of the republic in France. It sets a bad example to her neighbours.'

Gontaut-Biron's diplomatic activity may be regarded as the first attempt to exploit Germany in the furtherance of French designs, in this case the restoration of the monarchy, by deluding her with hopes of more cordial relations. The failure of this scheme was brought about, as I have said, mainly by the Comte de Chambord and to a lesser degree by Bismarck. But French diplomacy retained and repeatedly put into practice the idea of gaining German support for difficult tasks or in difficult situations, by leading the German Government to hope that French national feeling would thus be appeased. And no one put into practice these attempts at appeasement with such energy and vigour as Prince Bismarck over the French acquisition of Tunisia and the conflict between France and China in Tonkin.

It was obvious that the African Mediterranean coast would gradually pass into the hands of European Powers. While Tripoli, and to a certain extent Egypt too, still had to be regarded as parts of the Ottoman Empire, Tunisia had become completely detached. The Bey had ceased to pay tribute and in 1859, although Turkey and Austria enjoyed the most peaceable relations, he had equipped a flotilla to support France and Italy, chiefly by privateering; because of the unexpectedly speedy conclusion of peace at Villafranca the ships were never used. Thus Tunisia owed allegiance to no one.

[1] From 21 to 26 May.

Italy's commercial interests in Tunisia were greater than those of any other European state, and the geographical situation was such that the occupation of Tunisia by another sea power constituted a strategic threat to Sicily. The Italian press devoted considerable attention to Tunisia, and one might say that the wish to acquire Tunisia was general throughout Italy, and was in the circumstances quite understandable. But the Italian Government failed to see this. Since the Government made no secret of its wish to extend Italy's sphere of influence, the suggestion was put by Germany and Austria that Italy should annex Tunisia. I was told that during the Congress of Berlin the Italian Foreign Minister Count Corti[1] flatly rejected a suggestion unmistakably hinting in that direction, and intimated that Germany would no doubt be glad to see a war between France and Italy. At this same period the Italian Ambassador Count Launay, no doubt with tacit allusion to the Tunisian suggestion, said to me: 'The natural direction for Italian expansion is Albania. It's so near to us that on clear days you can see it from the Italian coast through a telescope.' I have always supposed that briefly outlined programme, which I received and passed on without comment, to have been suggested to the Ambassador by his Minister. It meant, in plain words: 'Not Tunisia but Albania.' Since this outlook revealed a complete lack of political judgement, I prefer not to attribute it to shrewd old Launay but to Count Corti, who was subsequently recalled from his post as Ambassador in London by Crispi, then Foreign Minister, for the characteristic reason: 'Either you do not understand me or you will not understand me.' Corti certainly did not understand the European situation in 1878 if he regarded an Italian annexation of Tunisia as dangerous and an Italian annexation of Albania as feasible. France in isolation was powerless to act if Germany, Austria and England favoured Italian penetration in Tunisia. As late as the summer of 1890 (June or July), that is, long after the declaration of the French protectorate, Lord Salisbury[2] gave the Prime Minister Crispi an assurance in

[1] Luigi, Count Corti. Italian Foreign Minister and plenipotentiary at the Congress of Berlin, 1878; Ambassador in Constantinople, 1880–6, in London, 1886–7.

[2] Robert Cecil, third Marquess of Salisbury. British Foreign Secretary in the Disraeli Cabinet, 1878–80; second delegate at the Congress of Berlin; Prime Minister, 1885–6, 1886–92, 1895–1902; Foreign Secretary, 1885–6, 1887–92, 1895–1900.

writing that he recognized that Italy had important interests to safeguard in Tunisia.[1] Beaconsfield, who had already, in 1875, revealed a particular interest in the Suez Canal and Egypt by buying up all the Suez Canal shares held by the Viceroy of Egypt, must in 1878 have thought it eminently desirable for Italy to gain a footing next to France on the northern coast of Africa and thus to check any French expansion eastwards. The anti-French emphasis in British colonial policy did not change until after the Krüger telegram. A few days after the publication of this telegram I was told by an English politician who is still fairly prominent now in 1907: 'Now England will be obliged to make sacrifices she never dreamed of in order to enjoy France's friendship.' At the Congress of Berlin England was not yet meditating such sacrifices, so that Italy would have run no risk if, with the approval of Germany, Austria and England, she had occupied Tunisia.

The question of an Italian move towards Albania was totally different. It is precisely because, as Launay quite rightly pointed out, you can see the Albanian shore through a telescope at Brindisi, where the sea is only forty-five miles wide, that an Italian occupation of the eastern seaboard is impossible. Austria, Hungary, Trieste and Fiume would be cut off from world trade and bottled up in the Adriatic. A famous Austrian writer, Baron Chlumetzky, says quite rightly that nowadays in the Adriatic it is Austria, not Italy, who puts into practice the political principles of old Venice. Venice retained her settlements on the eastern shores of the Adriatic, which cost more than they yielded, solely to prevent both shores from falling into the same hands. Thus the Spaniards, when they possessed Brindisi, were for centuries a greater danger to Venice than the Turks.

The attitude adopted by Italian diplomacy in 1878 towards the Tunisian and Albanian questions showed that Italian policy was still controlled by French advice and the French point of view, just as it was before 1870. For it was then and is today important to France that Italy's attention should be diverted from North Africa to Albania.

Bismarck's observations on this occasion confirmed the view he

---

[1] Salisbury's letter of 4 August 1890 is published in *The Memoirs of Francesco Crispi* (English edition, London, 1912), vol. II, pp. 454–5.

had held since 1866 of the insecurity of our relations with Italy and were hardly likely to make him pay particular heed to Italy's wishes. Thus he was in no way committed with regard to the Tunisian question when, some time after the Congress of Berlin, Count St Vallier[1] intimated that it would certainly have a favourable effect on Franco-German relations and on the attitude of the French people if Prince Bismarck were willing to place no obstacle in the way of the absorption of Tunisia in the French sphere of influence. The Chancellor showed himself amenable. Now that the attempt to use Tunisia as a means of bringing Italy and Germany nearer together had failed because of Count Corti's refusal, there was nothing to prevent an attempt to improve Franco-German relations by furthering French designs on Tunisia. In view of the contemporary world situation Germany's attitude was of decisive importance to the French plan. But Bismarck also, by frequently inviting the French Ambassador to Varzin and Friedrichsruh, made it plain that he did at least think it possible that German co-operation in this important question would have a conciliatory effect on the temper of the French people. That Count St Vallier took this line I became quite convinced, particularly on one occasion— probably in the autumn of 1879—when I delivered to him an invitation to Varzin. As little as possible of these Franco-German discussions found its way into the files; the preliminary negotiations were conducted verbally.[2] Their effect became clear when the French plan of action gradually matured and the other Powers tried to discover in Berlin what the German attitude would be. When it became known that France's action caused Prince Bismarck no misgivings, the success of the French undertaking was assured. But French animosity towards Germany remained unchanged.

The Tunisian episode had shown the French diplomatic world that Germany, even Prince Bismarck himself, could be induced to make considerable concessions in the hope of a reconciliation with France. It is therefore not surprising that Count St Vallier's successor, Baron Courcel, a man of outstanding character and intelligence, took this line as soon as the occasion arose. The occasion, a most urgent one, was provided by the conflict between

[1] Charles, Count de St Vallier. French Ambassador in Berlin, 1877–81.
[2] See *Grosse Politik*, vol. III, nos. 656, 657, 667, pp. 388–9, 399–401.

France and China over Tonkin.[1] It was a war without a declaration of hostilities, rendered costly because of its distance, productive of heavy casualties because of the climate, with in addition the possibility that England would intervene at the critical moment. In the important question of whether rice should be regarded as contraband of war the British Government had already adopted the opposite view from the French. The French Government therefore greatly desired to reach an agreement with China, and Baron Courcel must be given the credit for bringing about this agreement through Prince Bismarck. I was able to follow closely Courcel's handling of the affair because I knew him quite well. We had been attachés together in St Petersburg. During my term in Paris I found he was *sous-directeur* in the Foreign Ministry and often came in contact with him professionally. Since 1882 he had been Ambassador in Berlin. When the Franco-Chinese conflict took a serious turn and showed signs of lasting some time, Baron Courcel at suitable points in his conversations stressed the difficulty of France's situation instead of concealing it. He then worked in remarks to the effect that it was urgently desirable for France *de sortir de ce guêpier chinois*, and that the French nation would be sincerely grateful to anyone who helped them to do so. During the winter of 1884–5 the French position deteriorated by reason of a defeat inflicted on General de Négrier's expeditionary force by the 'Black Flags';[2] the General was wounded in the encounter. This first Chinese success, insignificant in itself, caused a great stir throughout the world and encouraged not only the Chinese but all who opposed an aggressive French colonial policy. At this point Courcel asked point-blank whether Prince Bismarck would prepare the way for a settlement between France

[1] Since 1801 Tonkin had belonged to the state of Annam. After gaining a firm footing in Annam as a result of the Treaty of Saigon in 1862, the French marched on Tonkin in 1873–4 and again in 1882. The King of Annam summoned the help of China, whose suzerainty over Annam still formally existed. In 1883 and 1884 regular Chinese troops were employed against the French, so that a *de facto* state of war existed between France and China. In the Treaty of Tientsin, 11 May 1884, China renounced her legal claims to Tonkin. Nevertheless war flared up again. On 28 March 1885 General Négrier suffered a defeat which resulted in the overthrow of the Ferry Ministry. By the Peace of Tientsin, 9 June 1885, China renounced Tonkin.

[2] Chinese rebels who fled to Tonkin after the T'ai-p'ing insurrection and founded a state in 1868 on the Red River. They put up a stiff resistance to the French in Tonkin.

and China. Of course he could promise nothing definite in advance, but the *caractère généreux* of the French could lead one to expect that such support at a critical moment would have a profound effect on their attitude towards Germany.

The most obvious and banal conception of German interests was no doubt that every weakening of France was a certain gain but the prospect of France's gratitude a problematic one. However, Prince Bismarck decided to help France out of her difficulty, and his entire personality is a guarantee that it was not without very good reason. The German Minister in Peking[1] was instructed to advise the Chinese Government that, as the weaker party, China should exploit her recent military victory on the diplomatic level, so as to obtain from France the most favourable terms possible.[2] At the same time a chance meeting was arranged between the Chinese Minister in Berlin[3] and Baron Courcel in the ante-room of Count Hatzfeldt, the State Secretary.[4] The Chinese Government followed Prince Bismarck's hint, chose the path of reconciliation and surrendered Tonkin. Some time later I asked our Minister, von Brandt, who happened to be home on leave, what impression his step had made in Peking. He replied: 'The impression that the Chinese are now convinced that despite the war of 1870 France is still stronger than Germany, and that the latter serves the interests of French policy through fear.'

France's gratitude, as everyone knows, was shown in the way Ferry,[5] the Prime Minister, was grossly insulted by Clemenceau[6] after the conclusion of the treaty with China,[7] for having had dealings with Bismarck. The Ministry to which France owed Tonkin and peace fell amidst the howls of the Chamber, and for years *Ferry le Tonkinois* was treated by the French Press as a second-rate Frenchman.

[1] Maximilian von Brandt. Minister in Peking, 1874–92.

[2] Cf. *Documents Diplomatiques Français (1871–1914)*, (Paris), Première Série, vol. v, no. 638, p. 660; *Grosse Politik*, vol. III, nos. 699–701, pp. 443–5.

[3] Li Fong Pao.

[4] Holstein has assigned the wrong date to this incident which in fact took place on 17 September 1884. (See *Documents Diplomatiques Français*, Première Série, vol. v, nos. 396–399, 401, pp. 405–13, 414–5.)

[5] Jules Ferry. French Prime Minister, 1880–1, 1883–5.

[6] Georges Clemenceau. French Deputy; Prime Minister, October 1906–July, 1909.

[7] The Ferry Ministry fell on 30 March 1885, before peace was made with China on 9 June.

Immediately after the fall of Ferry I met Courcel in the Pariser Platz. 'Well,' I said, 'you didn't expect this turn of events, did you?' 'No', he replied, 'The Ferry Cabinet has had *une mauvaise sortie*, and I can't understand how it happened. I think the explanation is Ferry's ugliness. The Frenchman is *très ami du beau*, and Ferry is one of the ugliest people you ever set eyes on. That's why the Chamber wanted to get rid of him.'[1]

Quite a clever way of getting out of a tight corner. I do not for one moment believe that Courcel took his reply seriously. In order to help his country out of a dangerous situation he had aroused hopes which were not fulfilled; he had not given any definite promise. As a French diplomat and patriot he had merely done his duty, even if he himself regarded the hopes he held out as illusory. I became convinced this was so after some remarks Courcel made to me during the last few months of his term in Berlin. In 1886 Courcel left his post in Berlin and retired temporarily from the Diplomatic Service. He continued to give the general impression that he disagreed with one of his Government's measures, probably the banishment of the princes.[2] Shortly before his retirement he may have thought it useful to explain to me what in his view were the necessary pre-conditions for genuine reconciliation between France and Germany. I am selecting from his frequent expositions some of the main points which I feel sure I am reproducing accurately:

'Louis XIV was once asked whether the German command in some of the regiments in his army, e.g. the *Royal Allemand*, should be regarded as an abuse and forbidden. "Certainly not," replied the King, "for German is one of the languages spoken in my kingdom". . . .

'France is united politically, but ethnographically it is more diverse than Germany. Take the Walloons and the Basques; what have they in common? The equilibrium which had existed between the various northern and southern races was destroyed by the Peace of Frankfurt. France feels very much this lack of equilibrium. . . .

[1] Cf. Holstein's memorandum of 22 February 1906. (*Grosse Politik*, vol. xxi, i, no. 7034, pp. 206–8.)

[2] In June 1886 a law was passed whereby the territory of the French Republic was forbidden to the heads of those families which had reigned in France, and to their direct heirs according to the law of primogeniture.

'*Rendez-nous la frontière du Rhin, notre frontière naturelle, et les deux peuples tomberont dans les bras l'un de l'autre.*'

Courcel uttered this opinion calmly and gravely during the last of my conversations with him in 1886.[1] His successor had already been appointed. This conception of the ideal France which is expressed in the statements outlined above made it hard to believe that Courcel can really have imagined that German support over a colonial question, however important, would suffice to conciliate France. Far more in keeping with the tenor of these ideas is the opinion Courcel is said to have expressed to Lord Salisbury ten years later when he was French Ambassador in London, immediately after the Krüger telegram: 'France has only one enemy, Germany. You can conduct your policy accordingly.'

Courcel's political outlook was based on the history of France. Ever since Richelieu and the Thirty Years War, that is from 1640 to 1870, France proved superior to any other Power alone. French advances had been successfully checked only when several Powers united to that end. And even then they were only partially checked. Louis XIV's reign considerably increased French territory, and also the France of 1814 was conceived on a larger scale than in 1793.

Soon after the outbreak of the Franco-Prussian War I was examining the protocols of the Congress of Vienna for publicist purposes[2] and came across a memorandum by the Russian plenipotentiary, Pozzo di Borgo, concerning the new frontiers to be given to France. It ran, almost word for word: 'Take care, do not go too far, or the French nation, *ivre d'amour-propre et de gloire*, will rise again as in 1793.' For a plenipotentiary to dare to express this to the Congress is remarkable enough. Still more so is the fact that the Congress took this advice to heart and in 1814, at a moment when the armies of the whole of Europe were or had been on French soil, decreed an extension of the French frontier of 1793. Historical events of this kind inevitably led the French, even educated Frenchmen like Courcel, to feel convinced that France and the French enjoyed some advantage over other nations. It was to counteract this superstition that Prince Bismarck told Jules Favre in 1871 that France's honour was no different from

---

[1] Holstein noted these ideas of Courcel's in a memorandum dated 1 September 1886, which is not being printed. Similar ideas may be found in his diary under the entry for 27 August 1884 (*Diaries*).

[2] See Rogge, *Friedrich von Holstein*, pp. 93–6.

the honour of other nations who had to agree to cede territory after defeat. To anyone but a Frenchman what Bismarck said was self-evident. But the French regarded it as brutal and, with history to support them, could for every Bismarck count several Pozzos who had all bowed before French power or prestige. Even today the educated Frenchman regards the seizure of Strasbourg in peace-time and the wars of plunder in which Louis XIV annexed whole provinces and laid waste vast areas—*vide* the Palatinate and the Heidelberg Schloss—as no more than the practical application of France's civilizing mission. But the *restitutio in integrum*, i.e. Germany's reacquisition of the German territories and of the frontier fortress at Metz as a check to further pillage and plunder, was called an act of barbarity for which the formula *La Force prime le Droit* was invented.

The Frenchman cannot be blamed for this. He is the product of his own history. But this peculiarity must be reckoned with if we do not wish to experience bitter disillusion. If we do allow ourselves to be deceived we have no excuse, because Germany's experiences a generation ago over Tunisia and China could and should be a lesson to the present generation. I have already said that Prince Bismarck probably had his own reasons for granting the French request to effect a peace settlement in 1885. He may well have thought: 'One of two things is possible. Either the French will be reconciled to us if I help them out of this *guêpier chinois* and they have convinced themselves that though Germany can be a formidable enemy she can also be a useful friend. Then we should save on our war budget. Or else they will refuse to be reconciled in spite of everything, in which case this experience is valuable for the future course of German policy. Even Tunisia was a valuable acquisition which would never have been made if Germany had opposed it. But the help we are now giving France by ending the war in China, with its lurking danger of further entanglements, is far more important. If, after two such herculean German services France does not bury the hatchet but still clings to the *revanche* programme, then we shall know where we stand, which is also an advantage.'

If Prince Bismarck by his magnanimous compliance with France's wishes over the war in China wanted to test her intentions, he succeeded. For no sooner had the German lackey done his duty and actually brought about peace, than the French Chamber, led by the present Prime Minister, Clemenceau, renounced Germany in unmistakably clear terms. And yet there was no prospect of a *revanche* at the time; the French Republic stood isolated and the Triple Alliance was still in its heyday.

After 1885 no particular efforts were made towards a rapprochement and no changes in the situation were noted. Ten years later, in 1895, Russia, Germany and France united to lodge a joint protest against the Sino-Japanese peace treaty of Shimonoseki.[1] The first to reach an agreement were Russia and Germany. France, faced with the choice of joining forces with them or of deserting her Russian ally at the first test of her sincerity and allowing her to stand alone with Germany, took the first course. France had beforehand done her utmost to dissuade Germany from interfering. The Foreign Minister, Hanotaux,[2] said to Count Münster: '*Vous voulez donc nous forcer à faire de la politique russe?*' When none of this had any effect, France came in. But the French attitude is pretty clearly revealed in a remark made by Herbette[3] to the head of another mission who repeated it to me. 'You can imagine my feelings when I think that now perhaps in the Far East our cannons and the Germans' will be firing side by side instead of at each other.'

Three years later, in June 1898, Münster was instructed to tell Hanotaux that there were a number of isolated problems, particularly in the colonial field, in which German and French interests were identical. The two Powers would both derive profit by acting in concert in such matters, without renouncing their fundamental national viewpoint. There was at the moment an unsettled dispute over the Portuguese colonies in which they might with advantage take joint action.[4]

When Münster delivered this message Hanotaux replied that he entirely shared this view concerning the treatment of isolated questions and would give the appropriate instructions to the French representative in Lisbon[5] for dealing with the case now

---

[1] 17 April 1895. See *Grosse Politik*, vol. IX, chapter LVII.

[2] Gabriel Hanotaux. French Foreign Minister in the Dupuy Cabinet, 1894–5, the Ribot Cabinet, 1895, and the Méline Cabinet, 1896–8.

[3] Jules Herbette. French Ambassador in Berlin, 1886–96.

[4] Bülow to Münster, 18 June 1898 (*Grosse Politik*, vol. XIV, i, no. 3813, pp. 266–7).   [5] Charles Rouvier, Minister in Lisbon, 1898–1906.

under discussion. As to the general principle of concerted action in cases presenting a community of interests, he must consult the Council of Ministers. This would be done in the next few days as soon as the present ministerial crisis was over.[1]

But the crisis ended in the fall of Hanotaux and the appointment of Delcassé.[2] After a week or two Richthofen[3] came to inquire whether he ought to ask the Ambassador, Noailles,[4] what had become of our suggestion of joint action in the Portuguese colonial dispute. I replied: 'No, don't ask him. His silence is answer enough. The new Minister probably has different views from Hanotaux.'

But Richthofen, a communicative soul, could not restrain himself from asking his question; he met with a complete rebuff. Noailles replied that concerted action by Germany and France could never be anything but *exceptionnelle et fortuite*. French public opinion was not yet ready for it. He, the Ambassador, had heard nothing about our proposal.[5] That was clear enough.

Again, two years later, in 1900, after the outbreak of the Boxer Rebellion, we approached France and other governments and asked 'whether the isolated problems connected with the Yangtse question, first and foremost the question of protecting Europeans, should be dealt with by the Powers in common, instead of devolving on one single Power?'[6]

This inquiry was directed against England, whose behaviour in the Yangtse question gave ground for suspicion. Delcassé declined to take up the suggestion, saying that these questions could only be judged properly on the spot, and were therefore the province of the diplomats in Peking.[7] This reply was not free from irony,

---

[1] Münster to the Foreign Ministry, 19 June 1898 (*Grosse Politik*, vol. XIV, i, no. 3814, p. 268).

[2] Théophile Delcassé. French Foreign Minister in the Brisson, Dupuy, Waldeck-Rousseau, Comtes and Rouvier Cabinets, 1898-1905.

[3] Oswald, Baron von Richthofen. Director of the Colonial Division in the Foreign Ministry, 1896–1900; Under State Secretary, 1897–1900; State Secretary, 1900–6.

[4] Emmanuel Henri Victurnien, Marquis de Noailles. French Ambassador in Berlin, 1896–1902.

[5] Bülow to Radolin, 2 September 1898 (*Grosse Politik*, vol. XIV, i, no. 3877, pp. 360–2).

[6] Holstein is not quoting directly from one single document. Cf. *Grosse Politik*, vol. XVI, nos. 4701–3, pp. 201–4.

[7] This account of Delcassé's reply is inaccurate. Cf. *Grosse Politik*, vol. XVI, no. 4704, p. 204. Delcassé had replied that the affair would best be dealt with by the

for just then the diplomats in Peking were having great difficulty in saving their skins. Meanwhile other Powers accepted and carried out the German proposal as suited to the situation.

Despite the unfavourable reception which Delcassé accorded the German proposals just mentioned, and others besides, it seemed right during the negotiations over the evacuation of Shanghai to treat the French Government with no less consideration than other interested Powers. And so the German Government informed Paris, as well as London, Tokyo and Washington, that before the evacuation it would require from the Chinese Government an assurance that China would not grant any Power special privileges in the Yangtse basin.

The British Government made it clear that it found the proposal unacceptable. In reply to the German communication it said it was unwilling to commit itself in respect of future eventualities. The Japanese said they approved of the idea in principle but that they would like to sound the other Powers first. When they discovered England's opposition to it they let the matter drop. France declared that upon the evacuation of the city she would notify the Chinese that if other Powers re-entered it she would proceed to reoccupy it too. Germany required of the Chinese Government the assurance, which was readily given, not to grant special privileges. Germany apparently stood alone in this and drew upon herself all the anger of the British Press. Meanwhile the inquiries of the German Chargé d'Affaires revealed that France had secretly obtained from China the same assurance not to grant special privileges as Germany had received. The aim of this secrecy was of course to direct all the odium against Germany.[1]

In the foregoing pages I have briefly summarized the experiences we had in our relations with France from 1880 up to the Moroccan Question.

commanders of the naval forces then off the Chinese coast. The same inexact account is to be found in a memorandum written by Holstein in April 1903 (*Grosse Politik*, vol. XVIII, ii, no. 5888, pp. 802–7).

[1] For the last two paragraphs, see *Grosse Politik*, vol. XVI, ch. CVIII.

CHAPTER VII

BISMARCK'S RUSSIAN POLICY[1]

Alexander II a friend of Prussia. Gorchakov's jealousy of Bismarck. The 1875 war scare. Bismarck's revenge at the Congress of Berlin. Resentment of Alexander II. Bismarck's policy of pin-pricks. Failure of this policy. The Reinsurance Treaty; political bigamy; a weapon in the hands of an unfriendly Russia; the Treaty not renewed.

PRINCE BISMARCK'S Russian policy after 1875 was governed by emotion and therefore unsound.

The Prussian royal family and the Prussian army have never had a better friend outside Prussia than Alexander II. His natural sympathies were strengthened and justified by the world situation as it appeared in the early 'sixties. Austria, by her behaviour during the Crimean War, had given practical proof of the ingratitude[2] prophesied by Prince Schwarzenberg.[3] England had emerged as Russia's principal opponent, had pressed for war, and during the peace negotiations had striven to prevent the concessions France was prepared to make. France in turn had alienated the Russian sympathies she had enjoyed after the war by the way Napoleon III sided with the Poles during the Polish insurrection, even though he did so only in his usual half-hearted manner. Prussia on the other hand, under Bismarck's leadership, expressed vigorous opposition to the insurgents and thereby helped to contain the Polish sympathies of other Powers within purely academic limits.

Tsar Alexander repaid Prussia's support by protecting our rear in the wars of 1864, 1866 and 1870. On learning of the capitulation of Sedan he drank General Werder's[4] health and then threw the glass against the wall.

But the brilliant conclusion of the Franco-Prussian War had the disastrous effect of awaking the envy, not of Tsar Alexander but

---

[1] This essay was probably written in 1898. The chapter-heading is the editors'.
[2] For the help Russia gave Austria during the revolution of 1848–9.
[3] Felix, Prince Schwarzenberg. Austrian Minister-President, 1848–52.
[4] Bernhard von Werder. Prussian Military Attaché in St Petersburg, 1869–86.

of Prince Gorchakov, who could not bear the idea that the German Chancellor, whom he had treated with condescension ten years before when he was Prussian Minister, had now surpassed him in world fame. Prince Gorchakov now sought an opportunity of reminding the world of his own and Russia's importance. He found this opportunity in the spring of 1875.[1]

Other people can no doubt give the details of the 1875 Franco-German crisis better than I can. I was then attached to the Paris Embassy. One day there appeared in the *Post* the famous 'War-in-Sight' article, written by Konstantin Rössler on Bucher's instructions, threatening the French with war. The threat was taken seriously in France; in well-informed circles it was affirmed that there were other unmistakable signs that 'Bismarck' wanted war. France dramatically exploited her alleged helplessness—exaggerating it still further for the purpose. The Minister for War[2] declared in public: 'France has no army. If they make war on us I shall go to the frontier with a corporal and four men and blow out my brains in full view of the enemy.'

The German Embassy in Paris knew nothing of this. We had only read the 'War-in-Sight' article, but without understanding it, for at the moment there was not a single question at issue between Berlin and Paris which could have been worked up into a pretext for war. We also learned from reliable sources that a junior German diplomat had told the French Ambassador in Berlin: 'It would be both politically and morally justifiable for Germany to attack France before she had finished rearming.'

This remark became the pretext for the uproar which now arose in the world of diplomacy. Gontaut-Biron reported to Paris, the Duc de Decazes[3] got in touch with London, and Queen Victoria asked Tsar Alexander to intervene.

I am firmly convinced that Prince Bismarck had no thought whatever of going to war. Not only are there no definite signs of such an intent, but later on, in every case when war really did seem possible, Prince Bismarck showed a most zealous love of peace. He used to say: 'You know where a war begins but you never know where it ends.' There is also another factor whose

---

[1] Compare Holstein's account written in 1907, pp. 93–4.

[2] Ernest Courtot de Cissey. Minister for War, 1871–3, 1874–5, 1875–6.

[3] Louis Charles Amadieu, Duc de Decazes. French Ambassador in London, 1873; Foreign Minister, 1873–7.

significance must not be overlooked in view of the strongly developed subjectivity of Bismarck's character. Bismarck's achievement—and so far as I know the case is unparalleled in world history—was that after three victorious wars he, the civilian, ranked first in fame and power, whereas the army commanders took second place. I will not go into the reasons for this unusual phenomenon, for there are several. One reason is undoubtedly the impersonal nature of our army command. But that situation might well be changed. In the next war a military figure might well have come to the fore, either through merit or by chance, and become the focus of the nation's enthusiasm. There would then arise an unwelcome rival to Bismarck for power and fame.

But, as I have said, the diplomatic world and in particular the diplomatic corps in Berlin believed in Bismarck's warlike intentions. 'Believe me, the Prince wants war', said Odo Russell to the Spaniard Rascon, who repeated it to me.

It was a psychological necessity for Bismarck to make his power felt by tormenting, harrying, ill-treating people. His pessimistic view of life, which had long since blighted every human pleasure, left him with only one source of amusement, and future historians will be forced to recognize that the Bismarck regime was a constant orgy of scorn and abuse of mankind, collectively and individually. This tendency is also the source of Prince Bismarck's greatest blunders. Here his intellect was the slave of his temperament and justified outbursts for which there was no genuine cause. Thus it had become a habit for Bismarck to seize every opportunity of threatening and alarming the French Government without any intention of going to war, merely because he was convinced of French military weakness at that time. But it suited Prince Gorchakov, who for some time had been awaiting the opportunity for a diplomatic *coup d'éclat*, to take the German threats in 1875 seriously, so that Prince Bismarck suffered the indignity of having the Cabinet in St Petersburg first bid him be more moderate and then publish this admonition in the Press, amongst others in a Karlsruhe newspaper.[1]

Bismarck never forgot this insult. From that moment his Russian policy changed. He no longer thought of the gratitude Germany owed the Tsar, in fact Russia for him ceased to exist

[1] See *Grosse Politik*, vol. I, ch. VII.

except in the person of Prince Gorchakov. If the determining factor in Bismarck's policy had been Russia, and not the Russian Chancellor, then he would either have had to support the Russians in the Russo-Turkish War—which he could have done by a mere diplomatic flick of the fingers, without the slightest risk to Germany—or else, if he wished to weaken Russia permanently, i.e. for a considerable period, he would have had to let things take their course and allow the war between England and Russia to develop. But he did neither; he allowed himself to be guided not by political but by personal motives. By convening the Congress in Berlin and as 'the honest broker' stressing his own role as mediator, he made Germany responsible for the outcome. The outcome was that Russia was not weakened, but deeply offended by the abrogation of the Treaty of San Stefano, while Bismarck posed as arbiter of the world.

One day, towards the end of the Congress, Bismarck invited *The Times* correspondent Blowitz[1] to lunch. The present Chancellor, Prince Hohenlohe, and I were also present. After the meal Bismarck said to Blowitz: 'Now Prince Gorchakov realizes the price he has to pay for having been so rude to me in 1875.' Prince Hohenlohe's memoirs, which are very complete, probably contain this remark too, for I have often spoken to him about it.[2] When, some time later, Blowitz reported Bismarck's remark in the Press, without even making it sound as blunt as it had been, Bismarck declared in the Reichstag: 'In future we shall say that so-and-so "lies like a *Times* correspondent".' But at my next conference with Prince Hohenlohe I said to him: 'What would we two have done if Blowitz had cited us as witnesses?'

I should like to insert here as a parenthesis that one of the greatest difficulties in dealing with Prince Bismarck was his complete contempt not only of mankind but of the truth as well, as is shown by the following example taken from a different political sphere. As I write this I cannot be sure from memory when the Reichsgericht was formed. But at the time when this question was being discussed—between 1876 and 1878[3]—it was of prime

[1] Heinrich Opper von Blowitz. For many years *The Times* correspondent in Paris.

[2] This remark of Bismarck's cannot be found in *Denkwürdigkeiten des Fürsten Chlodwig zu Hohenlohe-Schillingsfürst*, 2 vols (Stuttgart and Leipzig, 1906).

[3] The Reichsgericht debate on the question of where the Reichsgericht should sit took place in March 1877.

importance for the parties supporting the Government to find out whether the Chancellor wished the Reichsgericht to have its seat in Berlin or elsewhere. But the Chancellor refused to be drawn. I can point to no definite reasons for his silence, but can only suppose that he begrudged the city of Berlin, with whose civic administration he was constantly at war, this increase in its importance and the material gain, but that he was unwilling to state his opinion directly and publicly because he thought it open to criticism. I do know that one evening Lucius,[1] who had not yet become Minister, tried his hardest to persuade Prince Bismarck to say which town would be most suitable as the seat of the Reichsgericht, but without any definite result. As we were coming away—we were just passing Holy Trinity Church, where we separated— Lucius summed the matter up by saying: 'He obviously has no objection to its being outside Berlin.' The morning of the day on which the question was to be voted on in the Reichstag I happened to go into the Reich Chancellery and there I found Helldorf-Bedra,[2] then leader of the Conservatives, in heated argument with Tiedemann.[3] Helldorf was determined to see the Chancellor and ask him where his preferences lay in this question of the location of the Reichsgericht; but Tiedemann, who had of course been primed, said he had orders to admit no one. Shortly afterwards the Reichstag, partly with the idea of conforming to the Chancellor's view, determined that the Reichsgericht be set up in Leipzig. Up and down the country and particularly in Prussia this vote met with no approval and Prince Bismarck, who would stop at nothing when it was a question of preserving his popularity, at once took refuge in the formula: 'I knew nothing about it, I was not even asked.' I was once sitting next to him at table during this period, when the conversation turned on the establishment of the Supreme Court at Leipzig. Some one mentioned that Helldorf had tried in vain to discover the Prince's opinion. Prince Bismarck replied, 'I didn't see Helldorf. If he had asked me

[1] Robert Lucius, later Baron Lucius von Ballhausen. Member and a leader of the Free Conservatives in the Reichstag, 1870–9; Prussian Minister for Agriculture, Crown Lands and Forestry, 1879–90. See *Bismarck-Erinnerungen des Staatsministers Freiherrn Lucius von Ballhausen* (Stuttgart and Berlin, 1921), pp. 105 *et seq.*

[2] Otto Heinrich von Helldorf-Bedra. Member of the Reichstag from 1871.

[3] Christoph von Tiedemann. *Vortragender Rat* in the Prussian Ministry of State from 1876; Head of the newly constituted Reich Chancellery, 1878–81; Head of the Administration in Bromberg, 1881–9.

I should have told him my opinion.' At this point I remarked: 'I beg your pardon, Your Highness, but I was present when Helldorf was trying to gain admittance to you, but Tiedemann would not let him in.' Prince Bismarck's only comment was: 'Now you're against me too.' His reply entirely achieved its purpose of silencing me but it did not alter the facts.

After this digression on the theme 'Bismarck and the truth' I return to the Congress of Berlin.

It is granted neither to me nor anyone else, except perhaps a mind-reader, to be able to define the complete range of Bismarck's ideas at the Congress of Berlin. It is possible only in exceptional cases to tell even what ordinary people think, and the assertions of the people themselves, being a species of special pleading, are usually the most unreliable indications the historian could have. But one can perceive in Bismarck certain guiding ideas. From 1878 until his dying day he reiterated with feverish energy that he had never wished to harm Russia; on the contrary he had supported all the claims of the Russian plenipotentiaries, and but for his efforts they would have obtained much less. This assertion is undoubtedly true, but it is equally true that Prince Bismarck could have gained more for the Russians had he so desired. The Russians themselves counted on this 'more' as the obvious return for the services they rendered in 1864, 1866 and 1870.

On the contrary, Prince Bismarck's main intention was to teach the Russians a lesson, to make it clear to them that their plans could not be executed without his consent, and that his consent depended on the good conduct of the Russian Government. That was why Gorchakov was treated badly and Shuvalov[1] treated well, and just to leave the Russians not the slightest doubt as to cause and effect, Blowitz was 'primed'. His choice was the guarantee for Prince Bismarck that the lesson he wished to teach the Russians by way of Blowitz would really reach its destination, for Blowitz as a naturalized Frenchman and overt anti-German naturally had an interest in rubbing salt into the Russian wound. Even so he performed this task with moderation, for when he published Bismarck's remark—which he did only after some time—it was much

---

[1] Peter, Count Shuvalov. Russian Ambassador in London, 1874–9; Russian plenipotentiary at the Congress of Berlin, 1878.

less outspoken than the original, so that he certainly did not deserve the brutal reproof which Prince Bismarck, with his usual contempt of people and of the truth, meted out to him.

While Prince Bismarck indulged in ridiculing Gorchakov before the whole of Europe, he neglected the fact that behind Gorchakov was the Tsar Alexander. The Tsar had approved of the Treaty of San Stefano, so that when with Bismarck's co-operation, or rather under his direction, this treaty was abrogated, he took it as a personal insult. I can still see Gorchakov as he sat diagonally across from me during a session of the Congress; I can still hear his exclamation during a discussion on some Article or other, when the scales were tilted *against* Russia: 'The Tsar is most indignant, I can tell you!' And he angrily flung his pencil on to the table. That was the triumph, the revenge, the rebuke—call it what you will—for which Bismarck had striven, as he himself told Blowitz.

Bismarck's confidant amongst the Russians was Shuvalov. Bismarck always came to an understanding with him beforehand as to how much could be obtained, i.e. how much Bismarck was prepared to allow the Russians to obtain. Within these limits Shuvalov then fought like a lion, occasionally seconded by Bismarck; he showed himself a debater of the first rank, while Gorchakov listened in sullen silence and once stayed away from several sessions so as to throw into even sharper relief the fact of Shuvalov's responsibility.

If Bismarck imagined, as he undoubtedly did, that his ill-treatment of Gorchakov and his favouring of Shuvalov would help the latter to become Russian Chancellor his belief proved to be a grave psychological error. Bismarck refused to take into account that not merely Gorchakov but also the Tsar had personally identified himself with the agreements reached at San Stefano. Consequently, when Shuvalov presented himself to the Tsar after the signing of the Treaty of Berlin, which dealt a mortal blow to the Treaty of San Stefano, the Tsar received him with the words: 'You have betrayed me.'

The two injured parties at the Congress of Berlin were Turkey, who forfeited territory, and Russia, whose prestige was diminished. The Powers who gained by it were Austria, who acquired two Turkish provinces, and pre-eminently England. England's gain is to be found less in the text of the Treaty of Berlin or the Treaty of Cyprus[1] than in the immense relief of knowing that from that moment the full weight of Russian national hatred was turned away from England, the overt enemy, and directed towards the 'traitor', Germany. I have often wondered in recent years whether the subsequent realization that by the Congress of Berlin he had helped England against his will and at Germany's expense may have partly contributed to the irrational, the hysterical hatred of England which is revealed in all Prince Bismarck's later utterances. Immediately after the Congress this realization and the enmity accompanying it had not yet been born; on the contrary Bismarck, so far as was compatible with his nature, was well disposed toward [Disraeli], who handled him very skilfully. This appears from the following incident.

In the second half of 1878 (or was it 1879?—at any rate, just before the English elections) an English journalist Lavino (Levi) came to me from Vienna with a letter of introduction and asked me to procure him an audience with the Chancellor. At that time Lavino was *Daily Telegraph* correspondent in Vienna; now he represents *The Times*. He said he hoped his interview with His Highness and a discussion of his views on England and particularly on Beaconsfield would provide material for an article which might help the Prime Minister in the elections. Prince Bismarck, whom I informed of this, replied that though he could not grant him an interview because otherwise he would be besieged by correspondents, he was nevertheless prepared to publish in the *Norddeutsche* one or more pro-Disraeli articles if Lavino thought they might be of use. The latter said the articles would certainly benefit Disraeli. Thereupon Bismarck himself dictated two eulogistic articles for the *Norddeutsche*.[2] In fact when the elections resulted in a resounding victory for Gladstone[3] the view gained ground in England that these articles had contributed to the Opposition's victory because they had provided the pretext for spreading the election slogan that Beaconsfield was Bismarck's

[1] By the Treaty of 4 June 1878 the Sublime Porte handed over the administration of Cyprus to Britain.

[2] Holstein is mistaken about the date. An article, whose draft was corrected by the Chancellor, appeared at Lavino's request in the *Norddeutsche Allgemeine Zeitung* of 28 March 1880. See Windelband, *Bismarck und die europäischen Grossmächte*, pp. 120, 668.

[3] William Ewart Gladstone. British Prime Minister, 1868–74, 1880–5, January–July 1886, 1892–March 1894.

lackey. Nevertheless Bismarck had done what Lavino wanted, thus giving practical proof of his goodwill. Shortly afterwards, and to greater effect, he gave evidence of this same goodwill towards the British Liberal Government over the Egyptian question.

Meanwhile Prussia's former friend, Tsar Alexander II, had died a wretched, lonely, broken man. For him the outcome of the Congress of Berlin spelt political bankruptcy. The support of Kaiser Wilhelm I had been the basis of his policy. Prince Bismarck once said to me after the death of the Tsar, in 1882, perhaps: 'The fact that the Russians let us annex Alsace-Lorraine was not Russian policy but the personal policy of Alexander II.' This policy of Alexander II's had proved a complete failure when in the hour of need it had become clear that the Germans did not believe in the principle of reciprocity. The realization of this created a complete estrangement between the Russian people and their sovereign, whose nickname of 'the Prussian Tsar' has stuck to this day; 'the liberator Tsar' was forgotten. Ever since then he was an object of loathing to his people, and even those who did not actually load mines or carry bombs awaited indifferently the catastrophe looming ahead.

The dispatches sent at the time by Schweinitz[1] show that the Tsar himself clearly expressed the bitterness of his disillusion. Prince Hohenlohe told me that the Tsar said to his brother-in-law, Adjutant-General Prince Peter Wittgenstein: '*J'aime mon oncle, mais Bismarck est une affreuse canaille.*'

Bismarck, who was well aware of the feeling in Russia, retorted by renewed pin-pricks, starting with the [anti]-plague campaign in the late autumn of 1878.[2] Feeling ran so high that I have since been

---

[1] Hans Lothar von Schweinitz. Prussian General; Ambassador in St Petersburg, 1876–92. A memorandum written by General von Schweinitz in autumn 1883 contains this passage: '[…] just as foolish and no less widespread than was the cry in France, "*revanche pour Sadowa*", is the desire in Russia to avenge the Treaty of Berlin. This mood was artificially created during the weeks immediately following the Congress, when the aged Chancellor on his return from Berlin stayed with the Tsar in Zarskoje Selo; it was heightened and fostered throughout the following year, when Commissions met at various points on the Balkan Peninsula to determine the frontiers and to constitute the new states; […]'. (*Denkwürdigkeiten des Botschafters General v. Schweinitz* (Berlin, 1927), vol. II, p. 40, n. *).

[2] Holstein is referring to the measures taken by the German Government to prevent the import of Russian goods in view of an outbreak of plague in Russia at the beginning of 1879. In February 1879 Oubril was instructed by Gorchakov to inform State Secretary Bülow that the Tsar was '*froissé*' by this ruthless embargo

assured by a reliable man who was well informed on contemporary events in Russia that we had never come so close to war with Russia under Alexander III as we did at the end of the reign of Alexander II. This same man also said to me: 'If Prince Bismarck wants to create an impression on the Russians he must deal them such a blow that they sink to their knees. If he can't or won't do that he should leave them in peace; these pin-pricks simply goad them further.' Bismarck, however, drunk with his sense of power, continued this system of harassing and worrying which corresponded to his temperament. The last pin-prick I can remember now was the order forbidding the German Reichsbank to discount Russian securities. This insulting vote of no confidence in Russian finances occurred at a time when Alexander III was staying in Berlin as a guest.[1] This measure marked the conclusion of the campaign generally called 'the expulsion of Russian securities'. Bismarck, with the whole weight of his authority, told the German holders of Russian securities that Russia was an unreliable debtor. He hoped to 'get Russia where he wanted her' by making it difficult for her to obtain money. Instead the only result was that France replaced us as Russia's chief creditor nation, and consequently Russian securities soared. And all this happened when the secret treaty[2] was already in existence. In 1890 it only had to be renewed. Despite the treaty Russia's justifiable susceptibilities were continually outraged and her material interests prejudiced. Bismarck's behaviour is well described by a saying of Goethe's that a complete contradiction is equally obscure to wise men and to fools. The only explanation of this contradiction is that as a result of his constantly increasing sense of power his intelligence had been gradually subjugated by his temperament.

Alongside a craving for power and a lust for revenge, one of the main elements in Bismarck's character was the desire to 'chop and

which was very detrimental to Russian trade. (Memorandum by Bülow of 2 February 1879: from the Foreign Ministry files.) In the memorandum of autumn 1883, quoted above, Schweinitz describes the circumstances leading to the deterioration in Russo-German relations and says: '[...] but more hatred was aroused by the security measures we were bound to take against the plague in Vebljanka than by anything else; they actually mark the turning-point in the attitude of the Russians against the Germans.'

[1] In November 1887. See *Grosse Politik*, vol. v, ch. xxxvi, app. A.
[2] The so-called Reinsurance Treaty of 18 June 1887 (*Grosse Politik*, vol. v, no. 1092, pp. 253–5).

change'. The concept 'friend', that is, someone attached to you with a claim to be treated with consideration as an equal, was distasteful to him. Relays of followers who were unharnessed and put out to grass as soon as their task was done—that was the system which suited Bismarck's character. In his dealings with men he followed the same tactics as a libertine does with women. Many years ago now, probably in the late 'seventies, I was saying to Princess Johanna how necessary it was for Bismarck to meet people so that he should not live entirely cut off from society. 'Oh,' she replied, 'he never keeps his friends long, he soon gets tired of them.' Part of the trouble was Prince Bismarck's habit of doing all the talking himself. Occasionally, of course, he sent for someone to question him closely on some specific subject. But apart from these exceptional cases he always monopolized the conversation. He therefore preferred people who had not yet heard his stories. But the main reason underlying this desire of Prince Bismarck's to keep ringing the changes was the wish to prevent people or parties from thinking they were indispensable.

I have mentioned this peculiarity here because I think it possible that, alongside his hatred of Gorchakov, Bismarck also felt that Tsar Alexander as a 'friend' was becoming a burden to him. In the course of their earliest meetings after the Franco-Prussian War[1] the Tsar had said to Bismarck: 'You are in my debt and can show your gratitude by a frontier adjustment in North Schleswig.' Bismarck, who mentions this incident in one of his reports from Gastein in 1879[2] as a point in favour of the Austro-German Alliance, refused to grant the Tsar his wish, and so he did not insist further. But I think it probable that the way the Tsar behaved, and particularly his repeated refusal to recall Oubril, the Ambassador Bismarck objected to, strengthened Bismarck's intention of once more bringing into play his system of relays and of making Russia jealous of Austria and England for a time.

This method of browbeating Russia by arousing her jealousy and treating her roughly did not prove a success either with Alexander II or Alexander III. Prince Bismarck asserts that

[1] 6–12 September 1872, in Berlin.
[2] Bismarck wrote: 'Quite soon after the war His Majesty [Alexander II] told me personally in Berlin: "Your Government is in my debt and could give me proof of it by ceding North Schleswig".' Bismarck to Wilhelm I, 24 August 1879 (*Grosse Politik*, vol. III, no. 447, pp. 16–20).

Alexander III had confidence in him. So far I have found nothing to support this assertion, though the contrary may be seen in a memorandum written by the State Secretary Count Bismarck, on the [   ][1] after a conversation he had with the Grand Duke Vladimir. According to this the Grand Duke told him plainly it was now a regrettable fact that his brother, the Tsar, had *no* confidence in Prince Bismarck.[2]

The secret treaty, nowadays called the Reinsurance Treaty, had existed since 1887. Prince Bismarck eagerly indulged in his treaty-spinning in every direction. The more tangled the mesh, the more difficult it was to find one's way about in it *without* Prince Bismarck. 'My father is the only person who can handle this business', Count Herbert Bismarck used to say.

The mere fact that we had a secret treaty with Russia, Austria's arch-enemy, the terms of which were unknown to Austria, was naturally bound to prejudice the Triple Alliance. The terms of the treaty were even more likely to do so. To the Russians the thought that they controlled the fate of the Triple Alliance may have proved the decisive factor in the conclusion of the treaty. It may have been thought in St Petersburg that by uttering threats of indiscretions—or 'disclosures' to use the modern term—Russia would acquire the whip hand over the Cabinet in Berlin. At this period, between 1887 and 1890, those few people who knew about the conclusion of the treaty sometimes discussed the question: 'When will Russia let something leak out in Vienna?' However, apart from the first few months of 1887, no acute situations arose during those three years which might have caused the Russian Government to resort to extraordinary measures. In addition the Foreign Ministry, so long as Bismarck was still there, persisted in its superstitious belief that if the need arose he would skilfully and successfully extricate himself even from a false position. But for those in the secret there was no altering the fact that the Reinsurance Treaty contradicted the terms of other still valid agreements. Nine years earlier Prince Bismarck, guided by emotion

---

[1] Holstein gives no date.

[2] The memorandum written by Herbert von Bismarck to which Holstein refers is probably that of 27 April 1888 (*Grosse Politik*, vol. VI, no. 1338, pp. 294–8). Herbert quotes Grand Duke Vladimir as saying: '*Mon frère* [Alexander III] *est malheureusement pétri d'un soupçon insurmontable envers Votre père: Il reconnaît son génie, mais il craint toujours d'être joué par lui.*'

and caprice, had sent Russia about her business, once she had done her duty. Now, in order to win Russia back, he committed political bigamy.

Kaiser Wilhelm is entirely blameless in the matter. No one could expect the ninety-year-old monarch to have made a critical comparison of the texts of the various agreements forming Bismarck's complex system. He was fully justified in his reliance on Bismarck's word. An additional factor was Bismarck's habit of replying to every protest the Kaiser made with his resignation, so that in his last years the Kaiser on that account alone avoided expressing doubts on Bismarck's proposals.

And moreover, each step bringing Germany closer to Russia again corresponded to the aged ruler's heartfelt wish.

Thus from the spring of 1887 until 1890 we were in the following anomalous position: Russia, whose Tsar openly proclaimed his unfriendly attitude and his mistrust of Germany by word and deed, i.e. by constantly massing his troops on our borders, found herself in possession of an agreement whose publication would brand the German Government as a breaker of treaty obligations, and show her up as an undependable ally now and in the future. Of course one could always hope that Bismarck's tremendous authority would conceal all this. But the affair took on a different aspect when the question arose of renewing the treaty at a time when Bismarck's resignation already was a *fait accompli*.

The 1890 treaty episode came about in the following way. Count Shuvalov[1] had gone to St Petersburg on leave during the winter to prepare for the renewal of the treaty. When Prince Bismarck noticed that his position *vis-à-vis* the Kaiser had become precarious, he pressed for the treaty to be concluded and, in the first half of March, sent a telegram to St Petersburg asking when Count Shuvalov intended to return.[2] He arrived, I think, on 18 March—when the crisis had already arisen. The first card the Bismarcks played was that Count Herbert informed the Kaiser in a memorandum that Count Shuvalov had arrived fully empowered to conclude the treaty. But now he had heard that His Majesty might not scruple to accept Prince Bismarck's resignation, the Ambassador must first make inquiries in St Petersburg before

---

[1] Paul, Count Shuvalov. Russian Ambassador in Berlin, 1885–94.
[2] No such telegram has been found in the files of the German Foreign Ministry.

embarking on negotiations, since his instructions did not provide for this contingency.[1]

Wilhelm II, who had taken over the treaty *bona fide* from his father and grandfather, was most eager to renew it. Moritz Busch's assertion that Prince Bismarck told him during the crisis that *the Kaiser wished to break with Russia*[2] is a monstrous and contemptible lie, originating either with Busch or, more probably, with Bismarck. It is only because of this despicable conduct that I am now, for the first time in all the years I have been anonymously slandered and persecuted, writing an account of those events. And I have now no scruples in including all kinds of secret information from our files, in so far as this may be necessary to clear the matter up; every means is justified if it is likely to help truth to triumph over the abominable lie I have mentioned. The Kaiser, then, after receiving Herbert Bismarck's memorandum, sent for the Russian Ambassador and negotiated with him in person.[3] These negotiations failed to make any real progress, partly because the Kaiser, being imperfectly acquainted with the problem, trod warily but mainly because Count Shuvalov wanted to avoid reaching an agreement without Bismarck's participation.

Meanwhile Caprivi was appointed and instructed by the Kaiser to inform himself of the details of the treaty as quickly as possible. One morning, rather early, the new Chancellor arrived at the Foreign Ministry when I was the only senior official present, and asked to be shown the draft of the secret Russo-German Treaty. I observed, unnecessarily in view of Caprivi's incontestable right to see it, that the State Secretary[4] was not present, to which Caprivi replied that the State Secretary had said he was to be shown all he wanted—which of course went without saying.

I sent a message to the Central Bureau requesting the Head[5] to bring over the treaty files. While Caprivi read them I notified, with his consent, the Under State Secretary[6] and two other senior

---

[1] Herbert von Bismarck to Wilhelm II, 20 March 1890 (*Grosse Politik*, vol. VII, no. 1366, p. 3).

[2] Busch, *Bismarck. Some Secret Pages of his History*, vol. III, p. 314.

[3] See Schweinitz to Caprivi, 16 May 1890 (*Grosse Politik*, vol. VII, no. 1373, pp. 19–21).

[4] Herbert von Bismarck.   [5] Gustav Mechler.

[6] Max, Count von Berchem. First Secretary in the St Petersburg Embassy, 1875–8, in Vienna, 1878–83; Director of the Economic Policy Division of the Foreign Ministry, 1885–6; Under State Secretary, 1886–90.

officials. When they arrived we discussed the treaty with the Chancellor, at whose wish we immediately set down our opinions in writing. The four memoranda are still in the files.[1] Mine contains the warning not to conclude the agreement with Russia *now*, i.e. in spring 1890. After this consultation Caprivi went to see the Kaiser and told him of these misgivings which he shared. The Kaiser said to him: 'Talk the matter over with Schweinitz and tell me what he says.'

And so a conference took place between the new Chancellor, Schweinitz and Berchem,[2] who had in the meantime taken over the direction of the Foreign Ministry after Herbert Bismarck's retirement. The relevant documents were produced and after examining them Schweinitz said they certainly contained things that were new to him. Under those circumstances he thought it impossible to conclude this treaty with Russia because it would place us in a position inconsistent with other treaty obligations that were (at that time) still valid. I was not present at the conference but was told of its result immediately afterwards by Caprivi, who had wasted no time in going to see the Kaiser. The Kaiser had said:

[1] The account given by Holstein of the circumstances of the non-renewal of the Reinsurance Treaty is inaccurate. As is apparent from a letter of Holstein's to Eisendecher of 16 April 1890 (*Correspondence*), Caprivi asked to see the text of the Reinsurance Treaty 'on Chapter Day' (the Chapter of the Order of the Black Eagle, i.e. on 22 March 1890). A consultation, at which Caprivi, Berchem, Raschdau, and Holstein were present, took place not on the same day, as stated by Holstein, but on 23 March. (See *Grosse Politik*, vol. VII, no. 1391, p. 47, n. ***.) The only memorandum of March 1890 is Berchem's (*Grosse Politik*, vol. VII, no. 1368, pp. 4–10). In a letter to Bülow of 3 June 1904, Berchem wrote: 'After Herr von Caprivi had expressed his agreement with my opinion which was identical with that of *Geheimer Legationsrat* Herr von Holstein, all question of signing the draft treaty, which the Kaiser did not desire either, was dropped.' (*Grosse Politik*, vol. VII, no. 1391, pp. 47–8.) The joint consultation which Holstein erroneously places in the month of March, took place on 20 May 1890. It was convened because of a dispatch from the Ambassador in St Petersburg, Schweinitz, of 15 May 1890, according to which Giers had again broached the question of renewing the Reinsurance Treaty even though in a modified form. (*Grosse Politik*, vol. VII, no. 1372, pp. 17–19.) The four memoranda dated 20 May 1890, and written by Marschall (not Berchem), Holstein, Raschdau and Kiderlen, are printed in *Grosse Politik* (vol. VII, nos. 1374–7, pp. 22–9). See also Holstein's memorandum of 10 June 1904, *Grosse Politik* vol. VII, no. 1392, pp. 48–9, in which, as here, he gives March 1890 as the date of the memoranda.

[2] The conference took place on 27 March 1890. (See Schweinitz, *Denkwürdigkeiten*, vol. II, pp. 403–5 and *Grosse Politik*, vol. VII, no. 1391, pp. 47–8.) Schweinitz thought the Reinsurance Treaty incompatible with the Triple Alliance and particularly with the Treaty with Rumania. See also *Grosse Politik*, vol. VII, nos. 1369 and 1392, pp. 10–11 and pp. 48–49.

'If Schweinitz is also against it then it cannot be done. I am extremely sorry, but I desire more than anything to pursue an honourable policy.'

The honourable policy was also the only possible policy, for by concluding the treaty the Kaiser would have been at the mercy of anyone who shared the secret. Judging by our experiences over the last few years the assumption is justified that we should not have had to wait long for indiscreet revelations which would *not*, like the 'disclosures' of autumn 1896,[1] have misfired but would have convicted the Kaiser's Government of political bigamy. The reactions such disclosures would have had on the Government's position both at home and abroad may well be imagined.

Count Herbert Bismarck, when he heard that the treaty files had been submitted to the new Chancellor, was in a towering rage. First he sent for the Head of the Central Bureau and asked him savagely how he dared to show anyone those highly secret documents without his, the Count's, instructions. He concluded with the threat: 'I'll deal with you on my return.' Next Count Bismarck called to account the Under State Secretary. The latter explained truthfully enough that he had not sent for the treaty files but that on his arrival the Chancellor was already reading them. Thereupon the Count sent for me and said, maintaining his self-control with difficulty: 'You have been guilty of something which in past circumstances I should have been obliged to punish most severely. Under present conditions all I can say is that you have been in too big a hurry to regard me as a back number.' I had no difficulty in justifying the professional propriety of my behaviour, and we parted, shaking hands for the last time. But when the discussions between Caprivi and Schweinitz resulted in a breakdown of the treaty negotiations, my relations with the Bismarck family were also at an end. The next time I met Count Herbert Bismarck, on the stairs, he gave a deep bow and passed by without a word. When I discussed the affair with one of the Count's close friends,

---

[1] In the *Hamburger Nachrichten* of 24 October 1896. An article composed or inspired by Bismarck describes the good relations that existed between Germany and Russia until 1890. 'Up to this point both Empires were in complete agreement that, should one of them be attacked, the other would remain a benevolent neutral. [...] This agreement was not renewed after Prince Bismarck's retirement. [...]' (Hermann Hofmann: *Fürst Bismarck*, 1890–1898 (Stuttgart, 1913–14), vol. II, pp. 370–3.)

he said: 'Well, why did you have to send for the documents? What could it matter whether the "old man" knew about the treaty twenty-four hours sooner or later?' I mention no name,[1] but I reproduce this remark because, just like what I have already described, it shows the contemporary mood: the Bismarck idea submerged everything else, swamping, though fortunately not in every quarter, the concepts of Emperor, Empire, and Service, whose place it had usurped.

[1] The remark was made by Wilhelm von Bismarck.

CHAPTER VIII

BISMARCK AND WILHELM II[1]

Marschall: his character; his mission to Darmstadt and the Battenberg marriage. The Bismarcks and Prince Wilhelm. Awaiting the succession. Crown Prince Friedrich Wilhelm: his illness. Puttkamer's dismissal. The Ninety-nine Days. Wilhelm II. Question of ministerial access to the Kaiser; Bismarck's and Wilhelm II's attitude towards the workers and Social Democracy. Incidents connected with Bismarck's dismissal. Crispi and the Tunisian Question, 1890. Kálnoky. Caprivi and the Tunisian Question. Britain's friendly attitude to Germany.
Appendix. Holstein warns Bismarck.

15 *January* 1908:

THERE is a concerted agitation on foot to make Marschall the next Chancellor. Hatzfeldt-Trachenberg,[2] though not averse to the post himself, says Marschall is the only possible candidate, the only one who would be able to set right the present situation. Ballin[3] told the Kaiser the same thing in person. Marschall's supporters are pressing for a decision; they say that if it were delayed Marschall's prospects would not be so bright in six months' time as today. His achievements at the Hague[4] (which are really Kriege's[5] achievements in any case), would already be half forgotten and also his status in Constantinople would have noticeably declined because the Sultan feels personally insulted by Marschall's behaviour and desires a change.

In my view Marschall's intelligence and eloquence would make him a better than average Chancellor, but he has not a strong enough character. You could almost say he has no character. That

---

[1] The chapter-heading is Holstein's.

[2] Hermann, Prince Hatzfeldt, since 1900 Duke of Trachenberg. Free Conservative Member of the Reichstag, 1878–93, 1907–11; Head of the Administration of Silesia, 1894–1903.

[3] Albert Ballin. Managing Director of the Hamburg-Amerika Steamship Company (Hapag), 1900–18.

[4] In 1907 Marschall was First German Delegate to the second Hague Peace Conference.

[5] Johannes Kriege. *Vortragender Rat* in the Foreign Ministry, 1900–11; Second Delegate to the second Hague Peace Conference.

is mainly what makes him absolutely unreliable in his personal relationships. When he became Minister for Baden in Berlin he at once attached himself to Bötticher,[1] spending nearly every evening as a guest in his hospitable house, but as his fortunes prospered he moved further and further away from Bötticher and finally dropped him completely in 1897.

Marschall first attracted notice in 1885 or 1886 when he undertook a secret mission to Darmstadt at Bismarck's request.[2] At that time the Crown Princess Victoria was very eager to marry her daughter Victoria to Prince Alexander of Battenberg, Prince of Bulgaria.[3] The royal families of Hesse and of England were working to bring this about; the old Kaiser and Kaiserin and Prince Bismarck worked against it.

The Crown Princess wanted to make Prince Alexander King of Bulgaria. This idea of hers acquired fresh impetus after the victorious Serbian war of 1885.[4] In a letter which I heard read out she developed the theme that Russian policy should aim not at the Balkans but in the direction of the Indian Ocean and should bring Persia into the Russian sphere of influence. The letter was sent to an English address, and the recipient commented bitterly that the noble lady's family interests had caused her to overlook the vital interests of the British Empire.

Prince Alexander himself, whom I never met, must have been far less ambitious than his would-be mother-in-law. A very handsome man of weak character, who regarded his good looks as his main asset. I once saw a letter he wrote to the Crown Princess when he was just recovering from a skin disease, smallpox I think. The Prince began by describing his appearance. He looked more or less the same, but the disease had left behind just one small scar (on his nose I think). Then he bemoaned his sad and lonely plight and sighed for his 'joy'. 'You can say that the interests of Europe

---

[1] Karl Heinrich von Bötticher. State Secretary in the Ministry of the Interior, 1880–97; Prussian Minister of State.

[2] Marschall's mission to Darmstadt took place in April 1888, as Holstein records in his diary, entry of 11 April 1888 (*Diaries*).

[3] Prince of Bulgaria, 1879–86.

[4] When Eastern Rumelia was united with Bulgaria, Serbia demanded some compensation for Bulgaria's territorial gain and on 13 November 1885 declared war on Bulgaria. The Serbs were defeated at Slivnitza (17–19 November) and Pirot (26–27 November). It was only Austrian intervention which saved Serbia from forfeiting any territory at the conclusion of the Peace of Bucharest (3 March 1886).

require me to remain here. But how can Europe compensate me if I lose my joy as a result?'

In the preceding passage the wording is a more or less faithful rendering, the shade of thought entirely so. I read this letter myself with the closest attention and impressed it on my memory. To me as a politician it was a human document which left me in no doubt that the Prince had only undertaken to play his Bulgarian role on his relations' persuasion, that when he wrote that letter, at any rate, he was already weary of his role, and that he regarded it as a means to an end, namely a life of peace and comfort. That is why after the *coup d'état* of 1886[1] during which his life was in danger for twenty-four hours, he could no longer be held in check despite the exertions of his English relatives.

But this scheming for a Battenberg-Hohenzollern marriage did not cease with the loss of Bulgaria, on the contrary it was carried on at even higher pressure by the Hessian and English royal families and by the Crown Princess. For in the meantime one of the Battenberg brothers had married a Princess of Hesse,[2] another[3] had married Princess Beatrice of England,[4] so why should not the third brother, the handsome famous Alexander, marry a Prussian princess?

His father, Prince Alexander of Hesse, and still more his mother, Princess of Battenberg, gave our Minister Stumm clearly to understand that it was not 'fair' to keep the Prince in suspense; he was thereby letting slip very favourable prospects which might well turn up elsewhere. Stumm asked, quite correctly, whether he might make use of this information. Certainly, was the reply. So Stumm sat down and wrote a dispatch which created a great stir in Berlin and earned for the House of Hesse-Battenberg the categorical declaration that there could be no question of this marriage with the Kaiser's granddaughter. Stumm was amazed when the next time he met Prince Alexander von Hesse the latter said: 'So far our relations have been cordial. I am the more sorry that they must now cease.' The fact is, Mama Battenberg was furious. When Stumm told me of the affair he said: 'I can't understand why they're so touchy. I had expressly asked whether

---

[1] During the night of 20–21 August Prince Alexander of Bulgaria was abducted by a band of insurgent Bulgarian officers and forced to abdicate. His definitive abdication took place on 7 September.

[2] Prince Ludwig von Battenberg married Princess Victoria of Hesse on 30 April 1884.   [3] Prince Heinrich von Battenberg.   [4] On 23 July 1885.

I could pass on the information they had given me.' 'Yes', I said with a laugh, 'but I expect they thought you would tell Seckendorff[1] maybe, but never Bismarck.' Stumm was taken aback and then admitted it might be so. But it is probably to this dispatch that he owes his sudden advancement in 1887 to the Embassy in Madrid.[2]

One of the methods employed by Bismarck to convince the Court in Darmstadt that a Battenberg-Hohenzollern alliance was out of the question for all time, was Marschall's mission mentioned above. He must have performed his task satisfactorily, for he was immediately decorated with the Red Eagle First Class or Grand Cross. This achievement made him *persona grata* with Bismarck, and Herbert designated him to me as one of the people to whom I was to give information on the contemporary situation, should he require it. As a result Marschall, though he can hardly be blamed, contributed in 1890 to Bismarck's downfall. For, as we subsequently learned, it happened repeatedly that information which Marschall obtained from me and passed on to his Grand Duke[3] was then discussed between the Grand Duke and the Kaiser;

[1] Götz, Count von Seckendorff. Chamberlain to the Crown Princess Victoria.

[2] The conversation between Stumm and the Princess of Battenberg, which Holstein describes, took place at the beginning of January 1885. Stumm gave a report of it in a private letter of 14 January, extracts from which were copied and transmitted by Rottenburg from the Reich Chancellery to the Foreign Ministry on 16 January. On the Kaiser's instructions, Stumm's letter was submitted to the Crown Prince. In the accompanying letter to the Crown Prince, Bismarck stated, among other things: 'His Majesty the Kaiser commanded me to add the expression of his conviction that an alliance with a Prince who is not of equal rank, not a reigning monarch, and whose future is uncertain, is deemed too unequal for the Imperial family to be acceptable.' By a dispatch of 26 January Stumm was instructed to inform the Princess of Battenberg that the marriage between Prince Alexander and Princess Victoria was impossible on account of the strained relations between Germany and Russia which would result. The dispatch continued: 'I [Bismarck] regard it under these circumstances as my bounden duty to Emperor and Empire to do what I can to prevent the occurrence of such an alliance, which may have been planned in England's political interests. English policy has an interest in our being on bad terms with the Emperor of Russia, and a Prussian Princess on the Bulgarian throne would be a fairly sure means of achieving this. [...] Their Royal Highnesses the Crown Prince and Crown Princess, of whom I had audience, expressed their astonishment at the Princess of Battenberg's statement that an "understanding" or "engagement" existed between the Prince of Bulgaria and Princess Victoria. [...] It was impossible to break off existing relations, simply because no such relations existed. [...]' (From the Foreign Ministry files.) The further development of this stage of the Battenberg marriage question is recorded in Holstein's diary, entry of March 7, 1885 (*Diaries*).

[3] Friedrich I, Grand Duke of Baden, 1856–1907. He was married to Luise, daughter of Wilhelm I.

it thus became clear that Prince Bismarck had given the Kaiser completely different information, and particularly that he had concealed things which in the Kaiser's view he should have reported. This rendered the crisis more acute, but I am convinced that the Kaiser was already quite determined to get rid of Bismarck. The Kaiser had become estranged from Bismarck since the conflict over the Stöcker meeting in 1886 [sic].[1] I think I have already written an account of the incident[2] but for safety's sake I will repeat it here.

In 1886 relations between Bismarck and Prince Wilhelm were most confidential, and between Herbert and the Prince they were completely cordial. The Bismarcks regarded the Prince as a bulwark against the liberalizing and other suspect tendencies of the Crown Princess, who in the nature of things would inevitably come to power before very long. But there were other people who planned to use the Prince's influence for their own ends and to win him over to their side in good time. Waldersee[3] and Puttkamer[4] displayed particular zeal over this. They both knew they were in bad odour with the Crown Prince and still more with the Crown Princess. Waldersee told me one day: 'If there is ever any question of a *coup d'état* against the Crown Princess you can count on me. You can tell that to the Chancellor,' which, incidentally, I did not.

Herbert, who claimed for himself the monopoly of Prince Wilhelm's favour, watched this 'unfair competition' as he regarded it on the part of Waldersee and Puttkamer with growing displeasure. This jealousy, which was finally turned against Bötticher too, led gradually to the crash, as one grievance piled on another.

The first incident, as I have said, was the Stöcker meeting in the autumn of 1886 [sic]. A few weeks previously Prince Wilhelm had gone to await the Chancellor in the garden-room of his palace

---

[1] At a meeting in support of the Berlin City Mission on 28 November 1887, the Court Chaplain, Adolf von Stöcker, made a political speech. Stöcker was the founder of the anti-Semitic Christian Socialist Party and violently opposed to the Social Democrats and Progressives. Prince Wilhelm, who attended the meeting with his wife, was sharply criticized in an article inspired by Bismarck which appeared in the *Norddeutsche Allgemeine Zeitung*. The basis for the attack was that the Prince's name was being coupled politically with Stöcker's as a result of the meeting.

[2] In an essay written in 1898.

[3] Alfred, Count von Waldersee. Quartermaster-general and Vice-Chief of the General Staff, 1882–8; Chief of the General Staff, 1888–91.

[4] Robert Viktor von Puttkamer. Prussian Minister of the Interior, 1881–8; Vice-President of the Prussian Ministry of State, 1881–8.

so as to be the first person to greet him in Berlin on his return from taking the waters. Such were the relations between them. Shortly afterwards Waldersee and Puttkamer arranged a meeting in the office building of the General Staff,[1] to which Prince Wilhelm was invited and which he attended, to hear Stöcker give a speech on political rather than spiritual matters. When Herbert heard of this 'intrigue' he was extremely annoyed and found it only too easy to arouse his father's anger. It was certainly necessary to instruct the Prince, to make him see that he should not have attended this meeting. The Chancellor had the choice of the most varied methods of bringing this home to the Prince. If he did not want to write to the Prince he could have invited him to come stag-hunting in the Sachsenwald and there explained the position to him. Or he could have sent Herbert with a message to the Prince. Anything would have been better than the method they (i.e. Herbert) actually chose. For both the meeting and the Prince were criticized in the *Norddeutsche*. Rottenburg[2] wrote the articles. They were pretty blunt. 'Our friend writes with a broomstick', the Chancellor said to me later on—in English because one of the clerks was in the room—when speaking of these articles and the resentment they had caused in the Prince. The latter sent Liebenau, his Court Chamberlain, to Herbert to register a complaint. Herbert protested he knew nothing about the articles. But that did not help him. For when I too attempted to give the impression that the origin of the articles was obscure, Waldersee said to me: 'You needn't trouble, I've seen [the] manuscript.' The energetic Puttkamer had asked the editors of the *Norddeutsche* for the manuscript, which had enabled him to determine the origin with ease. It is clear beyond question that Waldersee and Puttkamer, particularly the former, for Puttkamer was not an intriguer, exploited this incident to sow doubts in the Prince's mind as to the loyalty and sincerity of the Bismarcks.[3]

Years later, when the situation was gradually nearing the critical stage, someone, I cannot remember who, but I do not think

---

[1] The meeting took place at Waldersee's house.

[2] Dr Franz Johannes von Rottenburg. Bismarck's assistant in the Reich Chancellery, 1881–90; Under State Secretary in the Ministry of the Interior, 1891–6.

[3] For the Stöcker affair see Bismarck, *Die gesammelten Werke*, vol. xv, pp. 458–60; *Denkwürdigkeiten des General-Feldmarschalls Alfred Grafen von Waldersee*, edited by H. O. Meisner (Stuttgart and Berlin, 1922–3), vol. i, pp. 338 *et seq.*

it was Liebenau, told me that the experiences the Prince went through over the Stöcker articles had a devastating effect on his temperament, colouring not only his attitude to the Bismarcks but his general estimation of mankind.

17 *January* 1908:

In 1886 [*sic*] Kaiser Wilhelm I's health was more precarious and gave rise to more immediate alarm than in the following year, which was his last. Everyone felt that a change of ruler was imminent. It had been slow in coming. I have heard Prince Bismarck say more than once that one of the factors that made his early days as Minister-President difficult had been the King's age. Politicians did not give him many more years to live, and so were unwilling to bank on him. 'If they could have foreseen that he would still be alive today, almost twenty years later, then I should have found ministerial colleagues easily enough.' But in 1886 the signs of his approaching end were unmistakable, and those concerned turned their thoughts to the succession. There was much talk of the plans and groupings of the Crown Prince's faction. But I shall not touch on this because I had no reliable sources of information. The question was ceaselessly discussed: will the Crown Princess continue to influence her husband, or will he realize his responsibility as a monarch and assert his independence? Some of the Crown Prince's immediate circle thought this latter course possible. But I took the view expressed in the legal axiom: No changes can be expected. Stosch,[1] who knew the royal couple extremely well, wrote on 31 July 1866 (p. 107 of his *Denkwürdig-keiten*):[2] 'The Prince is first and foremost his wife's husband. She has the most far-reaching influence on his thoughts and opinions.' The prevailing view was that this state of affairs would persist after the succession, and so, each in his own way the opponents, not to say enemies, of the Crown Princess—the Bismarcks, Waldersee, Puttkamer—set about fashioning Prince Wilhelm for his role in opposition.

Then the whole situation was suddenly changed by the news that the Crown Prince had cancer of the throat. The specialist

[1] Albrecht von Stosch. Prussian Minister of State and Head of the Admiralty, 1872–83.
[2] *Denkwürdigkeiten des Generals und Admirals Albrecht von Stosch*, edited by Ulrich von Stosch (Stuttgart and Leipzig, 1904).

Dr Tobold[1] had been called in and had said in the ante-room before leaving: 'Oh, it's horrible, horrible!' The German doctors wanted to excise part of the larynx. Mackenzie[2] and the Crown Princess were against it. Both of them were severely blamed for this because it was said that the tracheotomy would have prolonged the patient's life. I believe these reproaches to be unjust. The Crown Princess acted for the best. No one had a greater interest than she in prolonging the sick man's life.

It has often been stated that Prince Bismarck had planned to exclude the Crown Prince from the succession on account of his illness, and to have Prince Wilhelm proclaimed his grandfather's successor. I know that some such suspicion had been awakened in the Crown Princess, which goes far to explain her conduct during the Mackenzie episode. But I can positively assert that nothing came to my ears which could have led one to conclude that Bismarck had such a plan.

But it became clear that another scheme existed, less with the Chancellor than with Herbert, namely of removing the Minister Puttkamer before Prince Wilhelm came to the throne. This is how the plan was carried out during the Ninety-nine Days. It was decided to make use of Kaiser Friedrich's prejudice against Puttkamer's conservative tendencies. After the elections to the Prussian Chamber of Deputies (or was it to the Reichstag?)[3] Herbert informed the Court Chamberlain Prince Radolin[4] that it was desirable for the Kaiser to write to the Minister to express his disapproval of certain election tactics. Radolin, who was perfectly prepared to support Bismarck's policy, but not that of his son, arranged to travel in the same train as the Chancellor from Berlin to Wildpark, and during the journey he submitted to Prince Bismarck the draft of the letter in question. The Prince altered one or two phrases and said with a smile: 'Otherwise Puttkamer might take them amiss.' But even after these altera-

---

[1] Dr Adalbert Tobold. Throat specialist.
[2] Dr, later Sir Morell Mackenzie. Throat specialist.
[3] Elections to the Chamber of Deputies.
[4] Hugo Leszczyc, Count von Radolin-Radolinski, from 1888 Prince von Radolin. First Secretary in the Embassy in Constantinople, 1876–81; temporarily employed in the Foreign Ministry, 1881–2; Prussian Minister in Weimar, October 1882–May 1884; Chamberlain to the Crown Prince Friedrich Wilhelm, 1884–8; Ambassador in Constantinople, 1892–5, in St Petersburg, 1895–1900, in Paris, 1900–10.

tions the letter was such that Puttkamer immediately drew his own conclusions and tendered his resignation.

Late in the evening of the day on which the matter was being decided Herbert called on Radolin in Viktoria-Strasse where the Minister Friedberg and I had been dining, called Radolin out and asked him whether the Kaiser had in fact sent the letter off.

At the next session of the Council of Ministers Prince Bismarck told the other Ministers, who were indignant at the way Puttkamer had been treated: 'I understand and share your feelings. But, as patriots, we must subdue them and remain at our posts.'

The accounts I was given by Bismarck and by informants at the Court of the conferences Prince Bismarck had during the Ninety-nine Days with the Kaiser or the Kaiserin certainly did not tally; to say the least, they diverged rather widely. So I shall not go into them further. However, everything went off without incident.

I heard some remarkable details about the campaign for the Battenberg marriage, which was now renewed for the last time. The Kaiserin tried to win over the Kaiser to the idea of such a marriage but either the Kaiser did not think Prince Alexander good enough now he had been hounded out of Bulgaria, or else Bismarck had presented the affair from his own point of view; at any rate the Kaiser refused his wife's request with unusual violence. By now he was unable to speak, so he finally stamped his foot and pointed to the door, at which the Kaiserin retired as white as a sheet.

But Prince Bismarck told the Kaiserin that once the marriage was a *fait accompli* there would then be nothing he could do about it, though he would naturally be obliged to cause a certain amount of fuss. The Kaiserin with her suspicious nature thought she detected the Chancellor's intention of using this marriage to discredit her in Germany, particularly in Prussia, so from that moment she pursued the matter no further.

One day when Prince Bismarck was issuing some instructions he told me the actual business of government was easier under Kaiser Friedrich than it was likely to be with his son. It may be doubted whether this remark conveyed Bismarck's views completely. Certainly it was easy to govern, but the danger of a sudden fluctuation resulting from the Kaiserin's interference was always present not only to the Chancellor but to other people. A man who was able to observe closely what went on at Court said to me: 'No one can tell, if the present situation continues, how long the Kaiserin will restrain herself.' In fact the Kaiserin was in two minds during this period. She was urged in many quarters to make her influence felt both at home and abroad, and to use her temporary power to the full to make sure she was long remembered by posterity. On the other hand she probably hesitated to do anything which might permanently antagonize her son, on whom, after all, she would later be dependent.

Prince Bismarck may have divined this inner discord and strove constantly to keep the Kaiserin in a good humour. Kaiser Wilhelm had left savings of about eleven million marks which were his personal property. Prince Bismarck arranged for the whole sum to be made over to Kaiserin Friedrich for herself and her daughters, a step entirely at variance with the practices of the Prussian Court, where a Princess had hardly ever received more than a hundred thousand thaler. The fact that the old Kaiser's widow and his daughter the Grand Duchess came away empty-handed may perhaps have been due to some good reason of state but it was hardly in the interests of these two ladies.

During the Ninety-nine Days Kaiserin Friedrich once went to Posen, where she held a reception in the castle for the ladies of the Polish nobility, who attended in great numbers. The Kaiserin conversed with them in French.

There is nothing else I should like to mention in connection with the Ninety-nine Days, except the innocent joke telling how Bismarck, during a visit made by Queen Victoria to her daughter, described her to his family as 'a jolly little body'.

24 *January* 1908:

I know little about the period from June 1889 up to the crisis of April [*sic*] 1890, and prefer not to set down what I do know because it is too fragmentary and would give a distorted picture.

Neither Bismarck nor the Kaiser behaved with complete honesty.

One facet of the Kaiser's character was revealed to me in an anecdote Waldersee told me in summer 1888, just before or just after the succession. He said: 'During exercises today the Kaiser (or was he still Crown Prince?) made fun of the way Wilhelm

Radziwill[1] and Lehndorff,[2] both of whom were there, seemed so eager to be of service. He treated them both with the utmost kindness but said to me in an aside: "They think I'm going to keep them on." I found it an interesting study in character,' said Waldersee.

Radziwill and Lehndorff were very soon dismissed. Surprisingly enough, considering the great discrepancy of age between them and the Kaiser, they had not foreseen this possibility, and I heard that Lehndorff spoke bitterly of this 'complete lack of respect'.

The Kaiser retained from his father's personal staff Winterfeld[3] and Kessel,[4] who had both, during Kaiser Friedrich's lifetime, abandoned the sinking ship and climbed on to the new one. All kinds of stories were told about that. But it must in justice be said that Kaiser Wilhelm never bore a grudge against Prince Radolin for his determined championhip of the Kaiserin Friedrich's interests during the dispute immediately following her husband's death, but always accounted it to his credit.

Herbert Bismarck, so far as I was aware, lived on good terms with the Kaiser until December 1889 and was not dissatisfied with the degree of influence he possessed. That, so far as I know, is why he wrote to Friedrichsruh as late as December 1889 to say there was no business on hand which could make it necessary for Prince Bismarck to cut short his stay in the country.

Other people, such as Bötticher, thought otherwise. He thought the Chancellor's speedy return was necessary and went to Friedrichsruh to say so. But that very journey spelt disaster. For Schweninger, who had a bitter hatred of Bötticher for personal reasons, happened to be staying at Friedrichsruh. At the time Schweninger told the following story which I was told in exactly the same form by the journalist Jacobi[5] quite recently, that is within the last two years. Jacobi had it from Herbert and from Harden,[6] who had learned it from Herbert himself. He, Schwenin-

---

[1] Evidently Holstein means Prince Anton Radziwill, Adjutant-General of Wilhelm I and Friedrich III. Prince Wilhelm Radziwill had died in 1870.

[2] Heinrich August, Count von Lehndorff. Adjutant-General of Wilhelm I.

[3] Hugo von Winterfeld. Adjutant-General.

[4] Gustav von Kessel. Military aide, later General.

[5] Hugo Jacobi. Editor of the *Berliner Neueste Nachrichten*.

[6] Maximilian Harden. Political writer; founder and publisher of the weekly periodical *Die Zukunft*.

ger, had entered the morning-room at Friedrichsruh just as the Chancellor was briefing Bötticher. The latter was standing up and pretending to take notes. But as Schweninger walked past he saw that Bötticher was not writing a single word. At this the idea flashed through Schweninger's head: 'If matters have gone so far that Bötticher can take *such* liberties, then the crisis over the Chancellor is not merely about to happen, it's already upon us.' As a result he cut short his visit, giving as a pretext some urgent business, and returned by the same train as Bötticher. During the journey Bötticher tried to extract from Schweninger an admission that the Chancellor was a morphia addict. The whole tone of Bötticher's references to Prince Bismarck was one of unconcealed contempt. So Schweninger went straight from the station to call on Herbert, who was still in bed or in his bath, and told him the whole story. It made such an impression on Herbert that he said: 'I'm expecting the Kaiser in an hour. I'll ring up at once to cancel the appointment. At the moment I can hardly contain myself. I'm not responsible for what I might say.'

As I have said, I only heard this story a short time ago. If I had had any idea of it before, I should have understood more clearly much of what happened between New Year 1890 and the Ides of March (to use Herbert's expression). I suddenly noticed that Herbert was furiously angry with Bötticher. I had very little contact with Bötticher, because there was a firm and lasting friendship between him and Rottenburg, whom I disliked. But Schweninger's long story seems to me a tendentious distortion of a harmless incident. Anyone who has been briefed knows that you only jot down the key-words, mainly because you cannot keep pace otherwise. I should need stronger proofs than Schweninger's word before I believed it possible that Bötticher tried to fool Prince Bismarck and spoke of him contemptuously, in front of Schweninger at that.

Since Herbert did not tell me this story, but only spread it after his father's dismissal, I failed to understand this sudden access of hatred for Bötticher. I refused to take part in the persecution and once I even invited Bötticher to a meal, though I have never accepted any of his luncheon invitations either before or after 1890. Herbert, who naturally heard of this next day, made some spiteful comment to me.

Bötticher, who soon noticed Herbert's antagonism towards him, attempted to strengthen his position by conferring with the Kaiser during the Chancellor's absence whenever the opportunity occurred. But this only increased Herbert's anger and provided him with an effective means of rousing the Chancellor's anger, for Prince Bismarck guarded jealously the monopoly of direct access to the Kaiser which was guaranteed him by a long-standing order in council. The break between Bismarck and Savigny in 1866 had come about because the latter, as Head of the Department of the Interior, had also asked to have direct access. And in the late 'eighties the Minister Gossler[1] told me that Bismarck said to some Minister, either Gossler himself or Puttkamer: 'Don't imagine you can use the Kaiser to shield yourself from me.' From this it is easily imagined how Herbert's information that Bötticher was thrusting himself on the Kaiser's notice aroused in the Chancellor suspicions that had not previously existed.

This question of whether any Minister whatever or the Chancellor and Minister-President alone, could hold consultations with the sovereign, was one of the main causes which provoked the crisis. Bismarck took his stand on his apparent right, that is, the old order in council, whereas the Kaiser claimed the right to hear any of the Ministers. While Bismarck openly ill-treated Bötticher on account of his alleged self-assertiveness, the Kaiser conferred on Bötticher the Order of the Black Eagle to make up for it. The so-called *Krachunterhaltung* between the Kaiser and Bismarck on 15 (or 16?) March[2] also turned mainly, so far as I can now recall, on the question of ministerial access. When the Kaiser related this conversation he took pains to show that Bismarck's manner towards him had been violent and disrespectful. On the other hand I heard that the Kaiser went out of his way to annoy the old man by summoning him from his bed at about nine in the morning and requiring his presence in the State Secretary's garden. It would certainly have been more fitting on such a serious occasion if the Kaiser had either summoned the Chancellor to the castle or if he had himself gone to the Chancellor's palace. I cannot now remember any details of this incident.

[1] Gustav von Gossler. Conservative Member of the Reichstag from 1878; President of the Reichstag, 1881; Prussian Minister for Ecclesiastical Affairs, 1881–91.   [2] On 15 March.

Another bone of contention between Kaiser and Chancellor was the Government's attitude to the workers and to the Social Democrats.

Since the attempted assassinations in 1878 Prince Bismarck had adopted the view that stern measures must be taken against the Social Democrats. I do not know the full extent of his plans in this connection. All I know is that soon after the anti-Socialist law had come into force he expressed his conviction that the Berlin garrison would not be strong enough to quell an insurrection, and he therefore demanded the erection of a larger military encampment on the Tempelhofer Feld. I prefer not to give any figure because I am not quite sure of it after so long an interval, but the projected reinforcement was really substantial. I was sent one day with a message in connection with this plan to our Minister for War, von Kameke,[1] but found him decidedly averse to this idea of a reinforcement and prepared to resign over the issue. The Berlin garrison, he said, was most certainly large enough for any contingency; within a few hours reinforcements could be brought in from all directions; an encampment in the immediate neighbourhood of the city would have a harmful effect on the discipline and morale of the troops. And the Tempelhofer Feld was indispensable as a drill-ground, etc., etc.

I advised the Minister to put on his helmet and call on the Chancellor. I said I thought it probable that during a *tête-à-tête* the Minister would be able to put his case, whereas at a session of the Council of Ministers the Chancellor would be most unlikely to give way. Kameke took my advice and discussed the matter with Prince Bismarck; since then I never heard another word about the projected encampment. In the 'nineties, that is about ten years later, Miquel[2] once told me he was convinced Bismarck had wanted to engineer a clash—or clashes—with the Social Democrats in order to bring about an open trial of strength. I have no opinion on the matter and am quite unable to judge Prince Bismarck's domestic policy as a whole. What I heard during the early part of 1890 did not seem free from contradictions.

[1] General Georg von Kameke. Prussian Minister for War, 1873–83.

[2] Dr Johannes Miquel. Lord Mayor of Frankfurt-am-Main, 1879–90; Prussian Finance Minister, 1890–1901; co-founder of the *Nationalverein*; one of the leaders of the National Liberals in the Prussian Chamber of Deputies and in the Reichstag from 1867.

For example the Parliament was prepared to turn the anti-Socialist Law, which had been passed in 1878 as an exceptional and temporary measure, into a permanent law; but the exceptional clause [*sic*][1] was to be omitted, that is, the right to expel from any town any persons who had been participating in Socialist activities, simply by administrative measures. Various parliamentarians have told me that there was a great deal to be said against this kind of expulsion, because the agitators who were forbidden the towns turned their attention to the country-side. All the parties of the Right were agreed that the retention of the entire remaining anti-Socialist Law was important to the security of the domestic situation. So it came as an even greater surprise when the Chancellor seemed lukewarm. When asked by party leaders whether he favoured retention of the anti-Socialist Law without the expulsion clause Bismarck replied that he was unable to take the initiative in yielding by recommending the omission of the clause. He must leave this step to Parliament. The Conservative leader,[2] from whom I heard this immediately afterwards, replied that unless the party had the Government's consent it could not renounce the expulsion clause. But unless this happened the Parliament would not give its consent to making the anti-Socialist Law permanent, and thus an opportunity would be lost that would never recur. Bismarck persisted in his view that in the realm of concessions he must leave the initiative to Parliament. The Government could under certain circumstances accept concessions to the Left which Parliament had decided on and voted, but it could not be the first to show leniency.

And so the inevitable happened: the anti-Socialist Law was defeated, to the jubilation of the Democrats and Social Democrats.[3] The Conservatives and also the moderate group were bewildered. People wondered what the Chancellor was really aiming at. One even heard the question raised, whether perhaps he wished to render the political situation more difficult so as to make himself indispensable.

On the one hand the Chancellor had renounced the means granted him by the anti-Socialist Law for the fight against revolution. On

[1] Should read: 'expulsion clause'.   [2] Count von Helldorf-Bedra.

[3] On 25 January 1890, at the third reading, the anti-Socialist Law was defeated by 167 votes to 98, because the Conservatives voted against the law in its restricted form.

10-2

the other hand he declared himself, now as before, in favour of an unyielding attitude towards the working-class movement. The Kaiser's plan of summoning a conference to Berlin to discuss the protection of labour was not to Bismarck's taste and he did all in his power to prevent the conference. But the Kaiser succeeded in holding it, impelled partly by the desire to show off his gifts as an orator. Before the conference met, the Kaiser wanted to publish two short manifestos showing sympathy with the workers.[1] Prince Bismarck was against this, but he had a couple of drafts drawn up. The Kaiser made one, but I do not remember who made the other.[2] But I do know for certain that Prince Bismarck went through both drafts and actually corrected them along lines of far-reaching social reform. For example he had added to the list of the conference's tasks the laying down of fixed hours of work, that is the normal working day; I can still see the correction in his bold handwriting. The Prince took the two manifestos to the Kaiser, laid them before him and said he advised him to burn both of them.[3] Of course the Kaiser published them, and these far-reaching plans for the future may well have disconcerted many of the 'bourgeois' members of the conference. The Chancellor's emendations could have only one purpose—to arouse suspicion of the Kaiser's social policy. Many years later when I inquired about these drafts that Bismarck corrected, so as to have another look at them, they were nowhere to be found. They may have been handed over to the Ministry of the Interior but it is probable that together with many other documents, they disappeared during the last days of the Bismarckian regime.[4]

It is only now, as I attempt for the first time after eighteen years to gather together my recollections of that period, that I realize

[1] An international conference for the protection of labour, in which all the European states except Russia and the Balkan states took part, was held in Berlin, 15–29 March. The Imperial manifestos to which Holstein refers were published on 4 February in the *Reichs- und Staatsanzeiger*, but without having been countersigned by the Chancellor.

[2] The Kaiser made known his proposals for the improvement of the workers' lot at the session of the Imperial Council on 24 January. Under State Secretary Dr Bosse drew up a manifesto based on the Kaiser's proposals which was revised by Bötticher. The other draft was made by Herbert von Bismarck. (Georg Eppstein, *Fürst Bismarcks Entlassung* (Berlin, 1920), pp. 44–52, 146–55, 168–72.)

[3] Cf. Bismarck, *Die gesammelten Werke*, vol. xv, p. 500.

[4] Additional details on Bismarck's dispute with Wilhelm II, from Holstein's essay written in 1898, may be found in the Appendix to this chapter (p. 157).

what an enormous amount I have forgotten. But I can vouch for the accuracy of my account of those incidents which impressed themselves on my mind because of their particular interest. For example I can still remember how, the day before Herbert resigned his post, *Geheimer Hofrat* Mechler, the Head of the Central Bureau, called on me looking pale and overwrought and told me he had just had a terrible scene with Herbert. During the last few days Herbert had had great piles of secret documents brought to his villa. Mechler, whose responsibility they were, had begun to feel worried and had asked Caprivi for instructions; Caprivi had ordered that before any similar requests were granted in future his permission must be obtained. When Herbert again asked for documents to be sent to the villa, Mechler explained he could not surrender them without the Chancellor's permission. Herbert then sent for him and fairly dressed him down, adding in conclusion: 'I'll make you pay for this when I get back.'

The entire Bismarck family shared the conviction that they would soon return to power, and communicated it to their adherents. Mittnacht,[1] who visited Prince Bismarck in Friedrichsruh soon after his dismissal, said when passing through Berlin on his return journey that the Prince's return was a question not of years but months.

I urged Herbert to remain at his post. The Court and the Government would handle him with kid gloves, and there might be all kinds of possibilities for him. But he went, and I heard it was mainly on the insistence of his mother, who was furiously angry.

Berchem, who told me during the crisis: 'I'm not neutral, I am entirely pro-Kaiser and anti-Chancellor' also said: 'The Bismarck family would like to return, not as Ministers, but rather as the Bourbons did in 1814.' 'Oh', I said, 'You mean *dans les fourgons de l'ennemi*?' 'Yes, more or less.' Berchem felt that the appointment of Marschall, a native of Baden, as State Secretary was a personal insult. And yet he was willing to remain in the Imperial service in case he were promised the first Embassy to fall vacant. But since the Kaiser only promised him 'a good post' in general, he took his departure and, as I was definitely assured, declared in Munich that as a Bavarian and as a Catholic he could not remain under such a regime.

[1] Hermann, Baron von Mittnacht. Minister-President of Württemberg, 1876–90.

I too had been opposed to Berchem's appointment as State Secretary. On economic questions he was unusually able, but politically he was less gifted and was also at times inclined to flaunt his Catholic tendencies so as to obscure the fact of his Jewish blood. One day he told me in all seriousness that he thought all our office staff, in case of illness, should be sent to the Catholic hospital because the nursing was best there. I pointed out that this would be rather a reflection on all the non-Catholic institutions.

With the coming of a new Chancellor I had myself stated that I would remain in the service but would not accept promotion. When Caprivi asked me who I thought would make a suitable State Secretary, I gave as first choice Alvensleben[1] and as second choice Marschall. Alvensleben declined on the grounds that he lacked the gift of parliamentary oratory, but there were doubtless other reasons that prevented him from boarding Caprivi's frail bark. Marschall unhesitatingly accepted Caprivi's offer, and this behaviour gave Caprivi a most favourable impression of Marschall's character. As soon as Bismarck heard that Marschall had accepted he sent for him and tried to dissuade him. Marschall told me immediately after their interview that Prince Bismarck had said: 'My son and I between us were hardly able to cope with the work of the Foreign Ministry, so how will you, with your lack of experience, bear this burden alone? Your future lies with the Ministry of Justice. The philosopher up at the top' (he meant Schelling[2]) 'can't hold out much longer. And then, in my judgement, you are the right man for the post.' The gist of Marschall's reply was that as a civil servant aged forty-eight he could not declare at the outset, when offered a post by the Kaiser, that his strength was not equal to it. He must at any rate make the attempt.

The idea of becoming Bismarck's successor and at the same time his enemy was a common source of alarm at this period. The Bismarcks did their best to increase this alarm still further and prepared for battle. There is no other explanation of Bismarck's removal of two hundred and thirty-one thousand (231,000) marks

[1] Friedrich Johann, Count von Alvensleben. Minister at the Hague, 1882–4, in Washington, 1884–6, in Brussels, 1886–1901; Ambassador in St Petersburg, 1901–5.

[2] Ludwig Hermann von Schelling. State Secretary of the Treasury, 1879–89; Prussian Minister of Justice, 1889–94.

from the *Welfenfond*. Humbert[1] paid out the money and Rottenburg took charge of it. This occurred during the last few days,
between the 17 and 20 March. Humbert told me this. The impro-
priety of this behaviour was that the Kaiser never learned where
the money went. The few people who knew of this kept quiet. One
day, at the time when the Bismarcks were attacking me through
articles in the Press, the Kaiser sent Kessel, his aide, to ask me
whether it was true that Prince Bismarck had abstracted money
from the *Welfenfond*. I replied in general terms to the effect that
even when I was acting State Secretary I had always refused to
take cognizance of the expenditure from the *Welfenfond*. When
the Kaiser made this inquiry both Humbert and Rottenburg were
still alive, so the matter could easily have been investigated.

The very fact that Bismarck rendered no account makes it
difficult not to assume that this money was put to journalistic uses.

My general impression is that Prince Bismarck contributed in
various ways to making things difficult for his successor.

Just before the crisis Herbert told me one day: 'If my father
goes, the Triple Alliance will collapse.' I said: 'Why should it
collapse?' He replied: 'Well, because of Crispi. You'll see.' (Or
'We shall see'.)

I was reminded of this remark when in the summer of 1890
Crispi suddenly instructed the Italian Ambassadors in Berlin and
Vienna[2] to make the following statement: He had definite infor-
mation that on a certain date in June a treaty of devolution had
been concluded between France and the Bey of Tunis, whereby
Tunisia would lapse entirely to France on the death of the Bey.
It was, Crispi said, his duty to forestall such a serious threat to
Italian interests. He therefore inquired what the Cabinets in
Berlin and Vienna proposed to do to prevent the execution of this
treaty, which was an act of force. He needed an immediate and
clear-cut statement from Italy's two allies according to which he
could direct Italian policy.[3]

Crispi simply required a declaration that the annexation of
Tunisia would be considered a *casus belli* by Germany and Austria.
It would depend on this declaration whether or not Italian policy

[1] Georg Paul Andreas Humbert. Official in charge of the Personnel Department
in the Foreign Ministry.
[2] Constantino, Count Nigra. Ambassador in Vienna, 1885–1904.
[3] See *Grosse Politik*, vol. VIII, no. 1871, pp. 244–5.

would be geared to the Triple Alliance in future. The situation created by this demand was already ticklish enough on purely objective grounds, but it was made even more difficult by the personal characteristics of the Ministers responsible, in part Kálnoky's[1] vanity and prejudice against Italy, in part Caprivi's timidity, for which his political inexperience was adequate cause.

These memoirs of mine do not treat of one single theme, but are meant to portray, without any strict order, those impressions of my life which I still remember clearly, just as they come into my head. So I should like briefly to interpolate here the picture of Count Kálnoky which has remained in my memory. 'Proud and discontented.' This phrase of Goethe's exactly catches his outward bearing even in the days when he was a bald-headed Attaché in Berlin and Second Secretary in London. He had previously been an officer in a regiment stationed in Vicenza. That was during the Schwarzenberg period, of which I heard Bismarck say later that Austria, after a period of weakness during the years of revolution 1848 and 1849, had under Schwarzenberg's leadership rapidly soared to a position of power she had never possessed before. I assume that the officers of that Hussar regiment in subject territory were at least as conscious of Austria's power as was the foreign observer, and that a feeling of superiority and a tendency to vanity were thereby developed and fostered in Kálnoky; corresponding as they did to his temperament, they formed the basic feature of his character throughout the changing years.

This tendency to *hauteur* was not peculiar to Count Kálnoky, but permeated the whole of Austrian diplomacy. Prince Bismarck's experience of it in the Frankfurt days converted him from being a supporter of Austria to a systematic opponent. I can still remember the courteous but condescending manner of the Austrian diplomats of the pre-1866 period. During the London Conference of 1864 Major (later General) von Stiehle said to me: 'I doubt whether we'll be able to avoid war with Austria. The Austrians look down on us too much.'

After the Austro-Prussian War the Austrians respected the strength of their German neighbour and the genius of Bismarck.

---

[1] Gustav, Count Kálnoky von Köröspatak. Austro-Hungarian Minister in Copenhagen, 1874–9; Ambassador in St Petersburg, 1880–1; Foreign Minister, 1881–95.

But their instinctive condescension remained. It was later employed in dealings with the Balkan States and at times with Italy. About 1880, when Haymerle[1] was Foreign Minister, Prince Bismarck addressed a dispatch to the Vienna Embassy stating his conviction that Austria would have less trouble with her Balkan policy if in her dealings with the Balkan States she respected so far as possible the youthful susceptibilities of these newly created entities.[2] But Viennese diplomacy did exactly the opposite, first under Kálnoky and later under Goluchowski.[3] In addition Kálnoky committed the quite unforgivable blunder of allowing the two trump cards of Austrian Balkan policy, Milan[4] and Stambulov,[5] to be removed without lifting a finger to prevent it. Clumsiness and unreliability, those were the characteristics of Kálnoky's Balkan policy. No wonder that dislike and suspicion of the Dual Monarchy gradually became the sentiment uniting all races and parties in the Balkans.

Kálnoky was also uncivil and incalculable in his relations with Italy. His defects of character conflicted with his intelligence. For it was mainly out of regard for the interests and wishes of the Cabinet in Vienna that Bismarck, who had become suspicious of Italian policy since his experiences between 1866 and 1870, had consented to Italy's joining the alliance between Germany and Austria. I often heard him express the view, that in fact Austria alone had an interest in Italy's becoming a member. But even when Italy had become Austria's ally Kálnoky did nothing to spare Italian susceptibilities. His lack of consideration revealed itself most clearly over King Umberto's visit to Vienna.[6] It would have been proper to give the Italians some hint beforehand that it would not be possible for the Emperor Franz Joseph to pay a return visit to Rome. Since no warning was given, the Italians had a right to count on a return visit of equal import, that is a visit

---

[1] Heinrich, Baron von Haymerle. Austro-Hungarian Ambassador in Rome, 1877–9; plenipotentiary at the Congress of Berlin, 1878; Foreign Minister, 1879–81.

[2] Bismarck to Reuss, 17 May 1881 (*Grosse Politik*, vol. III, no. 530, pp. 172–3).

[3] Agenor, Count Goluchowski. Austro-Hungarian Minister in Bucharest, 1887–94; Foreign Minister, 1895–1906.

[4] Milan Obrenović I. Prince, later King of Serbia, 1868–89.

[5] Stefan Stambulov. Bulgarian Prime Minister and Minister of the Interior, 1887–94.

[6] 27–31 October 1881.

to their own capital. When this did not come about the whole of Italy felt humiliated, and King Umberto was placed in a false position *vis-à-vis* his people. Count Kálnoky had thus brought grist to the mill of the irredentists. Admittedly the Italian royal visit to Vienna had been suggested by the Italian Minister, Count Robilant. But when the suggestion of a visit was accepted unconditionally by the Austrians, the Cabinet in Rome was entitled to assume that the Emperor Franz Joseph would pay a return visit to Rome. Here Kálnoky acted not only in bad faith but also against Austria's interests. But the urge to humiliate the Italians and to make them feel his contempt for them proved stronger than his intelligence—which in any case was not outstanding.

And so it can be well imagined how, in the summer of 1890, Count Kálnoky reacted to Crispi's notion of making Italy's Tunisian interests into a *casus belli* against France. Kálnoky informed Berlin: 'Austria-Hungary is standing guard over the Balkans' (I can remember the phrase) 'and so is not in a position to come to the help of Tunisia.'[1]

Caprivi took the view that it would mean political bankruptcy for him if, a few months after taking office, his first act of diplomacy were to plunge the German nation into war over Tunisia. Caprivi cannot be blamed for not having learned to think like a diplomat. He thought it was only a step from complete inactivity to total mobilization. All the intermediate stages of diplomacy between these two extremes seemed to him insignificant. His composure entirely deserted him during this first diplomatic 'case' that came his way as Chancellor. Normally so correct, one day he came bare-headed across the courtyard from the Chancellor's palace to see me in my office. I had difficulty in persuading Caprivi to use evasive tactics instead of replying to the Italian proposal with a simple refusal. For then there would have been a definite danger that Crispi might shatter the Triple Alliance without a moment's hesitation 'for the alleged non-fulfilment of those pledges which for Italy constituted the value of the treaty'. But the Triple

[1] On 4 August 1890, the Austro-Hungarian Ambassador delivered to the Foreign Ministry a copy of the letter sent him by Count Kálnoky on 29 July, which contained the above communication, Count Kálnoky took the opportunity of reminding Berlin of the 1887 negotiations for prolonging the Triple Alliance, during which he had adopted the same attitude. (From the Foreign Ministry Files. See also *Grosse Politik*, vol. IV, no. 845, pp. 231–7.)

Alliance had become a household word amongst the public. Its dissolution so soon after Bismarck's departure would have been a serious fiasco with incalculable results. The suspicion that Crispi was pursuing some ulterior motive forced itself upon me the more because I doubted the existence of the alleged treaty of devolution. It had been established through our Consulate in Tunis that on the day in June when the agreement was supposedly concluded in Tunis, the French *Résident Général* was not even there, but had gone on leave to France weeks before.

Since Caprivi was not to be moved from his intention of giving a straight refusal, the affair would probably have turned out badly for the Triple Alliance without Hatzfeldt's co-operation. I turned to him in my need, explained the position to him both in official and private communications,[1] and suggested that he should prevail on Lord Salisbury to smooth down Crispi. This was done. Salisbury wrote Crispi a private letter[2] in which he recognized that Italy had important interests to protect in Tunisia, but added at the same time that these interests did not seem to him to be endangered at the moment. Those were roughly the contents of the letter. Its effect was miraculous. The day after he received it Crispi merely remarked to our Ambassador, Solms: '*L'affaire de Tunis est réglée*'—or some such laconic phrase. Neither through Solms nor Launay did he ever proffer any further explanation, and this silence strengthens my suspicion that the story of the treaty of devolution was a fraud. Crispi's respect for England, whose ships had made possible the landing of the Thousand at Marsala, was as firmly rooted as his dislike of France. Even so I rather doubt whether Crispi would have made so complete and immediate a *volte-face* because of such a slender letter as Salisbury's, had he not been afraid that a continuation of the discussion might prompt a request from Salisbury for more precise information about the treaty of devolution to which he, Crispi, would have no satisfactory answer. That is why I have always regarded that Tunisia incident of the summer 1890 as the last ripple of the Bismarck crisis. I was thinking more of Herbert than his father.[3]

In those days the foremost British Minister thought he was

---

[1] See *Grosse Politik*, vol. VIII, nos. 1888–90, pp. 263–5.
[2] See p. 106, n. 1.
[3] For the Tunis Question, see *Grosse Politik*, vol. VIII, chapter LIII b.

serving British interests by preventing the Triple Alliance from being endangered and helping Germany out of a difficult dilemma.

And a year later, in 1891, Salisbury showed that he was prepared to oppose directly France's Moroccan policy. At the time there was talk in the French Press of 'frontier adjustment', obviously aimed at the acquisition of the great Tuat oasis. At Germany's suggestion Lord Salisbury declared his willingness to make a diplomatic move in Paris, together with Italy and Spain, to dissuade the French Government from the extension of the eastern frontier of Algeria on which it seemed intent. The idea of German participation had been given up because we had pointed out that Germany's co-operation, in view of the peculiar relation between Germany and France, would inevitably make the projected diplomatic move in Paris particularly pointed. The Italian and Spanish Governments both expressed willingness to join with England in this diplomatic move to preserve the Moroccan frontier. But at the last moment Spain backed out. The Spanish Foreign Minister[1] had presumably been influenced by France, for he suddenly came out with the declaration, flatly contradicting his previous statements, that Spain would not take part in any undertaking directed against France, for Spain would always be the first to bear the brunt of any French attack. This Spanish defection wrecked the Tuat move. But it deserves mention, if only as a fragment of diplomatic history, because it stands as a historic monument of traditional British policy before the Krüger telegram, the German naval agitation and the speeches by the Kaiser and Prince Bülow brought about that enormous swing which has since made England the centre of the anti-German camp.[2]

[1] Carlos O'Donnelly Abreu, Duke of Tetuan. Spanish Foreign Minister in the Canovas Cabinet, 1890–2.
[2] On this paragraph cf. *Grosse Politik*, vol. VIII, nos. 1914–43, 1946–7, pp. 293–317, 319–20.

APPENDIX TO CHAPTER VIII[1]

When Prince Bismarck finally brought himself to leave Friedrichsruh on 22 or 23 January 1890 and came to Berlin, Herbert
Bismarck called on me the day he arrived. I happened to be ill in
bed. Herbert Bismarck told me of the disagreements between his
father and the Kaiser and said it was high time his father stepped
in and settled the matter. Their plan to drive the Kaiser into
a corner was extremely distasteful to me and gave me a sleepless
night. At six in the morning I turned on the light, sat up in bed
and wrote a letter to Herbert Bismarck, a sure instinct warning
me to make a copy immediately.[2] In it I cautioned him against
acting too rashly and advised him to give way to the Kaiser on
isolated points. By the time I, in my exhausted condition, had
finished writing and copying the letter, eleven o'clock had struck.
I then sent the letter to Herbert Bismarck, but he never said a word
to me about it. The letter did no good, for that very afternoon the
session of the Imperial Council took place at which the sparks
really flew for the first time. I think, though I cannot be certain
from memory, that labour questions were being discussed; but the
actual agenda is unimportant, what matters is the way it was
treated. First the Kaiser developed his point of view in detail.
Briefly, and without stating his reasons, Bismarck declared it to
be unacceptable and put the matter to the vote. The Ministers,
with I think the exception of the War Minister,[3] voted as usual
with Bismarck. At this the Kaiser relinquished his position but
added: 'I am being forced to give way.'

This session of the Imperial Council clearly revealed the position or, rather, the battleground. From that day the conflict never
abated. Another part of Bismarck's plan of campaign was to
withhold from the Kaiser information that did not fit in with it.
Bismarck's rudeness remained unchanged. It may have been the
middle of February or the beginning of March when I went one
day to see von Kessel, then aide, now General. I told him how
worried I was lest the conflict should lead to a complete break and
indicated where in my opinion Bismarck's tactics towards the

[1] From the essay written in 1898.
[2] Letter to Herbert von Bismarck of 24 January 1890 (*Correspondence*).
[3] Verdy du Vernois.

Kaiser were mistaken. The prime mistake was Prince Bismarck's habit of staging the *public* discomfiture of his opponents, particularly the Kaiser, instead of trying to win them over in private. Apart from this it must have annoyed the Kaiser that he was never deferred to even on secondary matters. Kessel entirely agreed with me and said he would go at once to the Chancellor's palace for lunch—he was related to the Bismarcks—to see what could be done. After a couple of hours he came to my office and said: 'It's a waste of time. Father and son listen patiently, and then, with a frigid smile, turn down every suggestion that they should give way or behave less harshly.'

This is another example of Prince Bismarck's temperament triumphing over his intelligence.

CHAPTER IX

THE BACKGROUND OF ANGLO-GERMAN HOSTILITY. GERMANY'S BOSNIAN POLICY[1]

Schlieffen's article: *Der Krieg in der Gegenwart*; his falsifications. Economic competition not the deciding factor in Anglo-German hostility. Chamberlain's offer of an alliance. The real reasons for England's hostility: the Krüger telegram and what preceded it; the Baghdad railway; the Navy League. Justification of Germany's Bosnian policy. Schlieffen's misrepresentation of the *Daily Telegraph* incident.

Appendix. Anglo-German relations: the war against Denmark; the Franco-Prussian War; Crown Princess Victoria; Wilhelm II; significance of the Krüger telegram.

13 *January* 1909:

COUNT Schlieffen's[2] article *Der Krieg in der Gegenwart*[3] which has been much talked of since the New Year, is a tendentious piece of writing serving a clearly recognizable aim and constructed on three falsifications of historical fact.

His first falsification is his assertion: 'The powerful expansion of Germany's industry and trade earned her another implacable enemy (England). This hatred of a formerly despised rival can neither be tempered by assurances of sincere friendship and cordiality nor aggravated by provocative language. It is not the emotions but questions of debit and credit which determine the level of resentment.'

That is the point of view of the Navy League, aimed at presenting the Kaiser's words and deeds for the last thirteen years, particularly the feverish naval activity he instigated, as harmless and insignificant. It was natural for our commercial rivalry to

---

[1] A new series of essays begins here, not written, but dictated, by Holstein. They were corrected by Holstein, and the one printed in this chapter was signed by him. The chapter-heading is the editors'.

[2] Alfred, Count von Schlieffen. Chief of the Army General Staff, 1891–1905.

[3] *Deutsche Revue* (Stuttgart and Leipzig, 1909), vol. I, pp. 13–24. The article is unsigned.

arouse a certain amount of antagonism in English commercial circles. But America is a far more formidable rival of England than we are. And the English know perfectly well that America would utilize a war between England and Germany to crowd out both belligerents from world markets as far as she could. His clear perception of this state of affairs led Joseph Chamberlain,[1] the most important champion of British commercial interests, to propose an Anglo-German pact, a formal alliance sanctioned by Parliament, to the then State Secretary Count Bülow, who accompanied the Kaiser to England in 1899.[2] The fact that this noble conception of an alliance between the greatest land power and the greatest sea power was never realized was neither Chamberlain's nor England's fault. Here at any rate is the proof that England considered her position in the world to be threatened by dangers beside which German commercial competition faded into insignificance. Chamberlain, in 1899, expressed in a public speech in Leicester his view that England had the greatest interest in a close co-operation with Germany,[3] so that Count Schlieffen, who as Chief of the General Staff at the time had also to keep an eye on the political horizon, was bound to know of this incident and take it into account, if he had any intention of being objective.[4]

But quite apart from this important single instance there still remain facts enough to convince the impartial observer that England, that rich and placid nation, was goaded into her present defensive attitude towards Germany by continuous threats and insults on the part of the Germans. The Krüger telegram began it all. I have noted elsewhere[5] that it was an expression of the Kaiser's annoyance, the result of disagreements of a personal

[1] British Colonial Secretary in the Salisbury and Balfour Cabinets, 1895–1903.

[2] A chronological error of Holstein's. Chamberlain had made a proposal to this effect on 1 April 1898 (*Grosse Politik*, vol. XIV, i, no. 3784, pp. 202–4). For the interview between Chamberlain and Bülow on 24 November 1899, which treated the general question of Anglo-German co-operation, see *Grosse Politik*, vol. XV, no. 4398, pp. 413–20.

[3] On 30 November 1899, Chamberlain, among other things, said: 'There is something more which I think any far-seeing English statesman must have long desired, and that is that we should not remain permanently isolated on the continent of Europe; and I think that the moment that aspiration is formed it must have appeared evident to everybody that the natural alliance is between ourselves and the great German Empire.'

[4] Holstein has more to say on Chamberlain's proposal of an alliance (see p. 181).

[5] Holstein wrote a separate account of the Krüger telegram episode in 1907 (see p. 163, n. 1 and the Appendix to this chapter, p. 168).

nature which had arisen between the Kaiser and Lord Salisbury a few months previously during a visit to England. Count Hatzfeldt had informed me in strict confidence in a personal letter that Lord Salisbury had suggested he should draw up a plan for the partition of European Turkey. Count Hatzfeldt had declined on the grounds that it was incompatible with his official position, at the same time promising Salisbury, at his own wish, to make no official report on his proposal. But since it was of the utmost importance to prepare the Kaiser for the possibility of the Eastern question being raised, Hatzfeldt informed me of what had happened.[1] So I sent Kiderlen[2] a personal telegram[3] which reached him in Heligoland before he left for England with the Kaiser, whom he was accompanying as the representative of the Foreign Ministry. The Kaiser had in fact scarcely landed before Lord Salisbury broached the Eastern question. I heard no details of this discussion. But we did learn immediately afterwards that the Kaiser had 'turned him down flat'.[4] This quite unnecessary brusqueness bore fruit. Lord Salisbury, unused to such treatment, avoided a subsequent interview requested by the Kaiser by pleading pressure of business and going to London.[5] The Kaiser took offence at this and instructed the Foreign Ministry to request an explanation from Lord Salisbury. The latter gave a coolly courteous explanation in which he made reference to his official business.[6] It was immediately obvious that the Kaiser was not satisfied with this method of settling the matter. Seeking an outlet for his resentment he seized on the first available opportunity, which was the Jameson Raid[7] and the Boer victory at Krügersdorp.

[1] Letter of 31 July 1895 (*Grosse Politik*, vol. x, no. 2372, pp. 10–13).

[2] Alfred von Kiderlen-Wächter. Secretary of the Embassy in St Petersburg, 1881–5, in Paris, 1885–6, in Constantinople, 1886–8; in charge of Balkan and Near Eastern affairs in the Foreign Ministry, 1888–94; Prussian Minister in Hamburg, 1894–5; Minister in Copenhagen, 1895–9, in Bucharest, 1899–1910; State Secretary in the Foreign Ministry, 1910–12.

[3] Telegram of 3 August 1895 (*Grosse Politik*, vol. x, no. 2377, pp. 19–20).

[4] See Hatzfeldt to the Foreign Ministry, 7 August 1895 (*Grosse Politik*, vol. x, no. 2385, pp. 25–7).

[5] Salisbury to Hatzfeldt, 6 August 1895 (*Correspondence*).

[6] Salisbury to Hatzfeldt, 8 August 1895 (*Grosse Politik*, vol. x, no. 2386, p. 27).

[7] Dr Leander Starr Jameson. Administrator of Rhodesia for the British South Africa Company. On 29 December he organized a raid on Johannesburg by which he hoped to raise a revolt against Boer supremacy in the Transvaal. On 1 January 1896 his force was defeated by the Boers at Krügersdorp.

I am sure that in Prince Hohenlohe's unpublished papers and notes there must be a description, doubtless shot through with dry humour, of that strange council that determined the wording of the Krüger telegram.[1] I think it was on 2 January 1896 that the Kaiser descended on his Chancellor (this seems the right expression for it) with a body of gentlemen representing the land and sea forces but without the slightest knowledge of politics. I can still remember Admirals Hollmann[2] and Senden[3] and the aide Schele[4] (formerly Governor of East Africa). I seem to recall one or two more who were present. Marschall was summoned. He requested Kayser,[5] the official in charge of colonial affairs, to wait with me in an ante-room in the Chancellor's palace which used to be Herbert's living-room, in case he needed us. After a considerable time Marschall came in, and in that laconic way of his instructed Kayser to draw up a telegram to Krüger,[6] at the same time telling him what to put in it. When I quite naturally expressed my misgivings he said: 'Oh, don't you interfere; you've no idea of the suggestions being made in there. Everything else is even worse.' That is how the world-famous telegram came into being.[7] The Chancellor and the State Secretary later referred with embarrassed reserve to what went on at that ill-assorted meeting presided over by the Kaiser. They were probably remembering with some shame the proposals discussed there in front of them, the two responsible representatives of international law and Imperial policy.

[1] All that is published is a brief entry from Hohenlohe's diary of 3 January 1896: 'At ten o'clock [yesterday] the Kaiser arrived with Hollmann, Knorr and Senden. Marschall was there already. The South African question was discussed. Marschall proposed sending a telegram to Krüger, which was accepted. Then a discussion of the possible support of the Boers. Colonel Schele was sent for and commissioned to go to South Africa and inquire what kind of help could be given to the Boers. Holstein, Kayser and Marschall are against this. We shall deal with the affair in a dilatory way.' *Denkwürdigkeiten der Reichkanzlerzeit*, edited by K. A. von Müller (Stuttgart and Berlin, 1931), p. 151.

[2] Friedrich von Hollmann. State Secretary at the Admiralty, 1890–7.

[3] Gustav, Baron von Senden und Bibran. Head of the Imperial Naval Cabinet, 1889–1906.

[4] Friedrich Rabod, Baron von Schele. Governor of German East Africa, 1893–1906.

[5] Paul Kayser. *Vortragender Legationsrat* in the Foreign Ministry, 1886–90; Head of the Colonial Division of the Foreign Ministry, 1890–6.

[6] Paul Krüger. President of the South African Republic, 1883–1900.

[7] In his 1907 account Holstein writes: 'And so the telegram was drafted by little Kayser and then stiffened by the big Kaiser.' (See also *Grosse Politik*, vol. xi, no. 2610, pp. 31–2.) For the text of the telegram see p. 170, n. 1.

Consequently I heard only a few of the ideas put forward. For example, Colonel Schele, a handsome man whose talents were generally considered very mediocre, was to disguise himself as a lion-hunter, present himself to President Krüger, and offer his services as Chief of Staff. Also German colonial troops, only one or two companies so far as I remember, were to be diverted from East Africa via Lourenço-Marques to the Transvaal. The Chancellor's or perhaps the State Secretary's remark that this would call out the British navy was met by the reply that the question of British sea power did not arise: they were only concerned with a colonial war and a colonial question. I have no doubt at all that this remark was made, for Hohenlohe had a good memory and his information could be relied on. Since he preferred not to remember who made this assertion I take it that it was the Kaiser himself. The remark is typical of that lack of seriousness and breadth of view, not to say sound common sense, which brought about the fateful switching of our foreign policy in the direction of hostility to England. The driving force was not reflection but the Kaiser's whim.[1] This was his first prank [*Streich*].[2] The second, so far as I remember, was the Baghdad railway project.

The idea of a railway connecting Constantinople with the Persian Gulf had already been mooted several years previously, probably by speculators. Caprivi spoke to me about it one day and linked this plan with the idea of German colonization and the extension of influence in Mesopotamia. Completely astonished at hearing the prudent Caprivi make such a suggestion, I vigorously opposed it and pointed out that there could scarcely be a more certain means of ranging against us Russia, England and the Mediterranean Powers in general, united by their common jealousy. Then I heard no more of the matter until the Kaiser's journey to the Middle East in 1898. On returning from leave that year I heard that the Baghdad railway project had been suggested by Marschall, accepted with enthusiasm by the Kaiser and forthwith

[1] Holstein's 1907 account of the origin of the Krüger telegram tallies in essentials with the version given above. He comes to the conclusion: 'This picture of events, the accuracy of which I do not doubt, gives the whole affair a childish appearance and shows it was not too badly intended. But the effect was bad, because of results in Germany, and in England.' Holstein's 1907 account of Anglo-German relations is continued in the Appendix to this chapter (p. 168).

[2] Holstein is quoting from the German humorist Wilhelm Busch: '*Dieses war der erste Streich, doch der zweite folgt sogleich.*'

sanctioned by the Chancellor. It had thus become a *fait accompli*, and has since contributed substantially to an Anglo-Russian rapprochement, in that both Powers imagined this plan concealed other far-reaching schemes which the Kaiser probably never entertained. *Pas si méchant*. He was only interested in the immediate effect. He wanted the world to ask itself in amazement: What will he do next? This, as I have said, was the second important political act by which England was alienated. I do not intend to give here a list of other acts that produced the same effect, but I should like to remind the reader briefly of that noisily proclaimed slogan: 'We shall wield the trident', which was bound to produce suspicion if not actual alarm in England, whose primary condition of existence is her status as a naval power. In addition to all this were the actions, speeches, proclamations and programmes of the Navy League which stated unequivocally that we must be strong enough to face England; and the official declarations of the Admiralty, for example the commentary to the naval statute of 1900,[1] were also pitched in the same key.

In the face of all these facts, all drawn from the most recent past, i.e. the last thirteen years, it is hardly possible to believe that Count Schlieffen is sincere when he tries to make his readers accept the view that England is and will remain our deadly foe *so long as the commercial rivalry continues.*

Schlieffen's second distortion of historical fact is his statement that the sudden emergence of the Bosnian question[2] had adversely affected Germany's position *vis-à-vis* the encircling Powers. This false assertion can quickly be disposed of. The Powers whose joint aim was to humble Austria because of her independent action in Bosnia and perhaps because of her alliance with Germany also, are those same encircling Powers whose primary aim had been to weaken Germany. In this Balkan question Austria, while pursuing her own interests, was fighting *our* battle. The joint efforts of Germany and Austria had aimed from the outset at proving by actions that the encircling Powers were not compact enough, nor their co-operation effective enough, to be able to risk conflict with Germany and Austria. This was the view put forward by Bülow

[1] Of 14 June. For a summary of the commentary see *The Naval Annual*, 1900 (Portsmouth), pp. 429 *et seq.*

[2] On 5 October 1908, Bosnia and Herzegovina were annexed to the Austro-Hungarian Empire.

and myself in September [*sic*] when he was in Norderney and I was in the Harz Mountains. Complete agreement was apparent in our correspondence.[1] The particular advantages of this conflict precisely over the Balkan question are twofold: for one, Austria fights in her own cause with greater energy and is a far more reliable ally than she would probably be if we were simply to call on Austria's loyalty as an ally in a *German* conflict; and then the interests of the encircling Powers in the Balkan question are widely divergent.

During this Balkan conflict England formally resumed, after a lapse of twenty years, her traditional role as protector of Turkey. Valentine Chirol,[2] the well-known English publicist, told me when he passed through Berlin at the end of October that this had been done out of consideration for England's Mohammedan subjects. I reminded him that I had told him fourteen years ago that the anti-Turkish swing in English policy would have evil results in India. (The fifty-four million Indian Mohammedans, almost exclusively Sunnites, recognize in the Sultan their spiritual head.) Chirol assured me that England's present swing back to Turkey was meant in earnest and would be lasting. That was why England was also defending Turkey's interests against Austria. Austria, like proud Russia thirty years ago, must be prevailed on to submit the Bosnian question to the decision of a congress of the Powers, and it was Germany's duty to see that her ally complied. When I treated this idea as a joke Chirol became very excited and shouted: 'Then Germany lays herself open to the suspicion that she's not so peace-loving as she would like to appear.' I replied, '*tant pis*', and we parted good friends, but in complete disagreement.[3] The Chancellor and I were agreed from the beginning that there was no danger of war and that England, like Isvolsky,[4] was only bluffing. The divergence of Russian, French and British interests was now brought out. Tsar Nicholas said some six weeks ago to someone on the staff of the German Embassy in St Petersburg

[1] See the Holstein-Bülow letters on this subject of October 1908 (*Correspondence*).

[2] Attaché in the Foreign Office, 1872–6; *The Times* correspondent in Berlin, 1892–6; acting Foreign Editor of *The Times*, 1896–9; Foreign Editor, 1899–1912.

[3] See Holstein's memorandum of 18 October 1908 on his conversation with Chirol (*Correspondence*).

[4] Alexander von Isvolsky. Russian Minister in Belgrade, 1896, in Munich, 1897–9, in Tokyo, 1900–2, in Copenhagen, 1903–6; Foreign Minister, 1906–10.

that Russia had now only *one* interest in the Balkan question: the Straits. Russia was striving to gain the front-door key, meaning that the Straits must be open for Russian warships but closed to the warships of other Powers.[1] This demand, which if granted would deliver Constantinople into the hands of Russia, is naturally being resisted to the uttermost by the Turks, behind whom there now stands England with her navy to protect the Young Turks.[2] England feels that Anglo-Russian friendship, made possible only by England's indifference to all Turkish interests hitherto, cannot last if England resumes her former role as guardian of the Straits. That is why, in the first phase of the present Balkan crisis, England tried to incite Russia against Austria, but Russia refused outright because the dangers of a major war both at home and abroad would not be outweighed by any advantage so long as England kept a watch over this 'front-door key'. Nor had France any inclination for a major war which, in addition to its inherent danger, would also imperil the twenty thousand million francs which France lent Russia and Turkey. Thus England had no other course than to adopt a more pacific attitude also and to urge the Turks to reach direct agreement with Austria. The Bosnian question is not yet settled but it has passed out of the acute stage. But one may wonder whether Count Schlieffen's unpatriotic and tendentious article, had it appeared four weeks earlier, might have complicated the Balkan crisis by discouraging Austria and perhaps certain elements in Germany also, and by encouraging our common enemies. But by the time the article was published the inaccuracy of Count Schlieffen's propositions had already been proved by events, and even the rumour that the Kaiser was said to have adopted the same view as the former Chief of General Staff could make no difference to the way things developed, i.e. the conciliatory attitude shown by Turkey on England's advice.

But the third and most flagrant distortion of history occurs in the concluding paragraph of the article. It points to the danger of internal dissension in the face of danger from without and culminates in the sentence: 'We have seen only recently how the same goal (sowing discord) may be attained in Germany by a short

[1] See *Grosse Politik*, vol. xxvi, i, nos. 9180–83, 9185, pp. 369–78, 380–3.

[2] The name of the revolutionary group which, on 24 July 1908, had persuaded Sultan Abdul Hamid II to restore the Turkish Constitution of 1876, and which had controlled the state since then.

newspaper article, by out-of-date accusations cunningly strung together.' This refers to the *Daily Telegraph* article and its sequel.[1] We have here a crude distortion which cannot possibly have been made in good faith. The Kaiser had blurted out to foreigners the most vital state secrets of the German Empire. Colonel Stuart-Wortley,[2] the recipient of the Kaiser's more important confidences, is Military Attaché in Paris and thus a political figure. The German nation was certainly not divided in its condemnation of the Kaiser's indiscretion, it was absolutely united. The Chancellor was requested by the Federal Council and the Reichstag to bring this to the Kaiser's notice, and the Kaiser solemnly promised to reform. That is what really happened. Count Schlieffen had to distort it in order to reach his conclusion: 'that in any future struggle, whether it is waged with weapons or by any other means, a "united nation of brothers" was necessary as was a vast and powerful army, *led by a firm hand* (i.e. the Kaiser's) *and inspired by absolute trust.'*

Comment is unnecessary.

Count Schlieffen has maintained all his life the reputation of an honourable man standing aloof from all intrigue. The whole construction of this difficult piece of tendentious writing, and its brilliant style, show he is not without talent. The fact that Count Schlieffen allowed himself to write this unpatriotic article—unpatriotic because of its undoubtedly harmful effects—is explained by his pliant character. The Count is a close friend of General von Plessen,[3] Chief of Imperial Headquarters. The pamphlet may have been inspired by him. And he was probably the 'General on intimate terms with the Kaiser' who gave the latter the article.

But, as I have said, this essay came too late to do any immediate harm abroad. [...]

---

[1] See below, Chapter x.

[2] Edward James Montagu Stuart-Wortley. British Colonel; Staff officer in the British War Office, 1904–8; Commander of the 10th Infantry Brigade, 1908–12. His description as Military Attaché in Paris is an error on the part of Holstein.

[3] Hans Georg Hermann von Plessen. Commander of Imperial Headquarters, 1892–1918.

APPENDIX TO CHAPTER IX[1]

In Germany the hostility towards England which had already been smouldering for some years was fanned into a bright flame. Actually England could not be surprised at this antagonism because for decades she had indulged in unfriendly and inconsiderate actions against Germany, and previously against Prussia.

During the Danish War her sympathies were with the Danes and she pursued a policy of what we call 'bluff' nowadays. Both before and during the war she uttered threats but never backed them up by deeds. Lord Palmerston, her foremost statesman, regarded France as England's most dangerous enemy on the Continent and avoided an active policy which might have increased French power and territory. The Emperor Napoleon's reply to England's suggestion that he should indulge in a little sabre-rattling on Denmark's behalf had been that he was certainly prepared to act if England would stand by him 'even if the worst happened'. That was far from Palmerston's intention, so after the breakdown of the London Conference at the end of June 1864 he made a speech in the Commons in which, though defending Denmark's position in theory, he did not lead the Danes to hope for any active intervention on the part of England. The Prince of Wales, who had listened to the speech from the Peer's Gallery, got up when it was over and stalked out uttering the one word 'Bosh'. At a dinner given about this time by the officers of a Guards regiment he proposed the toast: 'To the confusion of Germany.' Of course it was all words, not deeds. But the words became known and lessened the sympathy we had felt for England since the days of the wars of liberation.

On the outbreak of the Franco-Prussian War England was for a short time oppressed by the fear that France would annex Belgium. But after the first French defeats there was a complete change of front and the long continuation of the war was only made possible for the French by the loan of English money (the Morgan Loan) and the delivery of English war materials, even including batteries already provided with horses. These were hostile acts and were regarded as such in Germany at the time.

[1] The Appendix continues Holstein's considerations on Anglo-German relations quoted above (p. 163, n. 1).

The annoyance which resulted might have gradually subsided but for the existence in Germany of an element which, to borrow an expression from modern medicine, worked constantly as an irritant. This irritant was the Crown Princess Victoria. She had been the idol of her father, who used to describe the political essays of the not yet seventeen-year-old Princess as political masterpieces. She had come to Berlin firmly bent on reforming Prussia to her own taste, that is on English lines. Her plans for reform were not always liberal in character; for example, she was convinced that birth must take precedence over professional rank. She thought it unheard-of that an old Field-Marshal ranked higher than some young upstart Prince. She had also a marked respect for wealth and thought everything in Germany poverty-stricken. The story was current that she had said there were countless families in England who each possessed more silver plate than the notables of a whole town in Germany. Prussia's relative poverty prompted the Princess to draw endless comparisons, all of which were damaging to Prussian self-esteem. The disagreeable aspects of her character were so obvious that even her marked inclination to extreme political liberalism was unable to win her the affection, still less the trust, of the broad masses of the people. She was disliked most because she remained an Englishwoman, always put English interests first, and regarded it as the main task of Prussian and German policy to act as cat's-paw to England. On every political question that arose she invariably sided with the English. Perhaps this exaggerated behaviour sprang from the knowledge that apart from a few drops of Stuart blood there was absolutely nothing English about her. Von Friedberg, the Minister, who knew her very well, used to sum her up in the words: 'Talent, but no common sense.' And speaking of the Kaiser [Wilhelm II], General von Sommerfeld,[1] who had been able to observe both the Crown Princess and her son, said: 'Just like his mother, just like his mother!'

Certainly the Krüger telegram reveals a lack of practical good sense in the Kaiser. He had intended, as was known to his close political intimates, to give the English a fright, especially Lord Salisbury by whom he thought he had been ill-treated. But when the British government, without saying a word, quietly held a

[1] Aide-de-camp of Crown Prince Friedrich Wilhelm.

'flying squadron' in readiness while the British Press and British people showed clamourous indignation; when the Kaiser's dragoon regiment took the portrait he had presented to them and turned its face to the wall; when satirical songs were sung every evening in the music-halls and greeted with loud applause, then the Kaiser saw the matter in a different light and occasionally let fall remarks about 'that cursed Krüger telegram'.[1]

Since neither Germany nor England wished to pick a quarrel with each other, both Governments turned their attention to calming public opinion. But I can still remember two remarks from that period which prove what importance was attached to the Krüger telegram abroad, though it was in fact only a naïve expression of bad temper. I have probably mentioned both remarks elsewhere in these memoirs.

In February or March [1896] information reached us via Copenhagen that the French Ambassador had told Lord Salisbury: 'France has only one enemy—Germany. You can frame your policy accordingly.' Kiderlen had obtained the information at the Danish Court, which was always accurately informed on events in London. That marked the first switch towards the present Anglo-French entente. It originated with France.

At about the same period I was told by *The Times* correspondent, Mr Valentine Chirol, a former diplomat and outstandingly shrewd politician: 'After our recent experiences of the mood both of the Kaiser and people in Germany the British government will be inclined to go much further than it hitherto intended in the way of concessions or even considerable sacrifices, in order to create better relations with France.'

This remark was a direct prediction of the Anglo-French entente. *The Times* and Chirol later played their part in bringing it about.

---

[1] The text of the telegram was: 'I express my sincere congratulations that, supported by your people, without appealing for the help of friendly powers, you have succeeded by your own energetic action against armed bands which invaded your country as disturbers of the peace, and have thus been enabled to restore peace and safeguard the independence of the country against attacks from the outside. WILHELM I.R.'

CHAPTER X

WILHELM II AND FOREIGN POLICY[1]

The *Daily Telegraph* affair. Holstein's guess about its origin. Criticism of Wilhelm II. Opposition of the Foreign Ministry, particularly Holstein, to the Kaiser's ideas. Chamberlain's proposal of an alliance in 1899. The negotiations with England, 1898–1902. Bülow's suspicion of England. The Kaiser's policy of intimidation.

1 *February* 1909:

THE November crisis resulting from the publication of the *Daily Telegraph* article, together with its subsequent manifestations, still continues to dominate the political scene in Berlin.[2] The foreign press too, particularly the sharply anti-German great Paris dailies, still keep reverting to the affair. In leading articles, and in their Berlin correspondences, dailies like the *Figaro* put forward the view that Bülow read the manuscript sent him by the Kaiser, realized perfectly well the effect it would have, and decided to 'let the Kaiser ride for a fall'. This idea is being circulated in Berlin by all those who would like to see a change in the Chancellorship.

I cannot say I have any firm conviction in the matter, but after a thorough investigation of all the circumstances known to me, I think the following is probably what happened: On the manuscript sent to the Chancellor by the Kaiser there were beyond question marginal notes which showed that the Kaiser expected the publication of his views as contained in the manuscript to have

---

[1] Holstein here begins a new essay. The chapter-heading is the editors'.

[2] By a letter of 23 September 1908, Colonel Stuart-Wortley submitted to Kaiser Wilhelm II the text of an article which he proposed to publish in the *Daily Telegraph*. It consisted of ideas expressed by the Kaiser during sojourns in Great Britain in 1907 and 1908. The article appeared on 28 October 1908, attracted considerable attention, and gave rise to a debate in the Reichstag on 10 and 11 November, in which the Kaiser's 'indiscretions' came under attack from all parties. (See *Grosse Politik*, vol. XXIV, ch. CLXXVIII.) For the text of the article and the alterations suggested by the Foreign Ministry, see Appendix III.

a beneficial effect;[1] thus Bülow was certain to put the Kaiser in the worst possible humour if he wrote and said that he thought publication, far from doing good, would be risky. The fact that he tried to evade this unpleasant necessity if he possibly could was in keeping not only with his character but also, quite objectively, with the requirements of his extremely difficult position. And so he did not read the document, rightly supposing that he would hardly be in a position to consider the contents unobjectionable. But wishing to exercise some sort of control he sent it to the Foreign Ministry with the broad general directive to check whether it tallied with the files and whether alterations, particularly *omissions*, seemed indicated. But the Foreign Ministry also had a pretty good idea of the Kaiser's views on the conduct of official business. So they handled the affair like a hot potato. When the manuscript arrived, Schoen,[2] who had been recalled from leave, was in Berlin for a short time. Stemrich[3] told me later that Schoen 'saw the document lying about' but did not read it. Stemrich, the acting State Secretary, read it with misgivings but was reassured by the responsible official, Klehmet,[4] who pointed out that according to the Chancellor's directive the Ministry had simply to make sure that the article did not contradict the files. One can accept this as sufficient excuse for Stemrich, a newcomer to politics. I do not question Stemrich's good faith, but am thoroughly suspicious of Klehmet. There was a certain justification for Stemrich in what he said to me: 'Klehmet, who has been in the Political Division for fourteen years, was bound to know political procedure, or so I thought.' But Klehmet, who is by no means a fool, naturally realized that the memorandum in front of him was pure dynamite. But he also noticed the Kaiser's marginal notes which showed he wanted it published. And so he interpreted the Chancellor's directive in

[1] Cf. *Grosse Politik*, vol. XXIV, no. 8249, pp. 167–8. The Kaiser's belief in the beneficial effect of the article is apparent from the cover-letter written by the Minister von Jenisch which was sent to Bülow with the draft of the article. The original draft is not in the Foreign Ministry files.

[2] Wilhelm von Schoen. Minister in Copenhagen, 1900–5; Ambassador in St Petersburg, 1905–7; frequently representative of the Foreign Ministry in the Kaiser's retinue; State Secretary in the Foreign Ministry, 1907–10. See Freiherr von Schoen, *Erlebtes. Beiträge zur politischen Geschichte der neuesten Zeit.* (Stuttgart and Berlin, 1921), pp. 94 *et seq.*

[3] Wilhelm Stemrich. Consul-General in Constantinople, 1905; Minister in Teheran, 1906–7; Under State Secretary in the Foreign Ministry, 1907–11.

[4] Reinhold Klehmet. *Vortragender Rat* in the Foreign Ministry, 1896–1908.

such a way as to lay decisive importance on checking the manuscript against the Ministry's files; in this way he considered he had dealt with the other question of possible cuts. To preserve some appearance of independence he allowed himself one or two trifling corrections. (If my memory of the files does not deceive me, he could have, or should have, made even greater corrections to bring the article into line with them, e.g. on the question of Russia's diplomatic intervention on behalf of the Boers—but this is not important.) Bülow told me later when the row came that it was precisely these little corrections of Klehmet's which had led him to assume that Klehmet, whom we had long known to be very sound on the files, had gone into the matter thoroughly, and so there could be no serious objections to the article. The Chancellor's story has a ring of truth because it seems to develop naturally from the circumstances and from Bülow's character. He said to himself: 'There's certainly a good deal in the manuscript I'd be obliged to object to if I read it, so I'd rather not. There can't be anything really bad, or Klehmet, who is so punctilious, would not have been content with a few trifling corrections.'

When Rücker-Jenisch,[1] as representative of the Foreign Ministry in the Kaiser's retinue, sent the Chancellor the fateful manuscript he had said something in an accompanying letter about the necessity of examining it carefully. At the same time he informed the Chancellor of the Kaiser's wish to keep the Foreign Ministry out of the affair. The Kaiser's dislike of the Foreign Ministry is almost pathological and recognized as such by the people concerned. Bülow treats it as sheer bad temper and I think in most cases does not act upon it for the simple reason that it is impossible without studying the files to decide the questions brought up for discussion by the Kaiser, which are usually most ticklish and intricate. The case I am now concerned with was just the type that necessitated an extensive examination of the files because of the variety of highly important diplomatic questions discussed by the Kaiser. So it really is impossible to try to maintain that the Kaiser seriously intended not to consult the Foreign Ministry. For if he gave the matter any thought and was not just talking at random he must

[1] Martin Rücker-Jenisch, from 27 January 1906 Baron von Jenisch. Minister, Consul-General and Diplomatic Agent in Cairo, 1903–6; Minister in Darmstadt, 1906–13; on several occasions Foreign Ministry representative in the Kaiser's retinue.

have realized that Bülow had not taken the Foreign Ministry archives with him to Norderney.

To sum up, what I think happened was that Bülow said to himself: 'To avoid a quarrel with the Kaiser there are some things I'm prepared to wink at. So it would be better not to read the document at all yet, but to get the Ministry to go through it. They won't let pass any really doubtful passages, and I shall then be able to point out to the Kaiser that the petty criticism—as he is bound to regard it—comes not only from me but mainly from the Foreign Ministry. This necessity to refer back to the Foreign Ministry even in defiance of the Kaiser's order can be readily justified in that an examination of the files was unavoidable.' So when the document came back from the Ministry with only a few insignificant criticisms Bülow thought he was covered; there could be nothing dangerous in the manuscript, and he had been determined from the start, if not to swallow camels, at least not to strain at gnats. This calculation would have fitted the facts if Holstein had still been sitting where Klehmet now sat. During my last fifteen years in the service, the most painful of my duties was to point out once or twice each year that some apparently fruitful proposal which the Kaiser had advocated with vigour was quite unrealizable, in fact impossible. On all these occasions the Kaiser found that I was the doubting Thomas, and so there gradually grew up a dislike culminating in the row[1] engineered by Tschirschky.[2] The dramatically worded phrase of the Kaiser's, 'If anyone opposes me, I crush him', means in plain words: 'I get rid of people in an official position if they contradict me.' This and the plan to create a navy equal to the British Navy are the two principles to which the Kaiser remained true throughout his reign. [...]

Kaiser Wilhelm II was determined from the start to be always proved right both at home and abroad. His attempts in this direction led to a series of fiascos in the realm of foreign policy.

[1] In a letter to his cousin Ida von Stülpnagel of 4 April 1906, Holstein said he had handed in his resignation 'because I can tell from the behaviour of the new State Secretary that the Kaiser wants to get rid of me'. (Rogge, *Friedrich von Holstein*, p. 246.)

[2] Heinrich Leonard von Tschirschky und Bögendorff. Secretary of the Legation in Athens, 1889; First Secretary in the Embassy in St Petersburg, 1894–1900; Minister in Luxembourg, 1900–2; Prussian Minister in Hamburg, 1902–6; several times Foreign Ministry representative in the Kaiser's retinue; State Secretary in the Foreign Ministry, 1906–7; Ambassador in Vienna, 1907–16.

But within Germany, particularly in Prussia, he generally enforced his wishes. A particularly effective method of attaining his ends was his habit of dismissing civilian and military personages who contradicted him and making his displeasure widely felt. It is well known that over the years he put on ice a number of our most capable generals because they refused to express agreement with his sometimes utterly hare-brained views. Waldersee was the worst kind of political intriguer, whose fixed idea was to become Chancellor rather than to be Chief of the General Staff of the German Armed Forces. But historical justice demands it to be stated that during the manœuvres held by the Kaiser in 1890 (I may be mistaken about the year, but certainly not about the facts)[1] he subjected the Kaiser's dispositions to a withering criticism in the presence of King Albert of Saxony, saying amongst other things: 'If this had been a real attack a whole division would have been wiped out.'[2] A few months later Waldersee was transferred from Berlin to Altona. He would have deserved a transfer in any case for his political intrigues against Caprivi, but he would hardly have been moved just for that. The list of military men the Kaiser put in their place for contradicting him is a long one. I should like to instance as a typical example of the mood and attitude produced in the generals by this behaviour the attested fact that the Chief of the General Staff, Count Schlieffen, a man of integrity but with no wish to lose his job, simply stood by and watched when during manœuvres the Kaiser, wishing to balance the forces, sent a regiment or a battery over to the enemy side during a mock battle to continue the fight from there.

The Foreign Ministry was the only civilian department exposed to the effects of the Kaiser's whims, because the Kaiser only took an occasional interest in other civilian matters, for example the construction of new waterways. But the Foreign Ministry, year in year out, had to resist the Kaiser's sudden inspirations, and I was chiefly responsible for this censorship. During my years in the service I never kept a diary because I had taken to heart an emphatic remark Bismarck had made in my presence intentionally a few months after my arrival in St Petersburg, though it was not aimed at me personally. 'A diplomat should not write memoirs

[1] In September 1890.
[2] Cf. Waldersee, *Denkwürdigkeiten*, vol. II, pp. 145–6.

because it is impossible to keep personal and official matters separate.' So I am now thrown back on memory, which retains only the tiniest fraction of life's rich experiences. Thus I can remember only a few of the Kaiser's notions. In my official capacity as Head of the Political Division, I had the credit, and earned the odium, for opposing them, and also discussed them personally with Philipp Eulenburg,[1] who probably inspired not a few of these ideas. Eulenburg was, incidentally, not the only harmful influence on the Kaiser. Naval officers and travellers in foreign parts, particularly Africa, with whom the Kaiser liked to hold detailed conversations, all in their various ways had a finger in foreign policy. To give a few examples:

A plan was mooted, I forget how long after Bismarck's departure, of occupying uninhabited Bear Island, lying roughly midway between Norway and Spitzbergen, and using it as a German fishing-station and naval base. The idea had been put forward by the Württemberg Prince von Urach, a friend of Eulenburg's, who supported it. The Foreign Ministry was in the unpleasant position of being obliged to explain that the advantages of this acquisition were insignificant compared to the trouble it would cause in our relations with Russia. For the only political significance possessed by Bear Island is that it commands all shipping to and from the White Sea.[2]

---

[1] Philipp, Prince zu Eulenburg-Hertefeld. Secretary of the Embassy in Paris, 1881; Secretary of the Legation in Munich, 1881–8; Minister in Oldenburg, 1888–90, in Stuttgart, 1890–1, in Munich, 1891–94; Ambassador in Vienna, 1894–1901. Frequently the Foreign Ministry representative in the Kaiser's retinue.

[2] On 2 August 1897 the following communication was sent to Chancellor von Hohenlohe: 'His Majesty the Kaiser commands me to inform your Highness in *strictest confidence* of the following: His Majesty intends to send a ship to Bear Island (south of Spitzbergen) to hoist the German flag there and take possession of it. His Majesty feels certain that the above-mentioned island is ownerless and that no nation lays a claim to it. His Majesty believes that this island, lying on the route from the White Sea to the Atlantic, could possibly become useful as a counter in negotiations with Russia. [...] B. v. Bülow.' On 1 January 1898, the German Fisheries League addressed a petition to Tirpitz asking him to secure the fishing grounds near Spitzbergen, Bear Island and Jan Mayen for the German fishing industry. Accordingly the Admiralty planned to dispatch S.M.S. *Olga* to these islands with the task of staking legal claims, 'which could, depending on circumstances, be represented either as a political act of the German Reich or as the action of a private company (i.e. the Fisheries League) with no political implications'. On 5 May 1898, Holstein drew up a memorandum on this question. He wrote: 'The Russian press is extremely nervous and is discussing every aspect of the question: what does Germany intend to do? Without exception the theme is dis-

The Navy, understandably enough, had constantly in view the acquisition of naval bases and was convinced that the policy of the German Empire should be adapted and subordinated to this special interest. I cannot illustrate this tendency better than by repeating a remark made by Admiral von Senden, who despite his notoriously mediocre intelligence always had the Kaiser's ear. 'It should be the task of a properly directed foreign policy', said the Admiral, 'to acquire an island in the Gulf of Mexico without straining our relations with America'—an impossible task at variance with the Monroe Doctrine and the ever-growing awareness in the United States that they are the leading Power in the whole of the American continent. Holleben,[1] whose expert opinion was sought on this question, declared that the possible consequences of Germany's gaining a footing near the American coast could not be foreseen. Here again it was the Foreign Ministry which opposed the intention of accepting Denmark's offer [of the sale] of St Thomas Island which, though only thirty-two square miles in extent, is of strategic and commercial importance.[2]

cussed in a tone of sharp antagonism towards Germany. In these circumstances it would be an act of political foolhardiness—or should one say frivolity?—to make gestures which look like the preliminaries to an annexation of Bear Island, without first coming to an agreement with Russia. [...] The question now arises by what channels such an agreement can be reached, whether through normal diplomatic machinery or by personal contact between the two Emperors. The outcome is extremely doubtful in either event, in view of the present high feeling in Russia and the short interval separating this act of territorial expansion from the annexation of Kiaochau. [...]' Holstein concluded with the recommendation that negotiations with Russia be opened by means of a personal letter from the Kaiser to the Tsar. According to a letter from Bülow to Tirpitz of 26 May, Wilhelm II had indicated the desirability of acquiring Bear Island as a naval base. The Kaiser preferred not to consult the Russian Government beforehand, but for the moment he was equally unwilling to proceed to an official annexation. He wished to dispatch a scientific expedition to examine the island with a view to its suitability as a naval base. This resulted in the sending of S.M.S. *Olga* to Bear Island on 22 June 1898. In the following year the Fisheries League sent a further expedition to set up a fishing station. This act provoked great indignation in Russia and in July 1899 a Russian cruiser was sent to the island, where its commander found traces of earlier Russian settlements, over which he hoisted the Russian trading flag. The scheme for establishing a German base on the island was thereupon abandoned. (From the Foreign Ministry files.)

[1] Theodor von Holleben. Minister-Resident in the Argentine and Uruguay, 1875–85; Minister in Tokyo, 1885–91, in Washington, 1891–3; Prussian Minister in Stuttgart, 1893–7; Ambassador in Washington, 1897–1903.

[2] On 24 January 1900 Tirpitz asked the Foreign Ministry what attitude to take towards a petition from the Pan-German League advocating the purchase by Germany of the Danish Virgin Islands. In view of the fact that the United States were already negotiating with Denmark about the purchase of these islands, the

Of the African adventurers, First Lieutenant Werther, a relative of General Hahnke, has left particularly unpleasant memories because of the trouble he gave us over a long period. He put forward the idea, which I think was supported by another African traveller, Major Morgen, that Germany should acquire as a coal depot the Farsan Islands, situated in the southern waters of the Red Sea. For some time the Kaiser was wildly enthusiastic about the project, so the Foreign Ministry agreed as a first step to propose to Constantinople that this coal depot be set up. The Sultan approached the affair with visible hesitation and reluctance. His political instinct told him that if Germany gained a foothold in the Red Sea, and moreover in the neighbourhood of Aden, it would attract the attention of other great Powers, particularly England, and would also have unpleasant consequences for Turkey. Even so he complied with the Kaiser's request, though begging the affair to be kept secret, and there was at least one consignment of German coal unloaded there. As might have been expected, the incident did not remain secret; the foreign Press raised the alarm and demanded the investigation of the circumstances. If the incident were proved true, it would justify the most far-reaching inferences as to the aims of German policy. Meanwhile the months had slipped by, the Kaiser had become interested in other things, and was content to let our claims to the Farsan Islands quietly sink into oblivion.[1]

The Kaiser displayed quite unusual tenacity and obstinacy over his scheme to gain a footing in the Far East, i.e. in China. This idea first emerged when by the Treaty of Shimonoseki China made territorial concessions to Japan. The Kaiser had formerly spoken sympathetically of the 'plucky little Japs', but now the picture of a future 'Yellow Peril' took root in his mind and gave rise to a definite programme which frequently hampered German foreign policy. The well-known picture sketched by the Kaiser, 'Nations

Pan-German League feared difficulties and so it recommended that the United States should be prevented for the time being from purchasing them. Then Germany ought to purchase from Denmark the exclusive right to establish harbour installations, coal depots and cable stations on the islands, so as to gain a footing there. On 16 June the Ambassador in Washington was asked for his opinion. On 30 June he reported that any step which the United States regarded as a violation of the Monroe Doctrine would have incalculable results. The petition from the Pan-German League was not followed up. (From the Foreign Ministry files.)

[1] Cf. *Grosse Politik*, vol. xiv, ii, ch. xciv, appendix.

of Europe, guard your most sacred possessions', was hung in the cabins of German passenger-boats by order of the Kaiser and can hardly have promoted German commercial interests in China and Japan. Doubtless the Kaiser was never afraid that Japan, surrounded by sea Powers like Russia, England, France and America, could ever become a menace to us in Europe. He was put out by Japan's inclination to acquire Chinese territory because a similar inclination had been aroused in him. The Sino-Japanese War had revealed to the world China's weakness, or more accurately her backward state of development, and the notion that China was disintegrating and that one only had to pick up the pieces spread like an epidemic throughout Europe, not merely in Germany. I remember a German consul called Feindel, a native of Alsace, writing reports from some Chinese port or other[1] to the effect that Germany ought to annex a Chinese province.[2] The Navy sent in similar reports. The main idea behind Germany's participation in the revision of the Treaty of Shimonoseki desired by the Russians, and in the expulsion of the Japanese from the Chinese mainland, had been that Germany deserved some reward for her part in coming to China's rescue. People had in mind a German Hong Kong, and both our Minister Heyking[3] and Admiral Tirpitz,[4] then commanding the German ships in Far Eastern waters, were invited to look about and make suggestions. Heyking always proposed some port in Southern China, in particular Amoy. That would have brought us right into the British sphere of influence and would certainly have led to conflict with Britain. Heyking, it was learned later, was completely under the thumb of the clever Russian Chargé d'Affaires Pavlov.[5] The Foreign Ministry declared these proposals to be unacceptable. Tirpitz, for his part, had suggested Kiaochau.[6] Our ex-Minister von Brandt, who was consulted

[1] Feindel was Consul in Amoy, 1890–8.

[2] In a memorandum of 31 March 1895, Feindel expressed the opinion that the partition of China was imminent. In that case Germany must be given the coast of Southern China as far as Shanghai and the hinterland as far as the lower reaches of the Yangtse. (From the Foreign Ministry files.)

[3] Edmund, Baron von Heyking. Consul-General in Calcutta, 1889–93, in Cairo, 1893–5; Minister in Tangier, 1895–6, in Peking, 1896–9.

[4] Alfred von Tirpitz. Commander of the Cruiser Division in the Far East, 1896–7; State Secretary at the Admiralty, 1897–1916.

[5] Alexander Pavlov. Secretary of the Russian Legation in Peking.

[6] Heyking telegraphed on 23 November 1896: 'Admiral Tirpitz agrees Amoy a suitable naval base. [...]' In a detailed personal letter, copied extracts of which

as an authority, declared himself in the main against any annexation of Chinese territory because we should thus sooner or later stir up national passions whose strength and intensity could not be calculated in advance. But if we were determined on territorial gain, then Kiaochau was preferable.

The Kaiser, who had made his decision accordingly, judged the moment ripe for action at the end of 1897 when news came through of the murder of some German missionaries. He immediately ordered the commander of the Far Eastern Squadron—I think Admiral Diederichs[1]—to occupy Kiaochau. To forestall any possibility of a counter order he is said to have contrived a temporary interruption of telegraphic communications, or at least such was Admiral von Senden's boast afterwards. Thus the Foreign Ministry had no hand in the occupation of Kiaochau.

As a typical example of Russia's world view at this time I should like to stress that Muraviev,[2] then Foreign Minister, tried to claim this port situated to the south of Shantung and near the mouth of the Yangtse as part of the Russian sphere of influence. He maintained that Russia had anchorage rights in Kiaochau. In the course of the negotiations Heyking, at Pavlov's prompting, suggested we should give up Kiaochau in exchange for a port farther south, to be decided on by subsequent agreement. This was a last Russian bid to wedge us in the British sphere of in-

were found in the files, Heyking gave the reasons for his opinion on the necessity for occupying Amoy. The letter goes on: 'The Admiral [Tirpitz] also agreed from the start that, failing Kiaochau, Amoy was the only possible choice. I think he had a certain preference for Kiaochau because of his jealousy of Russia, but that is all over now. In my view and that of the Russian Navy we have lost nothing by it. [...]' (Cf. *Grosse Politik*, vol. XIV, i, nos. 3668 and 3669, pp. 43–6.) In a memorandum of 9 January 1897, for a personal report to the Kaiser, Admiral Knorr wrote that Tirpitz had reached the following conclusions in his reports: 'There can be no doubt that the Russians have acquired a special right to Kiaochau. [...]' Tirpitz had visited several ports and looked into their suitability as German bases. On the strength of these observations Tirpitz had written: 'Only the Yangtse area is formally unoccupied and at the same time full of promise. If we wish to achieve great things here in the Far East we must aim at this.' That required the occupation of Wusung, and Berlin must judge whether it was politically feasible. Admiral Knorr recommended that it should first be ascertained whether Kiaochau could not in fact be acquired by Germany. On 17 February 1897, the State Secretary at the Admiralty informed the Foreign Ministry that the Kaiser had ordered a plan to be submitted for the occupation of Kiaochau Bay. (From the Foreign Ministry files.)

[1] Otto von Diederichs. Rear-Admiral; Commander of the Cruiser Division in the Far East, 1897–8; Chief of the Naval Staff, 1900–2.

[2] Michael, Count Muraviev. Counsellor of the Russian Embassy in Berlin, 1884–93; Minister in Copenhagen, 1893–7; Foreign Minister, 1897–1900.

fluence. I conducted these negotiations under Prince Hohenlohe (during the critical phase of the Kiaochau affair Bülow was in Rome) and I followed von Brandt's view that if we really must have something, then Kiaochau was the least risky. But the whole idea of and insistence on territorial gains emanated from the Navy.[1]

It was probably because he noticed that both the Kaiser and a section of the German Press made constant and open reference to the desire for territorial gains outside Europe that Chamberlain in the autumn of 1898 [sic] made his proposal for an Anglo-German agreement which I mentioned briefly on p. 1 of these memoirs.[2] I can still remember clearly from what Bülow told me that Chamberlain had said England had enough and would be satisfied to retain what she already possessed; she would therefore not hinder Germany's schemes for expansion but under certain circumstances might even assist them. The negotiations carried on between 1898[3] and 1902 with Chamberlain and the British Government are the subject of an article published in the *Berliner*

[1] For Germany's acquisition of Kiaochau cf. *Grosse Politik*, vol. XIV, i, ch. XC. The following should be noted: In 1925 a research student inquired of the Foreign Ministry whether he might be allowed access to the files covering Germany's Far East policy with a view to writing a doctoral thesis. Dr Thimme, one of the editors of the *Grosse Politik*, remarked in this connection: '[...] In their choice of documentary material on German policy in the Far East (vols. XIV, XVI, XIX of the *Grosse Politik*), particularly as regards the acquisition of Kiaochau, the editors went to the limits of what is desirable in view of present political interests. If a young student, whose political discretion is an unknown quantity, were now to "re-examine" the files and then make use of some unpublished item, there would be a danger of our official publication being accused of incompleteness, and the whole undertaking would be gravely prejudiced. [...]' Accordingly the Foreign Ministry from then on refused on principle all requests by researchers for access to these files. (From the Foreign Ministry files.)

The German Foreign Ministry files dealing with the Far East have been filmed by Florida State University and the University of California (Berkeley). These films are also available in the P.R.O., London.

[2] See p. 160. Holstein means the 1899 proposals.

[3] Holstein describes Chamberlain's offer of an alliance in 1898 in the essay on Anglo-German relations which he wrote in 1907. 'But we were offered one more chance of conciliation. Chamberlain, then the most powerful man in the government, instead of taking fright at the Krüger telegram, told our Ambassador Count Hatzfeldt quite candidly his opinion that England and Germany should co-operate as allies. The discrepancy between Chamberlain's remarks and the abuse in the English periodicals etc. was so considerable that even I wondered for a time whether Chamberlain honestly meant what he said or whether he was only wanting to trick us into some act of co-operation which could then be exploited before the world, particularly in St Petersburg. And so an attitude of reserve was adopted towards Chamberlain's proposals.' (See *Grosse Politik*, vol. XIV, i, ch. XCI and the Holstein-Hatzfeldt letters, 1898, *Correspondence*.)

Tageblatt of Monday, 8 February, the salient points of which were printed in Monday evening's *Neueste Nachrichten*. The article publishes one or two facts which can be known only to a few people, which makes certain omissions and inaccuracies seem the more surprising; I wonder whether the sole aim of publishing it was to set the latter circulating. Chamberlain's offer is reproduced more or less as Bülow told it me. Bülow had received the information with his usual affability but, according to him, without committing himself to the plan.[1] Chamberlain had mistakenly assumed that Bülow would also support the idea of an Anglo-German alliance and so had made his speech in Leicester, warmly recommending an Anglo-German partnership. Naturally Chamberlain, and judging by the Press the entire British nation too, felt hurt in their pride when Bülow seized the earliest possible opportunity in the Reichstag of rejecting the Chamberlain plan coldly, almost ironically.[2] But this did not prevent the British Government from reverting with vigour and tenacity to the idea of an alliance. But it is incorrect for the leading article in the *Tageblatt* to state that England wished to join the Triple Alliance. That is precisely what she did not want. But that is exactly what Bülow insisted on. He said it was impossible and dishonest towards Austria and Italy for Germany to enter upon an alliance to which they were not parties. But Britain emphasized that it would be dangerous for her to join the Triple Alliance, for she had no desire to take sides in the chronic Balkan dispute between Austria and Russia. I pointed out that Germany's entering upon an alliance with England would not be an act of disloyalty towards Austria and Italy because, judging by the world situation, the aims of the Anglo-German

[1] In the 1907 essay Holstein wrote: 'On his return Bülow told me what Chamberlain had said, without passing any criticism of it. He just said we could probably expect concrete proposals from England soon because Chamberlain was powerful enough to impose his view on his ministerial colleagues. Bülow had obviously left Chamberlain under the impression that the idea of an Anglo-German rapprochement was well received by Germany.'

[2] In the 1907 essay Holstein wrote: 'Just then—autumn, 1899—our Reichstag was in session, so Bülow replied there to Chamberlain's speech by pouring scorn on it and on the whole idea of an Anglo-German alliance, which he declared suspect. He had avoided seeing me for a few days before the speech. His refusal therefore was as much a surprise to me as to the British Colonial Secretary, who was naturally outraged.' Holstein is referring to Bülow's Reichstag speech of 11 December 1899, recorded in *Stenographische Berichte über die Verhandlungen des Reichstags*, x. Legislaturperiode, i. Session 1898/1900 (Berlin, 1900), vol. iv, pp. 3292–5.

alliance would presumably never prejudice Austrian or Italian interests. It was no use. One had the impression that Bülow seized on every obstacle standing in the way of the alliance. This was perhaps connected with memories of his youth (as I have noted elsewhere).[1] In 1864, when he was fifteen or sixteen, he had seen how England, after promising Denmark her staunch support —Lord Russell[2] as Foreign Secretary had declared that when the first cannon was fired Denmark would not stand alone—nevertheless stood by and watched while the Duchies were severed from Denmark. The Bülow family was thus rendered homeless. Bülow's father, who had held an attractive and important post in Frankfurt as Minister to the Federal Diet representing the Danish Duchies, was compelled to look around for employment elsewhere and had to be satisfied with the considerably inferior post of Mecklenburg Minister in Berlin, which he obtained on Bismarck's recommendation. I noticed more than once that this experience produced its after-effect on Bülow. For instance I clearly remember how one day when we were discussing the English proposals for an alliance the remark slipped out: 'Some people still firmly believe that if you make friends with England you're sure to be let down.' Even so I am certain that Bülow would not have persisted with such determination in so markedly a hostile attitude if he had not been certain that this accorded with the Kaiser's views and intentions. The latter, who had already decided on an anti-British act at the time of the Krüger telegram because he felt annoyed with Lord Salisbury, had naturally not been appeased by the resultant torrent of anger and ridicule which the British had directed against him for years. In the London music-halls a song ridiculing the Kaiser was the hit of the evening, and one read in the Press that the officers of his dragoon regiment had taken the portrait he had given them and turned its face to the wall. It may be assumed that these incidents, which were all known to him, had not put him in the right frame of mind for contracting an alliance. But I must add that Bülow never said a word in direct confirmation of this assumption. Altogether I learnt little of Bülow's dealings with the Kaiser throughout the years. I avoided asking questions and Bülow, in

[1] In the 1907 essay, which is almost identical with the version given below.
[2] Lord John Russell, from 1861 Earl Russell. Foreign Secretary in the Palmerston Cabinet, 1859–65.

contrast with his usual communicativeness, was reticent about his conversations with the Kaiser. Even so, other people apart from me who knew Bülow felt quite sure he never put forward any definite opinion unless he knew he had the Kaiser's backing.

For the sake of completeness I must mention here Eckardstein's[1] statement that when he once referred with regret to the breakdown of the negotiations over an alliance with England, the Kaiser said: 'What negotiations? I don't know anything about them.' But from what I learned elsewhere I really cannot treat this exclamation with the respect due to historical fact. On questions of responsibility, as in many other respects, Wilhelm II is very different from his grandfather. Bismarck was chary of praise, but I have several times heard him say that once the old man had finally approved some political step, even though reluctantly and after stubborn resistance, he regarded it from that moment as his own and defended it as such. But his grandson, as many of us know only too well, invariably saddles other people with anything that has turned out badly or even begun to look dubious. All the negotiations on the English alliance, from Chamberlain's original overture to their breakdown in January 1902, coincide with the Boer War, that is, with a period of English weakness. I have no evidence whether, and in what way, the Kaiser intended to exploit this state of weakness, unless evidence can be found in Bülow's Reichstag speech of January 1902.[2] I shall never forget it. The brusque and in my view quite unnecessary rebuttal of a misconstrued statement by Chamberlain about the behaviour of German soldiers during the Franco-Prussian War does not seem the main point of this speech; that, I thought, was Bülow's pronouncement on world policy and on Germany's right to have a say in it. To leave no doubt as to his meaning he named the chief trouble centres, Morocco, the Persian Gulf and the Far East.

Bülow had told me beforehand when I was trying to dissuade him that he had no alternative but to attack Chamberlain, out of consideration for the army's 'legitimate indignation'. One is led to think that in this case too the Kaiser posed as the army's

[1] Hermann, Baron von Eckardstein. First Secretary in the London Embassy, 1899–1902.

[2] Of 8 January, recorded in *Stenographische Berichte über die Verhandlungen des Reichstags*, x. Legislaturperiode, ii. Session 1900/03, vol. iv, pp. 3209–10 (see p. 186, n. 1).

champion and informed the Chancellor of its 'legitimate indignation'. And the section on world policy with its insistence on German interests in Morocco, the Persian Gulf and the Far East seems much more likely to have been inspired by the Kaiser than to have been initiated by the unenterprising Bülow. I have still not decided what can have been the real purpose of that completely superfluous speech. My first impression was that Bülow suddenly decided to pick a quarrel to put an end once and for all to the British proposals that were so distasteful to him personally. But when it is borne in mind that it would have been quite foreign to Bülow's nature to take such a momentous step, so capable of endangering his own position, without consulting the Kaiser, whose own mood at the time was exactly suited to such a course of action, then a different conclusion is reached. The Kaiser wanted to intimidate England by browbeating or 'bullying' as the English say. He used the same method in his action of 2 January 1896 when he planned to support the Boers with German colonial troops but then allowed himself to be persuaded by Hohenlohe and Marschall into doing no more than sending an expression of sympathy to President Krüger. I am told that Admiral Hollmann has now been instructed by the Kaiser (and indeed makes no secret of it) to make it widely known that the account given of the Krüger telegram in Stein's book[1] is correct in stating that it emanated from the Foreign Ministry. This assertion is a distortion of the truth. Marschall dictated the Krüger telegram to Kayser so as to restrain the Kaiser from still more rash actions which would have made war with England inevitable. In fact despite the Krüger telegram, or rather in addition to it, an official inquiry was sent at about this time to the Portuguese Government to see whether it would allow German troops to pass through Lourenço-Marques *en route* for the Transvaal.[2] I know that Soveral,[3] the Ambassador, has since discussed this very point with other people and said that Portugal could have done nothing about it if the Germans had staged a surprise attack on Lourenço-Marques and thus forced their way through. But, as he said, formal inquiry could only be met with

---

[1] Adolf Stein, *Wilhelm II* (Leipzig, 1909). In an unpublished paragraph of this essay Holstein expresses the opinion that Stein's book was approved by the Kaiser, despite the author's affirmation to the contrary.

[2] See *Grosse Politik*, vol. XI, p. 20 n. *.

[3] Luiz Marie Pinto de Soveral. Portuguese Minister in London, 1897–1910.

formal refusal. Obviously the Portuguese Government had no reason to keep the German inquiry secret. And so the Kaiser is gratuitously weakening the authority of his own statements by trying to present the German demonstration after the Jameson Raid as a crime on the part of the Foreign Ministry. There is an unmistakable similarity between these tactics and his denial of all knowledge of the British alliance proposals in 1900. The Kaiser, by championing the 'legitimate indignation' of his army and by emphasizing his right to have a say in Morocco, the Persian Gulf and the Far East, had no more desire to force a quarrel with England than he had at the time of the 1896 demonstration. He only wanted to warn England, while she still had her hands full with the Boers, that she must realize Germany was not to be had as an ally without very favourable terms. On both occasions, January 1896 and January 1902, the Kaiser justified the verdict of an Englishman who told me some years ago: 'The Emperor is half English and thinks he understands us, but he completely misunderstands the English character; if he so much as touches the English he hurts, and when he means to stroke us he rubs us the wrong way.' The outcome of that Reichstag declaration about 'biting on granite'[1] and world policy was the breaking-off of negotiations with England, which the Kaiser certainly did not wish. Had any doubts still remained as to the effect of that speech they would have been dispelled when Valentine Chirol, with whom I had been corresponding for several months on matters bearing on a rapprochement, wrote me a formal letter in which he stated all was over.[2]

The *Berliner Tageblatt* article referred to above, in trying to show that the raising of Chinese import duties was the reason for the breakdown of the alliance negotiations, is guilty of a childish attempt to divert attention from the facts.[3] The raising of the Chinese import duties bears no possible relation to the question

[1] Holstein refers to Bülow's speech of 8 January 1902, in which he replied to alleged criticisms by Joseph Chamberlain of the German army by citing a remark of Fredrick the Great: 'Let the man be and don't get excited, he's biting on granite.' (See p. 184, n. 2.)

[2] Letter of 12 January 1902 (*Correspondence*).

[3] The article says: 'The German government, on Waldersee's instigation, wished to withdraw German troops from Peking as quickly as possible, and, so as to make sure of her war reparations in advance, it recommended the immediate raising of Chinese import duties. England, seeing a threat to her exports, quite understandably put up a vigorous opposition, and in the dispute over these side-issues this most important plan broke down. [...]'

of an Anglo-German alliance. Neither that nor any other isolated problem would have caused the breaking-off of negotiations by which England obviously set great store. For this to happen it was necessary to bring out the heavy artillery as Bülow did when he openly insulted England's leading statesman in the Reichstag, an action almost without precedent in the history of the Great Powers except in time of war; at the same time he stressed that three points in which England was vitally interested had come within the German sphere of interest. The attempts to blame the Chinese import duties and the Pan-German movement for the breakdown show that the apparently motiveless *Tageblatt* 'disclosure' comes from a quarter wishing to clear Bülow from all blame and *ipso facto* the Kaiser as well. Flotow[1] is an acquaintance of Theodor Wolff's.[2]

Thus the Kaiser and the Chancellor are equally to blame for having guided German policy towards a possible war with England. But whereas the Chancellor wished to put an end to the idea of collaboration with England because of the suspicion he still retained from the Danish affair, the Kaiser had the one overriding idea of intimidating England to make her more docile. It is well known that every individual has not only his characteristic personality but also a characteristic way of thinking. The following very recent incident shows that even today intimidation as a means to an end still plays a part in the Kaiser's thought processes.

Count Zeppelin[3] had been asked during his recent visit to Berlin to give a lecture on the efficacy of his airship in peace and war. He had composed his lecture most carefully, omitting everything which could cause offence or give away official secrets to foreign Powers.

---

[1] Hans von Flotow. Secretary of the Embassy in Paris, 1904–7; *Vortragender Rat* in the Foreign Ministry, 1907–10.

[2] Paris correspondent of the *Berliner Tageblatt*, 1905; editor of the *Berliner Tageblatt* from 1906.

In his 1907 essay Holstein wrote: 'The period between January 1896 and February 1902, between the Krüger telegram and the 'biting-on-granite' speech, is the transitional period which in the field of foreign policy marks the beginning of English ascendancy and of the—let us hope only temporary—German decline. Germany now finds herself in the position she herself created, namely of directing her world policy and her colonial policy against England. The methods we envisage, namely, feverish naval construction and an understanding with France are childish in their simplicity. That is the path that leads to the regulation of armaments and the revision of the Peace of Frankfurt.'

[3] Ferdinand, Count von Zeppelin. Inventor of the rigid type of airship.

The Kaiser then invited him to breakfast and requested him afterwards to repeat his lecture. The Kaiser had invited a small number of soldiers and just one civilian to hear it. The latter looked absolutely German and spoke the language fluently. This time Zeppelin held nothing back but discussed in detail the possibility of war with England, dwelling particularly on the invasion of the country. He inquired later who the civilian was. 'The British Ambassador, Sir William Goschen.'[1] If one can credit the Kaiser with any directing idea, it can only have been to acquaint the English with our means of destruction in order to intimidate them. The fact that all kinds of official secrets were thus revealed to our enemies seemed to him of trifling importance, just as it did when he was at Highcliffe.[2]

[1] Ambassador in Berlin, 1908–14.
[2] Col. Stuart-Wortley's estate.

CHAPTER XI

THE KAISER'S RELATIONS TO POLITICS AND TO THE CHANCELLOR[1]

Relations between Bülow and Wilhelm II. The consequences of the *Daily Telegraph* interview. Wilhelm II congratulates Radolin on Morocco. Kiderlen ignored. The Press links Radolin with Holstein. The Press on the Holstein-Hohenlohe-Eulenburg-Hatzfeldt bloc. Holstein's comments on Hohenlohe, Hatzfeldt. Holstein, Bülow, Kiderlen and Germany's Bosnian policy. Holstein's advice to stand by Austria. Collaboration of Kiderlen and Holstein. Bülow's insecurity when dealing with the Kaiser, and *vice versa*. Opposition of the Kaiser's sons.

24 February 1909:

[...] The Kaiser, who had refrained from direct intervention in foreign policy since the events in November and had restricted himself to marginal notes on Foreign Ministry reports, reasserted himself for the first time after the conclusion of the new Morocco agreement.[2] Meanwhile, his relations with the Chancellor had been markedly cool. The Kaiser's morning visits, the strolls in the Chancellor's garden, were not resumed. The Kaiser did not dine with the Chancellor, nor was Bülow ever the Kaiser's guest except at large banquets; he had audience of the Kaiser only occasionally when business required it.

The Kaiser's inner dissatisfaction was revealed in the notes he made in the margin of newspaper cuttings. I thought particularly expressive the marginal note to an article criticizing the sale of royal castles: 'On that point nobody can tell me my business, not even Bülow.'

Another of the Kaiser's remarks shows how carefully he notices

[1] The chapter-heading is Holstein's.
[2] The Franco-German Morocco agreement of 9 February 1909. France reaffirmed her recognition of Moroccan independence and integrity. Germany confirmed her determination not to encroach on France's special interests, while France confirmed her decision to respect Germany's parity of economic rights. (See *Grosse Politik*, vol. XXIV, no. 8490, pp. 489–90.)

everything that can be regarded as indicative of his relations and standing abroad. Speaking of New Year greetings he said to one of his confidants: 'I have had several new ones I didn't expect, but many old ones I had counted on have failed to arrive.'

In the New Year there appeared those two publications by Schlieffen and Stein mentioned above, which aimed at presenting to the world the figure of the Kaiser in the most favourable light possible. Now they are joined by a third literary production, a book by *Regierungsrat* Rudolf Martin entitled *Fürst Bülow und Kaiser Wilhelm II*.[1] Whereas Stein attempts to shift the blame equally from Kaiser and Chancellor on to the bureaucracy, Martin lays all the blame on Bülow and says (I quote): 'Never before in the history of the world has a minister so dared to throw the blame for his own misdeeds on to his sovereign. That is all the gratitude shown to Kaiser Wilhelm II for having raised Bernhard von Bülow in rapid succession to the rank of Count, then Prince, in exchange for no particular services.' This is the last sentence of Martin's article in the *Gegenwart* in which he recommends his book to the public.

Like everyone else who takes up his pen in the Kaiser's defence, Martin treats the Kaiser's habitual indiscretions, his broadcasting of state secrets, as a secondary matter. The main emphasis is ingeniously placed on the fact of publication. Not only in Martin's work but elsewhere too the idea is expressed in the most varied ways that Bülow did not defend the Kaiser strongly enough last November.[2] I should like to give the following as my own opinion: in view of the Kaiser's indiscretions no defence was possible. That the Kaiser, who was well beyond the age of youthful exuberance and had reigned more than ten years, lacked, and one must regretfully say still lacks, all sense of what is fitting, is a misfortune both for him and for the German Reich. Future historians will compile a long list of the Kaiser's sudden impulses in conversation, in writing, in telegrams, which collectively and singly have had the effect of gradually diminishing the prestige of the Kaiser and the Reich, of wrecking diplomatic negotiations and even of provoking immediate danger of war. The misfortune and the mistake lay in the remarks themselves. The full effect of the Kaiser's remarks

[1] (Leipzig-Gohlis, 1909.)
[2] In the Reichstag debate on the *Daily Telegraph* affair.

was felt from the moment he confided a state secret to a foreigner. When the *Daily Telegraph* published in November [*sic*] a selection of these utterances they produced a sensational *after*-effect which bore the same relation to the real effect as thunder does to lightning. Anyone trying to defend the Kaiser at this stage would have provided his detractors with all too favourable opportunities of saying things better left unsaid.

Even so I wonder now, when I try to reach an impartial opinion, whether it would not have been possible for Bülow to have defended some other point in the Kaiser's interests, even though a subordinate one. I think every single speaker in the Reichstag, whether on the Right or Left, expressed his regret that at a time when the German nation was disconcerted and disturbed by the *Daily Telegraph* article the Kaiser should be enjoying himself in Donaueschingen, instead of watching the development of events from his official residence. When discussing this aspect of the affair with Bülow at the end of November I asked him: 'Did you, as many people are saying, dissuade the Kaiser from returning to Berlin?' He replied: 'No, I said nothing either way.'

Meanwhile more and more people were saying the Chancellor had in fact dissuaded him, and I am now told that Admiral Hollmann, who enjoys the Kaiser's confidence, is positively asserting that the Kaiser received in Donaueschingen a lengthy code telegram[1] from the Chancellor stating that it was quite unnecessary for him to return and that the Reichstag debate would pass off without incident. I informed Bülow through an intermediary that Hollmann was spreading this story, but I do not know how he has taken the news. And so I shall not ask again. The person to whom I gave this information at once replied that Hollmann was known for periodically displaying a cavalier disregard of the truth. But unless his version of events is contested it will soon be the only one current, much to Bülow's disadvantage. If he had in fact advised the Kaiser in the way Hollmann claims, then by remaining silent he missed a golden opportunity both for the Kaiser and for himself. If at the mention of Donaueschingen he had said: 'Gentlemen, I must accept full responsibility for His Majesty's absence. I expressed my view that His Majesty need not return because I felt convinced that the Reichstag would deal with this matter, so

---

[1] Not found in the Foreign Ministry files.

painful for all concerned, in the most proper and the most loyal way possible', he would then have stuck to the truth, paid the Reichstag a compliment and shown at the same time that he was prepared to defend the Kaiser when it seemed at all possible. Bülow's silence, always assuming he really had said the Kaiser need not return, was a serious tactical mistake with consequences which will, I think, make themselves felt more and more. The less possibility there was of saying anything on the main issue which could effectively defend or condone the Kaiser's misdemeanours, the more it was Bülow's duty to prevent unjust attacks being made on him over a side-issue which had nevertheless attracted the widest attention.

The Kaiser first emerged from the reserve he had imposed on himself since November when he sent a telegram to Radolin acknowledging the conclusion of the most recent Morocco agreement. Since the telegram was sent to Paris *en clair* it would be a waste of time trying to maintain that it was not intended to be made public. The Kaiser wanted to create an effect. He must of course have known that all the negotiations had been carried on here in Berlin between Cambon[1] and Kiderlen,[2] who kept in touch with Bülow, and that to avoid confusion they had not asked for Radolin's co-operation (which had led to some expression of annoyance on the part of the Paris Embassy). In sending his telegram the Kaiser wished to show pointedly his goodwill towards Radolin, and to ignore Kiderlen equally pointedly (or can Bülow and Schoen have concealed Kiderlen's activities from the Kaiser? I can hardly think so, but most improbable things happen). Of course the telegram became known in Paris and was published in the *Matin*.[3] Radolin made a short colourless statement on it, while an anonymous writer (Groeben,[4] I assume) added a lengthy commentary, malicious in tone towards me. This led to a controversy between the French Press and the semi-official Press in Berlin, the latter using the opportunity of dealing a blow to Radolin. I cannot say I find this sort of behaviour very attractive. The article of the *Neue Gesellschaftliche Correspondenz* of 24 February is obviously

[1] Jules Cambon. French Ambassador in Washington, 1897–1902, in Madrid, 1902–07, in Berlin, 1907–14.
[2] Kiderlen was acting State Secretary in the Foreign Ministry from November 1908 to March 1909.
[3] 17 February 1909.
[4] Unico, Count von der Groeben. First Secretary in the Paris Embassy, 1903–4.

inspired by the Press Bureau, despite the attempt to imitate Harden's style, particularly in the first two paragraphs. The purpose is to break Radolin. I had nothing to do with the affair but my name is brought in because it is hoped to discredit Radolin with the Kaiser by pointing out that I am a friend of Radolin's. It is both pointless and mean to speak of an anti-Bismarck group consisting of Holstein, Hohenlohe, Eulenburg and Hatzfeldt. That I am described in the tone the Bismarcks adopted in their time, is understandable. But Hohenlohe's one wish was to stay on quietly in Strasbourg, and Hatzfeldt, I can state most definitely, never intrigued against anyone all his life. So far as I could observe, it was to his unswerving political loyalty, even more than to his diplomatic acumen, that he owed the unshakable position of trust he enjoyed wherever he went. First of all he went as Minister to Madrid in 1873 or 1874, when he immediately gained the confidence of the republican government and the Regent Serrano.[1] When at the end of December 1874 Martinez Campos[2] set Alfonso XII on the throne by the *Pronunciamento* of Sagunto, the Spanish royalists suggested to Prince Hohenlohe, our Ambassador in Paris, that Hatzfeldt, having been so intimate with the republicans, would be hardly likely to win the confidence of the new legitimist government. On my advice Hohenlohe declined to pass on to Berlin this unofficial approach. Hatzfeldt stayed in Madrid and before six months were out he enjoyed the King's confidence to a far greater extent than he had ever done the republicans'. The King took Hatzfeldt with him on a tour of Spain, which created difficulties for him professionally in that the Foreign Minister Vega de Armijo[3] was jealous of him ever afterwards.

Hatzfeldt won the same position of trust with the Sultan. In 1879 he was sent to Constantinople. At that time the question was being discussed, and was gradually growing more acute, of ceding Turkish frontier territory to Greece. The Congress of Berlin, at

[1] Francisco Serrano y Domingues. Spanish leader in the revolutionary struggles, 1868–74; Regent, July 1869–January 1871; President of the Cabinet under King Amadeo, May–June 1872; President of the Republic, January–December 1874.

[2] Arsenio Martinez de Campos. Spanish general and statesman; appointed Captain-General of Catalonia and Commander-in-Chief of the Army of the North by Alfonso XII. In March 1876, at Peña de Plata, he won the decisive victory over the Carlists.

[3] Antonio Aguilar y Correa, Marquès de la Vega de Armijo became Spanish Foreign Minister only after Hatzfeldt had left Madrid.

the instigation of the French Foreign Minister Waddington, had formulated this *vœu*, and it was now a question of putting it into effect. Since the Koran forbids the cession of Turkish territory except after defeat in war, the Sultan was in a delicate position, for this particular surrender of territory could scarcely be regarded as a direct result of the Russo-Turkish War. There followed, it will be remembered, a joint naval demonstration by the Congress Powers. An internal upheaval in Turkey—with incalculable consequences abroad—already seemed possible when Hatzfeldt succeded in persuading the Sultan to give way. This put an end to the crisis, and Lord Ampthill wrote to someone in the Foreign Ministry: 'Bravo, Hatzfeldt.' But even the most unsuspecting reader could tell from the whole tone of his letter that a crisis would have suited the aims of British policy better. Perhaps Ampthill's dislike of Hatzfeldt, which was often apparent to his immediate circle during his term as State Secretary, dated from this incident. Other differences in their characters may have also played their part. What is certain is that my friend Courcel (as I have already noted elsewhere) said after Ampthill's death more or less these words: '*C'est curieux que cet homme d'ordinaire si sérieux devenait presque un gamin toutes les fois qu'il entrevoyait la possibilité de faire une niche à Hatzfeldt.*'

Ampthill's dislike was not shared by Lord Salisbury or any of the English statesmen. This was shown when Hatzfeldt was appointed Ambassador in London in 1885. I must mention briefly that in 1895 I was told by someone with reliable inside knowledge of the Foreign Office that there was some dissatisfaction there because Salisbury attached too much weight to Hatzfeldt's opinions. Needless to say, the Krüger telegram put an end to this state of affairs.

I have devoted this excursus to the memory of my old friend to show how monstrous was the semi-official insinuation that he too, along with such intriguers as Holstein and Eulenburg 'had been a little previous in taking an interest in the person of a second Chancellor'.[1] This insinuation is clumsy to the point of stupidity.

However, Hatzfeldt played only a minor role in this affair. The main figures are Radolin and Bülow. The following sentence is worth picking out: 'And it has been established for some time that

---

[1] Holstein is again referring to the article in the *Neue Gesellschaftliche Correspondenz* of 24 February 1909.

over the Morocco question the Chancellor was not for one single day a mere tool of Holstein's, and on this occasion too he read every detail of the instructions on which Cambon and von Kiderlen based their draft of the Morocco agreement.' Why could Prince Bülow's office not have issued a similar statement in 1906 when the whole of the Press was saying the Moroccan policy was my handiwork and I was to blame for everything? At that time the policy of firmness and calm, which I have never denied having advocated, was regarded by the public as mistaken, whereas nowadays public opinion no longer approves the principle of constantly giving way. This is the only explanation of the Chancellor's suddenly claiming as his own the so-called Holstein policy on Morocco. And with every justification, for until 12 March 1906, while I was doing the main work on Moroccan affairs, nothing was sent out unless it had first been fully approved by Bülow. Now Hammann's[1] bureau is falling into the opposite error by representing Kiderlen and myself as Bülow's tools, mere instruments to do his bidding. It makes no difference to me, but it most improperly reduces Kiderlen's status. Last autumn (I don't remember when, but I expect the copy of my letter is still about somewhere), I wrote to Bülow that it was impossible for me, as a sick man, from a distance, to be morally responsible to him for seeing that no isolated points were neglected while the Balkan question was under review. I therefore regarded it as vital to the Chancellor that Kiderlen should prolong his stay in Berlin. No one in the Reichstag or elsewhere would blame the Chancellor if he employed Kiderlen for a time as a specialist for the Balkans, for he had spent twelve years in Constantinople and Bucharest.[2] Bülow took my advice, just as he had at once come round to my view in September when I wrote to him in Nordeney from the Harz Mountains that there could be only one policy for Germany in the complications now developing in the Balkans: we must stand by Austria calmly and resolutely, imposing no restrictions or conditions, for in defending her *own* cause she was fighting *our* battle against the encircling Powers, England, Russia and France (and Italy). This basic principle must take precedence over all other considerations, particularly consideration for Turkey.[3]

[1] Otto Hammann. *Vortragender Rat* in the Foreign Ministry, 1894–1916. In charge of the Press Department.

[2] Holstein to Bülow, 5 December 1908 (*Correspondence*).

[3] Holstein evidently refers to his letter to Bülow of 8 October 1908 (*Correspondence*).

I gladly give Bülow his due and state that he accepted this idea at once and wasted no time in reversing with a single stroke the policy of friendliness towards Turkey and animosity towards Austria which had been initiated by the joint efforts of the Kaiser, Marschall and the Press Department. When, very early on, Russia and England put forward the idea of a European Congress to decide Austria's case, I advised Bülow to ask Schoen to inform the Ambassadors of the Powers concerned at the next reception, 'that Germany had no objection on principle to a congress, provided all the signatories of the Treaty of Berlin took part, including Austria. A partial congress, which would inevitably be an affront to Austria, would not suit German interests.'[1] Bülow replied by return that this formula had been passed on to the Embassies unaltered both by Schoen and himself.[2] Thus the German Government had taken up its position in the affair, and the other governments knew where they stood. But the question still appeared confused to the European public, for Hammann's bureau continued to print articles criticizing Austria's behaviour. The semi-official Press was particularly fond of reprinting material from the *Hamburger Nachrichten*, which was known to be subsidized by Russia, was the mouthpiece of Russian policy, and emphatically insisted that no German statesman who knew his duty would side with Austria in this question. Although I drew Bülow's attention to this scandal several times both in writing and by word of mouth, he could not bring himself to issue any forceful instructions to Hammann. Finally Erzberger,[3] the Deputy, published an article in the *Roter Tag* entitled, 'Is a revision of the Austro-German Alliance under consideration?'[4] That worked, and the semi-official Press was obliged from that time to follow in the wake of Government policy. But this occasion too had shown the same remarkable coincidence of Hammann's Press policy being in line with the interests of French policy. France could wish for nothing better than for Austria, grown suspicious of Germany, to decide to ally herself with the encircling Powers.

[1] Letter of 13 October 1908 (*Correspondence*).
[2] Bülow's reply was not found in the Papers. (See *Grosse Politik*, vol. xxvi, i, no. 9046, p. 177.)
[3] Matthias Erzberger. Member of the Reichstag (Centre Party) from 1903.
[4] A copy of Holstein's letter to Bülow of 22 October 1908, criticizing Erzberger's article, was found in the Papers.

But this time the policy of the German Government cannot be accused of uncertainty or ambiguity. I can truly say of Bülow that during all our written and oral communications during those first months of the Balkan question, I never saw in him the slightest inclination to leave Austria in the lurch. Then our collaboration was interrupted by the November crisis and a recurrence of my illness, but Kiderlen had meanwhile taken over and in conjunction with me—we met twice a week—he directed the progress of the affair. But to avoid behaving like many other people and claiming all the credit for myself I must emphasize that Kiderlen was by no means dependent on my ideas alone. His sound knowledge of the subject, his determination and assurance impressed me afresh each time we met. Recently, when the French and British Ambassadors proposed that Germany should join with them in working for the cause of peace in Vienna, Kiderlen put forward, quite on his own initiative, the counter suggestion: 'In Vienna, no, but by all means in Belgrade, for peace is being threatened not by Austria but by Serbia.'[1] This was a very good move both for Germany and for the cause of peace. The credit is due to Kiderlen alone, whether he made this declaration on the spur of the moment or whether he had first obtained the Chancellor's approval. And so Bülow could have allowed him just a modest share of the credit.

At the moment the Chancellor is doubtless mainly concerned with his relations with the Kaiser, to which I now return. Bülow obviously feels insecure. But from all the information reaching me that is also true of the Kaiser. Hans Oppersdorff,[2] who with his wife was breakfasting with the Kaiser recently, tells me that he seems in bad health, appears nervy, and affects a forced cheerfulness. Another person who spoke to the Kaiser the other day was struck by the way he steered clear of politics and did nothing but crack jokes one after the other. I attribute his sense of insecurity to the possibility that the Kaiser occasionally meets someone who alludes, though in veiled terms, to the mistrust that has recently arisen in many quarters of his personal rule and the consequences to be feared from it. I also hear from what I consider a thoroughly

---

[1] See *Grosse Politik*, vol. XXVI, ii, no. 9383, pp. 607–9.
[2] Hans Georg, Count von Oppersdorff. Member of the Reichstag, 1908–18 (Centre Party until 1912, then Independent). Brother-in-law of Prince Radolin.

reliable source that recently the Crown Prince drew aside Herr von Oldenburg-Januschau[1] and asked him the reasons for the Kaiser's diminished prestige and dwindling popularity. Oldenburg first asked: 'Does your Royal Highness really wish to hear the truth?' When he assented, Oldenburg went on to give him a list of grievances which included the way Bismarck was dismissed, the Krüger telegram, the constant trips, Phili Eulenburg, and finally the *Daily Telegraph* article. Oldenburg concluded by saying: 'If this goes on there is no guarantee that your Royal Highness will even come to the throne. This growing dissatisfaction is paving the way for Socialism.' The Crown Prince was dumbfounded and said he had no idea things had reached such a pass.

The same person from whom I learnt all this also told me it was significant that the Kaiser's sons, who used to be far from united, had several times, together with their wives, formed a solid front to resist the Kaiser and Kaiserin. According to my informant, what lies behind this phenomenon is that they all have a feeling of anxiety about the Kaiser's 'sudden sallies' and their reaction on the family. And it was, similarly, the joint influence of the sons and daughters-in-law which resulted in the Kaiserin's appearing at the last *Ordensfest* in an afternoon dress and hat instead of in court dress and coronet. The Kaiserin strongly resisted the idea but her sons obliged the Kaiser to accept the innovation. The younger generation were obviously making a well-meant attempt to modernize the ceremony. In fact, all the accounts that reached me gave me the impression that the effect produced on the public was far from favourable.

[1] Eland von Oldenburg-Januschau. Member of the Reichstag (German Conservative Party), 1902–12.

NOTES ON THE TEXT

Chapter I: Holstein wrote three separate accounts of his period of service in St Petersburg (cf. Introduction, p. xxiv). Because each of the three versions tells the same story and repeats substantially the same anecdotes, the editors have printed the most detailed memoir only, that written after Holstein's dismissal in 1906. Additional material of historical interest from the memoirs written in 1883 and 1898 has been interpolated so as to preserve the greatest possible narrative continuity. The interpolations occur as follows: p. 2–p. 5 (line 18) from the 1883 memoirs; p. 6 (line 16)– p. 9 (line 8) from the 1898 memoirs; p. 9 (line 32)–p. 10 (line 4) from the 1898 memoirs; p. 11 (line 32)–p. 12 (line 22) from the 1898 memoirs; p. 16 (line 14–end of page) from the 1883 memoirs; p. 19 (line 15)–p. 20 (line 26) from the 1883 memoirs.

Chapters II, III, and IV continue the memoirs written after Holstein's dismissal.

Chapter IV: Part of a separate essay entitled 'Bucher and Abeken', written by Holstein in 1898, has been interpolated as follows: p. 52 (line 29)–p. 56 (line 16); p. 60 (line 15)–p. 62 (line 14).

THE IMPERIAL GERMAN
FOREIGN MINISTRY

The German Foreign Ministry (*Das Auswärtige Amt des Deutschen Reiches*), established by the Constitution of 16 April 1871, was simply an expansion of the Prussian Foreign Ministry. There was no organic division between them. The Foreign Ministry conducted negotiations between Germany and foreign states, and between Prussia and the other states within the German Empire. A single central bureau dealt with reports from Dresden or London, and diplomats could be transferred between a royal Prussian post like Munich and an imperial German post like Rome.

At the same time, the individual German states continued after 1871 to maintain their own Foreign Ministries, as well as their diplomatic representatives at other German courts and abroad. The functions of the diplomatic representatives of the non-Prussian German states in foreign countries were largely social; but the representatives at the various capitals within the German Empire dealt with important internal problems, such as trade and transport, and were frequently called upon to settle delicate personal matters among the German rulers.

German foreign policy was directed by the Imperial Chancellor, a Minister appointed by the Kaiser and responsible only to him. The Chancellor was at the same time Prussian Foreign Minister, a dual role purposely created by Bismarck to give him control over the relationship between Prussia and the states within the German Empire as well as over German foreign policy.

At the head of the Foreign Ministry was the State Secretary, a civil servant responsible to the Chancellor. In 1881 the office of Under State Secretary was established to provide a regular deputy for the State Secretary and to release the State Secretary from all non-political work. In practice it was found that the decision of the State Secretary was still needed for important non-political matters, and that the Under State Secretary tended to become almost totally involved in the work of the Political Division.

In 1871, when the Foreign Ministry was established, it consisted of two Divisions: I. Political, and II. Legal-Commercial. In later years these Divisions were further subdivided as follows:

1879: The Personnel Section, except for the Consular Service, was separated from Division II, and was made an independent Division.

1885: Division II was broken down into Division II (Economic Policy, including the Consular Service) and Division III (Legal).

1890: The Colonial Section was separated from Division I, and was made an independent Division.

1895: The Personnel Section for the Diplomatic Service was separated from the Personnel Division and was placed under the Political Division.

1903: The Consular Service was separated from Division II and placed under the Personnel Division.

1907: The Colonial Division was taken out of the Foreign Ministry and made into an independent office.

The Political Division of the Foreign Ministry was in charge of the general problems of foreign policy, of press affairs (until 1915), of colonial affairs (until 1890), and, after 1895, of the Personnel Section for the Diplomatic Service. The other Divisions of the Foreign Ministry were obliged to submit all matters touching on general foreign policy to the Political Division for counter-signature. As a result, the Political Division often took over questions such as foreign loans or railroad construction which ordinarily would have been dealt with by other Divisions.

Unlike other Divisions of the Foreign Ministry, each of which had its own Director, the Political Division was directly under the State Secretary and his deputy, the Under State Secretary. The Division was staffed by a number of *Vortragende Räte* (Counsellors) and *Hilfsarbeiter* (Assistants). Work among the *Vortragende Räte* of the Political Division was normally divided according to geographical area, but the system was fairly flexible. Incoming documents ordinarily went to the responsible *Vortragender Rat*, and were then sent on or personally submitted by him to the State Secretary or the Chancellor. Under Bismarck, the *Vortragender Rat* was usually told how to reply, but later it was the *Vortragender Rat*, as the expert on a particular subject, who drafted instructions or replies, which were sometimes revised and usually signed by either the State Secretary or the Chancellor.

The Kaiser, as the head of the state, was automatically responsible for all German policy. The extent to which he took over the direction of foreign policy depended largely on the personalities of the Kaiser and the Chancellor. The Chancellor, as the minister responsible for foreign policy, invariably maintained a close supervision over the daily work in the Foreign Ministry. All the important instructions went out under his name. On important questions, it was the Chancellor himself who worked out the policy, usually in close collaboration with the Foreign Ministry specialist on that question, that is, the *Vortragender Rat*. It followed that the State Secretary or the Under State Secretary might be altogether excluded from certain negotiations. On the other hand, a forceful State Secretary, particularly when there was a weak or inexperienced Chancellor, could himself take over the direction of foreign policy. The influence of the *Vortragender Rat* in either case depended on how much the Chancellor or State Secretary needed to rely on his advice, and on the personal relationships between the men involved. The hierarchy of influence and power within the German Foreign Ministry was therefore in many ways a matter of personality more than position.

The career of Friedrich von Holstein showed how great an influence could be attained by a *Vortragender Rat*. From 1886, when he became senior *Vortragender Rat* in the Political Division, Holstein worked on all the more important problems of foreign policy, and could take over any problem when it became important. After the fall of Bismarck, his close personal relations with successive Chancellors and the most influential of the State Secretaries, his grasp of political problems as compared with theirs, his industry and ability made it possible for him to exercise an influence on German foreign policy out of all proportion to his rank.

THE 'DAILY TELEGRAPH' INTERVIEW[1]

We have received the following communication from a source of such unimpeachable authority that we can without hesitation commend the obvious message which it conveys to the attention of our readers:

Discretion is the first and last quality requisite in a diplomatist and should still be observed by those who, like myself have long passed from public into private life. Yet, moments sometimes occur in the history of nations when a calculated indiscretion proves of the highest possible service, and it is for that reason that I have decided to make known the substance of a lengthy conversation which it was my privilege during the present month to have with His Majesty, the German Emperor. I do so in the hope that it may help to remove that obstinate misconception of the character of the Kaiser's feelings towards England, which, I fear, is deeply rooted in the ordinary Englishman's breast. It is the Emperor's sincere wish that it should be eradicated. He has given repeated proofs of his desire by word and deed. But, to speak frankly, his large stock of patience is giving out, now that he finds himself so continually misrepresented and has so often experienced the mortification of finding that any momentary improvement of relations is followed by renewed outbursts of prejudice and a prompt return to the old attitude of suspicion.

As I have said, His Majesty honoured me with a long conversation and spoke with impulsive and unusual frankness. 'You English', he said, 'are mad, mad as March hares. What has come over you that you are so completely given over to suspicions quite unworthy of a great nation? What more can I do than I have done? I declared with all the emphasis at my command in my speech at the Guildhall that my heart is set upon peace, and that it is one of my dearest wishes to live on the best terms with England. Have

---

[1] The version printed here is the one submitted to the Kaiser by Colonel Stuart Wortley. The changes recommended by the Foreign Ministry and embodied in the version printed in the *Daily Telegraph* are given as footnotes.

I ever been false to my word? Falsehood and prevarication are alien to my nature. My actions ought to speak for themselves, but you listen not to them but to those who misinterpret and distort them. That is a personal insult which I feel and resent. To be for ever misjudged, to have my repeated offers of friendship weighed and scrutinized with zealous, mistrustful eyes taxes my patience severely. I have said time after time that I am a friend of England, and your Press, or at least a considerable section of it, bids the people of England refuse my proffered hand and insinuates that the other holds a dagger. How can I convince a nation against its will?'

'I repeat', continued His Majesty, 'that I am a friend of England but you make it hard for me to remain so. My task is not of the easiest. *The prevailing sentiment amongst my own people is not friendly to England. I am in a minority*[1] in my own land, but it is a minority of the best elements, just as it is in England with respect to Germany. That is another reason why I resent your refusal to accept my pledged word that I am the friend of England. I strive without ceasing to improve relations and you retort that I am your arch-enemy. You make it very hard for me. Why is it?'

Thereupon I ventured to remind His Majesty that not England alone but the whole of Europe had viewed with disapproval the recent action of Germany in allowing the German Consul to return from Tangier to Fez, and in anticipating the joint action of France and Spain by suggesting to the Powers that the time had come for Europe to recognize Mulay Hafid as the new Sultan of Morocco.

His Majesty made a gesture of impatience. 'Yes,' he said, 'that is an excellent example of the way in which German action is misinterpreted. First then as regards the journey of Dr Vassel. *The German Government had nothing whatever to do with his leaving Tangier. He started for Fez entirely on his own account to look after his belongings in that city, from which he has been so long absent. And why not? Are those who charge Germany with having stolen a march on the other Powers aware that the French Consul has already been in Fez for two weeks when Dr Vassel set out?*[2] Then, as to the

[1] For the words printed in italics, the Foreign Ministry recommended: 'The prevailing sentiment amongst large parts of the middle and lower classes of my own people is not friendly to England. So I am, as to say, in a minority....'

[2] For the words printed in italics, the Foreign Ministry recommended: 'The German Government in sending Vassel back to his post at Fez was only guided by the wish that he should look after the private interests of German subjects in that city, who cried for help and protection after the long absence of a consular

recognition of Mulay Hafid? The Press of Europe has complained with much acerbity that Germany ought not to have suggested his recognition until he had notified to Europe his full acceptance of the Act of Algeciras, as being binding upon him, as Sultan of Morocco and the successor of his brother. My answer is that Mulay Hafid notified the Powers to that effect weeks ago, before the decisive battle was fought. He sent, as far back as the middle of last July an identical communication to the Governments of Germany, France, and Great Britain containing an explicit acknowledgement that he was prepared to recognize all the obligations towards Europe incurred as Sultan by Abdul Aziz. The German Government interpreted that communication as a final and authoritative expression of Mulay Hafid's intentions, and therefore they considered that there was no reason to wait until he had sent a second communication, before recognizing him as de facto Sultan of Morocco, who had succeeded to his brother's throne by right of victory in the field.'

I suggested to His Majesty that an important and influential section of the German Press had placed a very different interpretation upon the action of the German Government and in fact had given it their effusive approbation precisely because they see in it a strong act instead of mere words, and a decisive indication that Germany was once more about to intervene in the shaping of events in Morocco. 'There are mischief makers', replied the Emperor, 'in both countries. I will not attempt to weigh their relative capacity for misinterpretation. But the facts are as I have stated. There has been nothing in regard to Germany's recent action with regard to Morocco which runs contrary to the explicit declaration of my love of peace which I made both at the Guildhall and in my latest speech at Strassburg.'

His Majesty then reverted to the subject uppermost in his mind—his proved friendship for England. 'I have referred to my speeches' he said, 'in which I have done all that a Sovereign can to proclaim my good will. But, as actions speak louder than words, let me also refer to my acts. It is commonly believed in England that throughout the South African War, Germany was hostile to her. German opinion undoubtedly was hostile, bitterly hostile. The Press was hostile, the private opinion was hostile. But official Germany—what of that? Listen. What was it that

representative. And why not send him? Are those who charge Germany with having stolen a march on the other Powers aware that a French consular representative has already been in Fez for several months when Vassel set out?'

brought to a sudden stop and absolute collapse the tour of the Boer delegates in Europe who were striving to obtain European intervention? They were fêted in Holland, France gave them a rapturous welcome. They wished to come to Berlin where the German people would have crowned them with flowers. They asked me to receive them. I refused. The agitation at once died away. The delegation returned empty-handed. Was that, I ask, the action of a secret enemy?'

'Or again when the struggle was at its height, the German Government was invited by the Governments of France and Russia to join with them in calling upon England to put an end to the war. The moment had come, they said, not only to save the Boer Republics, but also to humiliate England to the dust. What was my reply? I said that so far from Germany joining in any concerted European action to put pressure upon England and bring about her downfall, Germany *would use her armed might to prevent such concerted action*.[1] Posterity will one day read the exact terms of the letter—now in the archives of Windsor Castle—in which I informed the Sovereign of England of the answer I had returned to the Powers which then sought to compass her fall. Englishmen, who now insult me by doubting my word, should know what were my actions in the hour of their adversity.'

'Nor was that all. Just at the time of your Black Week, when disasters followed one another in rapid succession, I received a letter from Queen Victoria, my revered grandmother, written in sorrow and affliction and bearing manifest traces of the anxieties which were preying upon her mind and health. I at once returned a sympathetic reply. But I did more than that. I bade one of my officers procure for me as exact an account as he could obtain of the number of combatants in South Africa on both sides, and of the actual position of the opposing forces. With the figures before me I worked out what I considered to be the best plan of campaign under the circumstances, and submitted it to my General Staff for their criticism. Then I despatched it to England, and that paper likewise is among the State papers at Windsor Castle awaiting the severely impartial verdict of history. And, as a matter of curious coincidence let me add that the plan which I formulated ran very much on the same lines as that which was actually adopted by Lord Roberts and carried by him into successful operation. Was

---

[1] For the words printed in italics, the Foreign Ministry recommended: 'Would always keep aloof from politics that could bring her into complications with a sea-power like England.'

that, I repeat, the act of one who wished England ill? Let Englishmen be just and say!'

'But, you will say, what of the German Navy? Is not that a menace to England? Against whom but England is it being steadily built up? If England is not in the minds of those Germans who are bent on creating a powerful fleet, why is Germany asked to consent to such new and heavy burdens of taxation? My answer is clear. Germany is a young and growing Empire. She has a world-wide commerce which is rapidly expanding, and to which the legitimate ambition of patriotic Germans refuses to assign any bounds. Germany must have a powerful fleet to protect that commerce and her manifold interests in even the most distant seas. She expects those interests to go on growing and she must be able to champion them manfully in any quarter of the globe. Germany looks ahead. Her horizons stretch far away. She must be prepared for any eventualities in the Far East. Who can foresee what may take place in the Pacific in the days to come, days not far distant as some believe, but days at any rate for which all European Powers with Far Eastern interests ought steadily to prepare. Look at the accomplished rise of Japan, think of the possible national awakening of China, and then judge of the vast problems of the Pacific. Only those powers which have vast navies will be listened to with respect when the future of the Pacific comes to be solved, and if for that reason only Germany must have a powerful fleet. It may even be that England herself will be glad that Germany has a fleet, when they speak together on the same side in the great debates of the future.'

Such was the purport of the Emperor's conversation. He spoke with all that earnestness which marks his manner when speaking on deeply pondered subjects. I would ask my fellow countrymen who value the cause of peace to weigh what I have written and to revise if necessary, their estimate of the Kaiser and his friendship for England by His Majesty's own words. If they had enjoyed the privilege which was mine, of having once spoken they would doubt no longer either His Majesty's firm desire to live on the best of terms with England or his growing impatience at the persistent mistrust with which his offer of friendship is received.

BIOGRAPHICAL INDEX

[*Note.* biog. = biographical sketch]

SUBJECT INDEX

Albania: Italian aspirations, 105
Algeciras Conference, 1906: 100–1
Anti-Socialist Law: 146–8
Austria: troops in Danish war (1864), 26–9; war with France (1859), 30; Franco-Prussian War, 43–4; 116; gains at Congress of Berlin, 122; Reinsurance Treaty, 127; *hauteur* toward Germany, 152–3; Balkan policy, 153, 164–6, 195–7; Italian policy, 153–5

Baghdad railway: 163–4
Bavaria: attitude toward Prussia (1870), 38
Bear Island: 176
Belgium: attitude toward Prussia (1867), 36; 168
Berlin, Congress of: 65, 66–7, 105, 106, 107, 119, 121–4, 193–4; treaty of, 156
Boer War: 173, 184
Bosnian question: 164–6, 195–7
Bucharest, Peace of (1886): 134

China: Treaty of Aigun (1857), 16; Tonkin war with France, 104, 108–10, 112–13; Treaty of Shimonoseki, 113, 178–9; Boxer rebellion, 114–15; German aspirations in, 178–81; import duties, 186–7
Crimean War: 32, 116

Daily Telegraph affair: 167, 171–4, 190–1, 198
Denmark: War of 1864, xi, 25–33; Schleswig-Holstein question (1863), 23–4; London Conference, 31–2, 168, 183; attitude to Franco-Prussian War, 36–7; sale of Virgin Islands, 177

Ems telegram: 41
England: London Conference, 31–2, 168, 183; relations with France after Krüger telegram, 106, 170; Tonkin incident, 108; Boxer Rebellion, 114–15; Crimean war policy, 116; Congress of Berlin, 122–3; Disraeli and Bismarck, 123–4; Hohenzollern-Battenberg marriage,

134–5; naval rivalry, 159, 174; origins of Krüger telegram, 160–3, 185; Baghdad railway, 163–4; in the Balkans (1908), 165–6; relations with Germany, 168–9; in the Far East, 179–81; Chamberlain's proposed alliance, 181–8

Farsan Islands: 178
France: view of Prussian army, 24, 27–9; Austrian war, 30; unpreparedness for war, 31; prestige in London, 1864, 31; hopes to acquire Luxembourg, 35; war scare of 1875, 93–4, 117–18; Tonkin war, 104, 108–10, 112–13; Courcel on relations with Germany, 110–12; Treaty of Shimonoseki, 113; Portuguese colonies, 113–14; Boxer Rebellion, 114–15; Crimean War policy, 116; replaces Germany as Russia's creditor, 125, 166; Tunis, 151–6; Moroccan policy, 156, 184, 186; Franco-German Morocco agreement 1909, 189, 192–3, 194–5; English Entente, 170
Franco-Prussian War: xi, 34–6, 116, 168; outbreak of, 36–42; Hohenzollern candidature, 39–41; Ems telegram, 41; Favre, Bismarck and the peace 1871, 80; siege of Paris and aftermath, 79–83; Paris Commune, 82–9; attitude after 1871, 93, 107; plans for Bourbon restoration, 95, 102–3
Frankfurt, Peace of: 102, 110

German Fisheries League: 176 n. 2
Greece: deposition of King Otto, 22–3; Turkish frontier settlement, 65, 66–7, 193–4

Hague Peace Conference, 1907: 101, 133
Hungarian Legion, 1866: 58

Italy: Holstein's mission (1870), 42–5; renewal of Triple Alliance, 76–7; interests in Tunis and Albania, 104–6, 151–6; Austria, 153–5; Moroccan policy, 196

215